ATTP 3-39.20 (FM 3-19.50)

POLICE INTELLIGENCE OPERATIONS

July 2010

HEADQUARTERS, DEPARTMENT OF THE ARMY

Published by Books Express Publishing
Books Express Publishing, 2011
ISBN 978-1-78039-961-4

Books Express publications are available from all good retail and online booksellers. For
publishing proposals and direct ordering please contact us at: info@books-express.com

Army Tactics, Techniques, and Procedures
No. 3-39.20

Headquarters
Department of the Army
Washington, DC, 29 July 2010

Police Intelligence Operations

Contents

Figures

Tables

Preface

Army Tactics, Techniques, and Procedures (ATTP) 3-39.20 is the manual for police intelligence operations (PIO) doctrine. This manual aligns with Field Manual (FM) 3-39, the Military Police Corps Regiment's keystone manual, and other Army and joint doctrine. Simultaneous operations that combine offensive, defensive, and stability or civil support operations are emphasized. PIO is a military police function that supports the operations process and protection activities by providing exceptional police information and intelligence to enhance situational understanding, protection of the force, and homeland security (HLS). This manual emphasizes that PIO supports, enhances, and contributes to the commander's protection program and situational understanding by analyzing, integrating, and portraying relevant criminal threat and police information and intelligence that may affect the operational environment (OE). This threat information is gathered by military police Soldiers as they conduct military police functions and by other Army Soldiers, Service policing forces, multinational elements, and security forces.

This manual is written for military police and United States Criminal Investigation Command (USACIDC) Soldiers and civilians conducting the PIO function. This manual is focused on establishing the framework of PIO, how PIO supports military police and Army operations, and how to integrate PIO within the other four military police functions: law and order (L&O), internment and resettlement (I/R), maneuver and mobility support (MMS), and area security (AS). In addition to the revisions already mentioned, this manual–

- Identifies the fundamentals of PIO and synchronizes PIO doctrine and task alignment to the Army Universal Task List.
- Refines and clarifies key PIO-related definitions.
- Highlights the critical integration of PIO throughout the other four military police functions.
- Clarifies the relationship of PIO to the Army's intelligence process and the other integrating processes of Army operations.
- Demonstrates the capability to collect and process relevant police information.
- Acknowledges the ability of military police and USACIDC personnel to collect, process, and analyze evidence (including forensic and biometric information) during full spectrum operations.
- Applies lessons learned through the conduct of recent operational experiences.
- Validates the application of PIO across the spectrum of conflict.

This publication applies to the Regular Army, the Army National Guard (ARNG)/Army National Guard of the United States (ARNGUS), United States Army Reserve (USAR), and Department of the Army (DA) civilian and contract personnel, unless otherwise stated.

The manual is organized into six chapters with three appendixes to provide additional details on selected operational topics. The first three chapters describe PIO aspects of the OE and the integration of police intelligence in military police functions and operations. The remaining chapters discuss sources of police information, analysis, production, and dissemination of police information and police intelligence. A brief description of each chapter and appendix is provided below–

- Chapter 1 describes the OE, with particular focus on the nature and scope of modern conflict as well as important variables of the OE as described in FM 3-39 and other doctrine. The discussion is not a repeat of the information in previous manuals but, rather, it is focused specifically on those aspects of the OE that generate requirements for PIO. The chapter also defines and establishes the framework for PIO and police intelligence support to full spectrum operations.
- Chapter 2 discusses PIO integration within the military police functions and highlights the critical role that PIO serves in relation to the other four functions.

- Chapter 3 discusses the application and integration of PIO in the operations process and the supporting integrating processes: intelligence preparation of the battlefield (IPB); targeting; intelligence, surveillance, and reconnaissance (ISR) synchronization (and the associated continuing activity of integration); composite risk management (CRM); and knowledge management (KM).

- Chapter 4 describes sources of police information used to support analysis.

- Chapter 5 focuses on the analysis of police information. This chapter discusses the critical thinking and predictive analysis techniques applied by trained police intelligence analysts to support the formation of a holistic common operating picture (COP) and continuously feed the operations process.

- Chapter 6 discusses the production of police intelligence products. This chapter provides a brief description of some of the more common products that may be produced by the military police or USACIDC staff and their associated analysts. The chapter also discusses police intelligence networks.

- Appendix A provides information on briefing and debriefing requirements in support of PIO.

- Appendix B addresses applicable laws, regulations, and directives most relevant to the PIO collection efforts. Additionally, it provides a summary of each document (with respect to its relevancy and applicability to the PIO function) and its restrictions and previsions to Army law enforcement (LE) and the conduct of PIO.

- Appendix C identifies initiatives used by other agencies in an effort to facilitate necessary interaction and the timely exchange of police information and intelligence.

This ATTP provides the operational architecture and guidance for military police commanders and trainers at all echelons for the integration and instruction of PIO for established curriculum in the Army's education system. It applies to all military police Soldiers in the Regular Army, ARNG, and USAR. This doctrine will help Army leaders and trainers at branch schools plan for, integrate, and teach the integration of PIO capabilities into Army and joint operations.

Terms that have joint or Army definitions are identified in the text. Terms for which ATTP 3-39.20 is the proponent manual (the authority) are indicated in the glossary. Text references: Definitions for which ATTP 3-39.20 is the proponent are printed in boldface and italicized in the text. These terms and their definitions will be incorporated into the next revision of FM 1-02. For other definitions in the text, the term is italicized, and the number of the proponent manual follows the definition.

Military police refer to their analysts as police intelligence analysts, while USACIDC analysts are typically referred to as criminal intelligence analysts (due to the focused criminal investigative mission of USACIDC). For the purpose of brevity, the term police intelligence analyst is used in this manual to refer to both military police and USACIDC analysts.

This publication applies to the Active Army, the Army National Guard (ARNG)/Army National Guard of the United States (ARNGUS), and the United States Army Reserve (USAR), and Department of the Army (DA) civilian and contract personnel, unless otherwise stated.

The proponent for this publication is the United States Army Training and Doctrine Command (TRADOC). Send comments and recommendations on DA Form 2028 (Recommended Changes to Publications and Blank Forms) directly to Commandant, United States Army Military Police School, ATTN: ATZT-TDD-M, 320 MANSCEN Loop, Suite 270, Fort Leonard Wood, and Missouri 65473-8929. Submit an electronic DA Form 2028 or comments and recommendations in the DA Form 2028 format by e-mail to <leon mdottdmpdoc@conus.army.mil>.

Unless this publication states otherwise, masculine nouns and pronouns do not exclusively refer to men.

Introduction

Since PIO was recognized as a military police function in the early 1990s, it has been inconsistently applied across the force. Military police leaders and units often relegated PIO to USACIDC elements and select military police Soldiers who recognized the value of linking individuals with locations, events, and objects to identify patterns, trends, and associations. Application of PIO was more recognizable and understandable in the conduct of LE and L&O operations, focusing primarily on supporting posts, camps, and stations. Previous PIO doctrine failed to fully frame PIO in a context outside L&O operations and reinforced this misunderstanding. This ATTP builds on the experiences of Soldiers in the Army and the Military Police Corps Regiment during years of operations in the former Yugoslavia, Iraq, and Afghanistan. Lessons learned from these and other experiences serve as invaluable tools to expand the understanding, appreciation, and complete application of PIO as an integrated function of the Military Police Corps Regiment that supports all activities of full spectrum operations. PIO is not solely applicable to LE and criminal investigations. It encompasses continuous analyses and production by military police and USACIDC personnel; information collected by military police, USACIDC, and others; and subsequent dissemination of police information and police intelligence (as appropriate) to police agencies, other military units, and the Army intelligence community. All Soldiers conducting L&O, I/R, MMS, and AS missions collect police information for further analysis. Although considered a military police function, PIO is used by and serves all commanders, at all echelons, across the spectrum of conflict.

A recent Center for Army Lessons Learned (CALL) study found, in conversations with maneuver commanders, that future warfare will not be too dissimilar to what coalition forces are experiencing in Iraq and Afghanistan. Recent history (in Bosnia, Kosovo, Afghanistan, and Iraq) indicated that as United States (U.S.) forces began ground operations, they were confronted with enemy forces dressed in local civilian attire; criminals released from prisons; populace control measures (such as vehicle licensing and registration and property registration) and government records management no longer in place; lack of functioning civil or governmental systems; and organized crime, terrorist, insurgent, common criminal, political, and ethnic groups (to include tribes) all vying for control of the population. These nontraditional organizations add to the complexity of the already multifaceted environment associated with warfare. (See the *Military Police and Counterinsurgency Operations, Operation Iraqi Freedom Initial Impressions Report.*)

Maneuver commanders recognize several key PIO enablers that greatly enhance the effectiveness and value of PIO products and their contributions to mission success. The expansion of PIO capabilities, to include the recent introduction of USACIDC personnel, LE professionals, biometrics, and modular forensic laboratories, have all contributed to the success of PIO by providing actionable police intelligence to attack insurgents and other organized criminal networks. Formerly static and primarily positioned in the continental United States (CONUS), reachback capabilities such as the United States Army Criminal Investigations Laboratory (USACIL) are now providing modular elements in-theater, thus ensuring expedient and dedicated analyses. These analyses are available not only to support evidence or potential evidence for use in criminal cases, but also to support targeting by conventional forces.

PIO focuses the collection efforts of military police formations to ensure that the proper police information is collected and forwarded. At times, this collection effort will be in response to a specific requirement from a commander request—possibly in the form of priority intelligence requirements (PIR) or intelligence requirements (IR)—to address an enemy course of action (COA). At other times, the information will come directly from an investigation or event, without any preconception of its value. This information feeds into the operations process, including the commander's targeting cycle to enable informed decisionmaking and targeting of people, groups, and networks for both lethal and nonlethal effects, depending on the commander's assessment and the selected engagement method. Targets may also be identified for further informational exploitation as a conduit to attack an enemy, criminal, or terrorist network. The end result of PIO may be an actual prosecution in a court of law. If the prosecution takes place in an emerging democracy, it will also serve as an example to the people of that nation as to the value of a professional police force operating within the rule of law. PIO activities also provide information critical to determining measures required to protect the force.

This page intentionally left blank.

Chapter 1
Operational Environment and Police Intelligence Operations

Threats to the United States will continue to evolve. States, nations, transnational actors, and nonstate entities will continue to engage in efforts to achieve positions of power and dominance and strengthen political, economic, or ideological interests. U.S. forces will face increasing threats from adversaries who will employ capabilities ranging from cutting-edge, emerging technologies to relatively crude and simple tactics. An increasing characteristic of threat elements faced by U.S. forces is the use of criminal enterprises to fund and organize threat activities. Combating this threat requires a focused and integrated use of the full capabilities of U.S. forces and our multinational partners. Many of these capabilities have not been leveraged extensively in an OE to counter belligerent forces; therefore, the tools are unavailable (or unknown) to commanders and Soldiers. The application of police intelligence capabilities to collect, analyze, and disseminate information regarding police organizations and criminal threat elements in the OE and the rapid proliferation of technologies supporting biometric data and forensic evidence collection, analysis, and dissemination to the Soldier and the tactical unit level have greatly increased the effectiveness of U.S. forces combating this evolving threat. The strength of PIO comes from ensuring that this function is integrated into the operations process and its integrating processes. This integration provides use for the exploitation of police intelligence and ensures that policing actions meet the commander's intent throughout operations.

UNDERSTANDING THE OPERATIONAL ENVIRONMENT

1-1. *Operational environments* are a composite of the conditions, circumstances, and influences that affect the employment of capabilities and impact the decisions of the commander. (Joint Publication [JP] 3-0) The environment includes all physical elements (such as enemy, adversary, and friendly) and neutral systems (such as infrastructure, geography, and weather) across the spectrum of conflict. An understanding of the physical environment and factors, such as the state of governance, technology, local resources, and local population culture, are critical to operating successfully in a specific OE. Even with the best analysis and knowledge management capabilities, the modern OE is complex and extremely dynamic.

1-2. The complexity of land operations is directly attributable to the large number of Soldiers and weapons systems generally involved, and the close combat is often a part of these operations. This complexity also results in frequent interaction with enemies and noncombatants dispersed across the area of operations (AO) and intermingled in close proximity to each other. Complexity is also a function of the combined arms nature of full spectrum operations, involving the interaction and mutual support of different arms and Services. Instantaneous global communications—readily available to friendly, hostile, and neutral parties—increase this complexity. The environment is often characterized by uncertainty and chaos.

1-3. This uncertainty is increased by the impact of irregular criminal and terrorist threats operating in and transiting the AO. Technology, intelligence, and the design of operations can reduce uncertainty. However, regardless of the effort allocated to intelligence and increased situational understanding, commanders still have to make decisions based on incomplete, inaccurate, and often contradictory information. An understanding of the OE underpins a commander's ability to make decisions and is essential to the successful execution of operations.

1-4. To gain a broad understanding of these influences, commanders typically consult with technical specialists in each area. Military police, with their technical expertise in policing, penal, and general application of the rule of law are among the specialists available to add breadth and depth to the overall understanding of the OE. Military police contribute to situational understanding, an enhanced intelligence picture, and a more complete COP through the application of PIO. PIO activities are integrated into the execution of L&O, I/R, MMS, and AS operations in support of the commander's strategic, operational, and tactical plans. The strength of PIO comes from ensuring that it is planned and integrated into each of the military police functions and that the resulting information and police intelligence is integrated into the operations process. This integration provides flexibility for the exploitation of police intelligence and ensures that police actions meet the commander's intent throughout operations.

NATURE OF THE THREAT

1-5. The struggle by external elements to challenge and redefine global and regional distribution of power remains a significant threat to the United States and its interests, at home and abroad. States, nations, transnational actors, and nonstate entities will continue to engage in efforts to achieve positions of power and dominance to further political, economic, religious, or ideological interests. Threats may be characterized in four major categories: traditional, irregular, catastrophic, and disruptive. While these characterizations are helpful in describing the threats, our enemies will not likely fit neatly into any one category. Instead, they will likely simultaneously use tactics consistent with multiple categories in an effort to keep U.S. forces off-balance and strike where we are least prepared. See FM 3-0 for further discussion of the changing nature of the threat.

1-6. The nature of threats against the United States will continue to evolve, requiring changes in our methods to counter those threats. Arguably, the most urgent threats in the modern OE come from unconventional state and nonstate actors—terrorists and criminals operating under the banner of ideological or religious fanaticism or the lure of illicit gains. Modern communications—satellite telephones and the internet—and the ease of travel allow groups of similar ideology to form associations, partnerships, and networks with fewer obstacles than in the past. These groupings, both formal and informal, while increasing the capabilities of opponents, also offer potential avenues for exploitation.

1-7. While the United States holds significant advantages over traditional or conventional threats, the ability of threat elements to rapidly adjust and attack us with nontraditional warfare will continue to be a challenge. Our enemies will continue to operate in and among the local populace, making traditional lethal engagement more constrained. Many enemy tactics will be consistent with traditional criminal behavior faced by policing organizations worldwide. Some of these threat organizations will operate with highly sophisticated criminal enterprises to organize, fund, and otherwise support their operations.

1-8. Even while U.S. forces are training and operating with host nation security forces to improve and increase force capabilities and apply the rule of law, threat organizations (criminal and terrorist) will likely attempt to modify their capabilities and modes of operation in reaction to changes in the OE and pressure from security forces. This recognition is critical to combating adaptive threat organizations.

THE CRIMINAL ENVIRONMENT

1-9. Criminals seek economical and political gain through illegal activities, to include trafficking in drugs, weapons, people, and other contraband. Violence is often a primary tool, either through intimidation or actual attacks to steal property, influence the population, and escape prosecution. While many criminals operate independently, today's technology facilitates criminal organizations with much less regard for physical and political boundaries than at any other time in history. Drug cartels can move money and gather information on their distribution network without any need to expose members to international travel. Known associates or clever imitators can repeat a crime committed in one country the same day on another continent.

1-10. Irregular threat elements are able to use the same tools to further their causes. Funding moves smoothly across time zones and borders, even changing from a base currency to a local currency almost instantly. Information gathering and planning can also occur without ever leaving safe houses and between personnel who have never had face-to-face contact (to protect identities). Terrorist organizations have always recruited and trained members and conducted operations; however, today's technology provides our adversaries with the ability to recruit, indoctrinate, conduct operations, and share information on a scale nearly unimaginable twenty years ago.

1-11. Similarities between criminal and many irregular threat organizations—in techniques and in the advantages they gain in chaotic political and degraded security environments—have led to many confirmed instances of threat elements joining forces or morphing from an enterprise with a single focus to multifaceted, international organizations with diverse holdings, intentions, and operating locations. Threat organizations may turn to criminal activities to fund their training and operations, while criminal cartels may use terror to further their causes or to retaliate against government and police actions. These criminal and terrorist activities may interfere with U.S. objectives.

SOCIAL ORDER

1-12. The social fabric of a community often dictates the ability of criminals and criminal organizations to operate freely or with minimal police interference. Military police must understand the social order to begin to understand the patterns that offer insight into what is happening in the community and the region in which they operate. Religious, political, economic, ethnic, and agricultural patterns are just some examples of what military forces must be attuned to, especially when operating in unfamiliar areas. These patterns are so well understood in parts of the United States that Americans may fail to recognize them. Examples of such patterns include–

- Traditional summer vacations for schools, traditional holiday breaks between mid-December until after the New Year, and spring break in March or early April.
- Friday and Saturday "weekends."
- Daylight saving time.
- Sport seasons.
- Thanksgiving weekend "black Friday" shopping.
- Election cycles for public office holders.

1-13. These same types of patterns are present around the world and can be important indicators of stability in the social order, either by their presence or by their absence. The challenge for military police and other U.S. forces is to recognize these patterns and social nuances so that disruptions can be identified. For example, if Saturday is normally a busy business day for the local economy and U.S. forces encounter a normally bustling market that is deserted, this is an obvious indicator that should be investigated. The absence of activity could be the result of an important religious holiday or some external criminal influence. The recognition of such an anomaly in the social order and the reasons behind it require understanding of specific religious, political, economic, ethnic, and agricultural patterns in local communities. Recognition of unexplained variations in the environment should lead to further observation and investigation to determine the cause. The cause may be innocent, but it may also lead to the discovery of criminal elements operating in the AO.

1-14. Another social phenomenon that may influence U.S. operations is the reluctance in some societies to cooperate with LE, even when civilians are victims of crimes. Fear of police and governmental officials, a desire to not be seen as cooperating with LE entities, or other cultural mores may play a role in these actions. Military police must investigate and understand such societal beliefs so that they can tailor police engagement strategies to overcome obstacles to ensure timely reporting.

1-15. Early and thorough understanding of the social dynamics of the societies in the OE is critical to achieving strategic and operational objectives. Failure to understand these dynamics can result in mistrust of U.S. forces or, worse, outright contempt that could drive the populace to sympathize or support criminal, terrorist, or insurgent forces operating or attempting to gain a foothold in the OE. Military police are positioned early in any operation due to their dispersion throughout the AO while executing MMS and AS missions, to engage with and gain information from the local population and informal authority structures (such as clan or tribal leaders). These activities are synchronized and integrated with civil affairs, command information engagement priorities, and IR. These interactions, if successful, can be the first steps toward building legitimacy in the eyes of the host nation population. Information gained through these interactions feed valuable information into the operations process and police intelligence activities. This early tactical information may not be directly applicable to policing operations or criminal investigations, but can be critical to a commander's COP, fulfilling operational and tactical IR, enabling decisionmaking, and developing additional IR required to increase situational understanding.

POLICE INTELLIGENCE OPERATIONS FRAMEWORK

1-16. *Police intelligence operations* is a military police function, integrated within all military police operations, that supports the operations process through analysis, production, and dissemination of information collected as a result of police activities to enhance situational understanding, protection, civil control, and law enforcement. (FM 3-39) Information gathered as a result of PIO (whether information directly supporting LE investigations or IR generated by a commander or staff,) is gathered while conducting military police operations and, upon analysis, may contribute to a commander's critical information requirement (CCIR) and focus policing activities required to anticipate and preempt crime or related disruptive activities to maintain order. Military police Soldiers and USACIDC agents develop PIO skills while supporting L&O operations at home camps and stations, enabling them to integrate these skills across all military police functions in support of full spectrum operations. Other key definitions that provide framework and understanding for police intelligence include the following–

- *Police information* is all available information concerning known and potential enemy and criminal threats and vulnerabilities collected during police activities, operations, and investigations. Analysis of police information produces police intelligence.
- *Police intelligence* results from the application of systems, technologies, and processes that analyze applicable data and information necessary for situational understanding and focusing policing activities to achieve social order.
- *Criminal intelligence* is a category of police intelligence derived from the collection, analysis, and interpretation of all available information concerning known and potential criminal threats and vulnerabilities of supported organizations.

1-17. USACIDC and provost marshal (PM) staffs provide criminal intelligence analysis to commanders that identify indicators of potential crimes and criminal threats against Army property, facilities, and/or personnel. Criminal intelligence is a subset of police intelligence focused on criminal activity and specific criminal threats. It is more focused in scope than police intelligence, which has a broader focus that includes police systems, capabilities, infrastructure, criminal activity, and threats. All criminal intelligence is police intelligence; however, not all police intelligence is criminal intelligence.

ROLE OF POLICE INTELLIGENCE OPERATIONS

1-18. In the Army Universal Task List, PIO is aligned within the intelligence warfighting function, although it is not an intelligence discipline. PIO is an integrated part of police operations and is resident in the operations section. In the Army Universal Task List, PIO is further aligned with task support to situational understanding. Support to situational understanding centers provides military information and intelligence to the commander, facilitating his understanding of the enemy and the environment. This task supports the command's ability to make sound decisions. PIO is essential to enhancing situational understanding, particularly where irregular threats (such as criminals, terrorists, or insurgents) threaten the security of U.S. forces and military operations. See FM 3-0, FM 2-0, and FM 7-15 for a more detailed discussion on the intelligence warfighting function and the critical tasks associated with that function.

1-19. Due to the complexity of the environment, units often need to respond to multiple threats. The commander must understand how current and potential threat systems organize, equip, and employ their forces. It is also vitally important that the commander understand how friendly elements organize, equip, and employ their organizations. This is especially true of host nation policing organizations responsible for police and prison systems critical to stability and security in the OE. Military police conducting PIO provide the capability to rapidly identify and assess these entities. PIO provides a unique police capability supporting military police operation and the missions and operations of multifunctional commanders. The result of PIO, when integrated into the operations process, helps leaders and commanders to better understand crime and criminal networks and how they leverage illicit activities to facilitate criminal activity, subversion, general lawlessness, and insurgency. This understanding and insight can facilitate Army operations designed to disrupt these actions by targeting criminal activities and criminal networks.

1-20. In support of full spectrum operations, PIO will occur as an integrated activity within all other military police missions. During offensive and defensive operations, police intelligence can enable the staff to identify organizations and networks (police and criminal) in the AO that may provide indications of disruptive activities and conditions requiring corrective action to establish stability. As operations become more protracted and conventional threat levels are reduced from a traditional military threat to an irregular threat, the lines between criminal, terrorist, and insurgent activities normally associated with stability operations become blurred. PIO planned and conducted by military police staffs and PM sections contribute to the operations process and enhance the commander's situational understanding. This is especially true during stability operations where the role of the military police focuses on developing a country's ability to protect its communities and establish or reestablish civil security and civil control. PIO planned and conducted in stability operations provides police intelligence key in shaping the OE and contributing to the success of civil security and civil control lines of operation.

1-21. PIO provides essential products and services in support of military operations at posts, camps, and stations. In particular, police intelligence provides the commander and PM with situational understanding necessary to reduce threats against Army installations; provide threat intelligence for in-transit security; and focus the development and implementation of threat countermeasures to safeguard Army personnel, material, and information. Regardless of the OE, PIO helps bridge the information gap between what a commander knows and does not know. PIO provides direct support to the intelligence cycle, with the most reliable information being obtained through effective PIO networks.

Bridging the Information Gap

1-22. PIO activities provide capabilities that can bridge the gap between traditional military intelligence (MI) and information focused on policing and the criminal environment. When the intelligence staff officer (S-2) or Army Chief of Staff, Intelligence (G-2) identifies a gap in the commander's knowledge of the threat and the current threat situation, that gap may be included as PIR or selected as indications and warnings (I&W). (FM 2-0 contains information on I&W.) The S-2 or G-2 will then develop a collection plan to help the commander in filling this information gap. Military police staffs and PM sections will also identify information gaps pertinent to policing activities and develop IR to fill those gaps. The IR findings may also be included in the PIR of the echelon commander.

Note. The S-2 and G-2 are restricted from collecting information on U.S. persons (see Department of Defense [DOD] 5240.1-R) and will not direct military police or USACIDC elements to conduct such DOD collection activities (see Army Regulation [AR] 381-10).

1-23. Part of the commander's collection strategy is to select the best collection asset available to cover each information requirement. After a thorough analysis—an analysis that includes availability, capability, and performance history—the collection manager identifies which collection assets can best be used. In military police brigades and battalions, military police commanders and their staffs identify information gaps; develop IR; develop, synchronize, and integrate collection plans; and task or coordinate for collection assets. In echelons above brigade, a brigade combat team, or a maneuver enhancement brigade (MEB) structure, the PM section (working as part of the Assistant Chief of Staff, Operations and Plans [G-3] or the operations staff officer [S-3]) will typically coordinate with the S-2 or G-2 to ensure that military police-related IR information is synchronized and integrated in the overall ISR plan. When military police or USACIDC assets are tasked with the police information collection mission, they are provided specific guidelines and a prioritized collection requirement.

1-24. In the United States or its territories, effective PIO can provide installation commanders with situational understanding and address information gaps to ensure that threat assessments are valid and reliable. PIO in support of posts, camps, and stations is conducted by PMs and their staffs responsible for LE operations. USACIDC elements conduct PIO in their AO to support investigative and other support requirements. PIO capitalizes on connectivity between installation LE and civilian domestic agencies. In this OE, the MI involvement is typically limited. According to Department of Defense Directive (DODD) 5200.27, excluding specific LE and protection-related missions "where collection activities are authorized to meet an essential requirement for information, maximum reliance shall be placed on domestic civilian investigative agencies, federal, state, and local." MI personnel may actively participate in PIO activities when assigned to an LE agency and supporting an LE function.

MILITARY POLICE AND POLICE INTELLIGENCE

1-25. For many years, military police and USACIDC personnel have conducted PIO targeting conventional criminals in support of posts, camps, and stations. Like our civilian counterparts, military police and USACIDC personnel have developed analytical techniques to identify and mitigate criminals and criminal activity. For years, these activities were largely dismissed as irrelevant to military operations external to U.S. territories. Reality in the current OE (and in OEs likely in the foreseeable future) is that the threats we face will rely heavily on irregular tactics. The likelihood of large conventional battlefields is largely diminished in the current geopolitical context and any conventional threat will likely use irregular tactics to complement their conventional operations and shape the environment.

1-26. The irregular threats faced in the modern OEs operate from positions intermingled in the population. The threat operates in small groups, cells and, occasionally, as individuals (depending on the specific mission). Many of the threat methods employed are, at their root, criminal activities that mirror organized criminal and terrorist methods and organizational characteristics. These realities increase the relevance of military police and USACIDC units with capabilities to assess the criminal threat environment, gather relevant police information, conduct analyses, and produce actionable police intelligence.

1-27. Military police and USACIDC LE and corrections expertise have become increasingly relevant at all levels of war as nation building and the establishment of the law in collapsed societies has driven the requirement for civil security and civil control to facilitate successful stability operations. Military police and USACIDC assessments, analysis, and recommendations regarding police and prison systems, police capacity and capability, and assessments of criminal environments are key enablers to long-term U.S. objectives. Police intelligence products enable USACIDC special agents in charge (SACs) to build criminal cases for potential use in prosecutions for war crimes, U.S. criminal courts, or in a host nation legal system. PIO provides enhanced situational understanding at the operational level, enabling commanders to anticipate enemy or criminal actions and take preemptive measures to decisively disrupt, dismantle, or prevent those actions.

RELATIONSHIP WITH THE POPULACE

1-28. Police information flows continuously through the interpersonal information network established during the conduct of military police operations in support of full spectrum operations and during LE operations in support of posts, camps, and stations. Information can originate from a multitude of sources and may be obtained through deliberate collection efforts or passive collection resulting from police engagement and observation. Whether collected for a specific LE purpose or as a byproduct of daily interaction and situational awareness by military police or USACIDC agents, information collected by police personnel provides valuable insight to the OE. Police information and police intelligence enhance situational understanding, provide critical information that can fill gaps in IR, and add to the overall COP.

1-29. The relationship between the police and the population is critical in the ability to interact with and operate around the local population. Just as mistrust and a weak social order can help criminals and terrorists, a strong relationship between the population, police, and security forces is critical to assisting with investigations, understanding the social order, and defeating criminal networks.

1-30. The relationship between the police and the populace in many OEs is often not as strong as it should be to enable full support to LE forces. Examples of police corruption, excessive use of force, preferential treatment, and evidence mishandling have received regional and national exposure. Evidence of these actions, even if they are very isolated incidents, can degrade that relationship. Rebuilding public confidence in police forces requires both organized public awareness efforts and continuous professionalism on the part of LE forces. Military policing and LE operations are guided by the principles of policing (FM 3-39 discusses the principles of policing). The principles of military policing are–

- Prevention.
- Public support.
- Restraint.
- Legitimacy.
- Transparency.
- Assessment.

1-31. Military police are subject to the same forces that build public confidence and erode it. On military posts, camps, and stations, military police should always be cognizant of the importance of a positive relationship with residents, installation workers, and the general public. During support to full spectrum operations, military police remain aware of the importance of establishing this same professional reputation with the local population. This difficult task requires a thorough understanding of the rules of engagement (ROE) and support at every level of leadership.

1-32. The history of security forces and their interaction with the local populace highlights the importance of special attention being applied to training during the predeployment phase of any operation. This knowledge will provide insight and understanding on policy implications to military forces participating in the operation. If the local police forces are regarded as professional and supporting of the rule of law, they may provide effective support to U.S. forces. If these police forces are regarded as unprofessional and not supportive of the rule of law (as was the case in Iraq before Operation Iraqi Freedom), reorganizing or disbanding and rebuilding police forces may be necessary.

SOURCES OF POLICE INFORMATION

1-33. Police information is derived from a myriad of sources. Military police Soldiers throughout the AO collect it while interacting with the population, including observations of the local population, discussions with community leaders and residents, and analyses of population registration data (such as vehicle and driver's licensing, real estate transactions, and school enrollment). Military police and USACIDC Soldiers actively look for variations in daily routines and actions falling outside of the expected social order. Sources of police information are covered in depth in chapter 4. Other sources of police information include–

- Military police patrols.
  - LE patrols.
  - Combat patrols.
  - Reconnaissance patrols.
- Military police surveillance.
  - LE surveillance.
  - Tactical surveillance.
- Criminal investigations.
- Interviews and LE interrogations.
- Police investigations.
- Police informants and LE sources.
- Forensic evidence and biometric data.
- I/R operations.
  - Passive interaction and observation of detainees, displaced civilians (DC), prisoners, or visitors.
  - LE interviews of detained, displaced, or incarcerated persons.
- Citizen complaints and emergencies.
- Other governmental agencies (OGAs).
- Nongovernmental organizations (NGOs).
- Host nation civilian, military, and police forces.
- Community leaders.
  - Neighborhood mayors and watch leaders.
  - Religious and tribal leaders.
- S-2 and G-2 sources, including signals intelligence (SIGINT), electronic intelligence (ELINT), and human intelligence (HUMINT).
- Coalition military and police forces.
- Open-source information (media and public information forums).
- Psychological operations teams.
- Civil affairs teams.
- Other military units.

1-34. USACIDC specifically conducts and disseminates information from the following activities:
- Criminal investigations.
- Forensic lab analysis and product production.
- Personal security vulnerability assessments.
- Crime activity threat analyses.
- Logistics-security threat assessments.
- Crime prevention surveys.

ANALYSIS OF POLICE INFORMATION

1-35. Thorough, timely analyses of police information collected in response to IR and investigative leads are fused throughout the operations process. Analysis should allow the developed police intelligence to answer IR or provide actionable police intelligence that drives operations and LE investigations. These operations and LE investigations are then more likely to be successful and support the intent and requirements of the commander or investigator.

1-36. The analysis of police information may begin with a technical examination of a piece of evidence. Physical characteristics of persons, equipment, written documents, weapons, chemicals, and explosives may not be observable without special training and equipment. Analyses may also include careful examinations of the associations between people, items (evidence), locations, and events. Military police Soldiers conducting PIO must be aware of and search for these associations through physical evidence and extrapolation from known points. The use of link diagrams can graphically demonstrate these associations, facilitate a rapid understanding of the known links, and highlight information gaps requiring further collection and targeting. See chapter 6 for a more thorough discussion of analysis.

PRODUCTION AND DISSEMINATION OF POLICE INFORMATION

1-37. Police information and police intelligence products are produced to inform commanders, PMs, investigators, and other LE personnel of exceptional information and actionable police intelligence. Dissemination of this information and police intelligence is also conducted through command and staff and functional channels, including interagency host nation agencies and organizations (within legal and policy constraints). This enables appropriate coordination, synchronization, and fusion of police information and intelligence. Chapter 6 discusses production and dissemination of police information and police intelligence.

POLICE INTELLIGENCE SUPPORT TO FULL SPECTRUM OPERATIONS

1-38. Military police and USACIDC elements conduct operations and perform L&O, I/R, MMS, and AS functions in support of posts, camps, and stations and when conducting full spectrum operations. PIO is integrated in all military police functions and during all military police operations. Police information and police intelligence enables increased situational understanding and informed decisionmaking by Army commanders and shapes the execution of all policing and LE activities. Military police commanders direct police intelligence activities in their respective operations sections and operational elements. PMs conduct police intelligence activities within their staff sections in support of their multifunctional commander and subordinate military police elements. Each military police operations and PM section should be manned with a trained police intelligence analyst. The Crime and Criminal Intelligence Analysts Course (CCIAC) at the United States Army Military Police School (USAMPS) is the approved course to train police intelligence analysts for military police and USACIDC units.

1-39. The military police support commanders, Soldiers, family members, and visitors to installations (in both CONUS and outside the continental United States [OCONUS] posts, camps, and stations) through comprehensive policing activities. L&O operations are normally the most visible aspect of this support, with military and DA civilian police forces providing for a safe and secure environment on installations and in training areas. PIO, when properly resourced and employed, also provides critical support to personnel on and near installations.

1-40. The training and experience that military police Soldiers receive while conducting LE and PIO at their home stations becomes invaluable assets when deployed. Military police capabilities developed in support of posts, camps, and stations are critical to successful military police support to full spectrum operations and support to maneuver commanders. When not supporting deployed operations, military police must be integrated into PM operations to develop and hone their LE skills. Likewise, police intelligence analysts must be integrated into garrison PM police intelligence sections to remain current and continue to develop their analytical skills. This provides key support to the installation and ensures that police analytical capabilities are relevant and effective during deployment and support to the operational commander.

OFFENSE

1-41. *Offensive operations* are combat operations conducted to defeat and destroy enemy forces and seize terrain, resources, and population centers. They impose the commander's will on the enemy. (FM 3-0) Military police support offensive operations with a focus on conducting maneuver and mobility support to regulate movement on main supply routes (MSRs) and alternate supply routes, allowing for the execution of plans and orders in the required sequence and timing methods. They support operational AS requirements throughout the AO and conduct I/R operations at detention (internment) and DC (resettlement) facilities. The tempo of offensive operations may not allow the time required to fully establish a police intelligence network necessary to integrate PIO across the entire AO. Military police Soldiers may be required to support site exploitation and collection of evidence or biometrics information that will be passed to follow-on units and retained for possible exploitation and/or future criminal prosecution.

1-42. The importance of PIO during offensive operations should not be overlooked. Enforcing rules of evidence, facilitating forensic examination of key items, obtaining biometric identity, and collecting information for criminal prosecution allow for a rapid transition to a formal court system and empower detention facility commanders by enabling them to make informed decisions. Information and police intelligence derived from PIO can play a key role in establishing civil security and civil control in the AO.

DEFENSE

1-43. *Defensive operations* are combat operations conducted to defeat an enemy attack, gain time, economize forces, and develop conditions favorable for offensive or stability operations. (FM 3-0) Military police support defensive operations by conducting support missions across the full range of mission sets. The maneuver commander will direct the priority of missions based on his assessment of conditions and mission variables. Generally, interior lines of communication (LOCs) are more stable during defensive operations. This relative stability in unit locations and operations in the AO allows for rapid and extensive development of police intelligence networks with host nation police, the local population, community leaders, OGAs, and NGOs, enabling the establishment of a more robust police intelligence capability.

1-44. As commanders seek to develop conditions favorable for offensive or stability operations, buildup of personnel and sustainment support is often required. During this time, criminals and terrorists may attempt to take advantage of the situation. Stockpiles of weapons, ammunition, food, fuel, and spare parts are valuable commodities, especially in areas affected by warfare. A successful attack against a U.S. sustainment hub may provide terrorists with levels of attention much higher than the actual value of what they attacked.

STABILITY

1-45. *Stability operations* encompass various military missions, tasks, and activities conducted outside the United States in coordination with other instruments of national power to maintain or reestablish a safe and secure environment, provide essential governmental services, emergency infrastructure reconstruction, and humanitarian relief. (JP 3-0) Military police support stability operations through the conduct of all five military police functions. Stability operations typically require military police units to focus significant effort toward building the capacity of host nation police, security, and military forces supporting efforts to restore public order and enable transition toward normalcy for the host nation.

1-46. PIO is a critical enabler in the early phases of any operation as military police and USACIDC elements gather, analyze, and disseminate critical information and police intelligence regarding police and prison systems, host nation capability, policing and prison activities capabilities, and criminal environment assessments in the AO. This information and police intelligence provides commanders and staffs with situational understanding required for planning and executing stability operations. This is especially relevant to civil security and civil control lines of operations. Throughout the conduct of stability operations, military police and USACIDC organizations continue to update their running estimates and refine data and recommendations, based on gathered police information, analyses, and the production of police intelligence.

CIVIL SUPPORT

1-47. *Civil support* is the Department of Defense support to U.S. civil authorities for domestic emergencies and for designated law enforcement and other activities. (JP 1-02) *Civil support operations* are conducted in the United States and its territories and are divided into the three broad categories of domestic emergencies, support of designated LE agencies, and other support activities. (JP 3-28) This includes responding during disasters and declared emergencies, support or restoration of public health and services and civil order, national special security events, and periodic planned support of other activities. Military LE personnel conduct PIO in support of protection operations during defense support to civilian authorities (DSCA) events through the development of U.S.-based networks integrated with local, county, state, tribal, and federal LE agencies. This information is combined with MI within applicable legal and policy constraints to provide a total threat picture for the tasked commander. This threat picture is essential to assessing the risk associated with the operation or task.

1-48. In CONUS, commanders must work closely with the staff judge advocates (SJAs) to ensure that they conduct PIO according to sensitive-information guidelines, intelligence oversight laws, privacy act rules, and DOD policy (see appendix C for information regarding legal requirements and authorities). In most cases, the collection, reporting, processing, and storing of information on non-DOD-affiliated U.S. persons or organizations is restricted to DOD LE personnel only—only regarding those matters with a clear military nexus or interest.

1-49. In Section 1385, Title 18, United States Code (18 United States Code [USC] 1385), the Posse Comitatus Act (PCA) specifically restricts the use of military forces to enforce civilian laws in the United States. There are exceptions to the PCA, which can be enacted by the President or Secretary of Defense during DSCA operations. The PCA applies to military personnel operating under federal authority (Title 10, USC). National Guard elements operating under state control (Title 32, USC) are not restricted by the PCA. Once National Guard elements are mobilized under federal authority, they become subject to PCA restrictions. See appendix C for additional discussion of the legal authorities controlling military police operations.

This page intentionally left blank.

Chapter 2

Integrated Military Police Function

PIO supports commanders at all levels through the integration of police intelligence activities within all military police operations. PIO enables military police and USACIDC staff and police intelligence analysts to identify connections and correlations between people, locations, events, times, and things, allowing for the identification of trends, patterns, and associations pertinent to activity and organizational structure that facilitate criminal behavior. This enables commanders, PMs, LE investigators, and other LE personnel to develop a thorough understanding of crimes, criminal threats, and other factors in their AO, allowing commanders to take decisive and coordinated actions. PIO is an integrated function that supports and enables all other military police functions. The integrated activities associated with PIO enhance L&O, I/R, MMS, and AS by increasing situational understanding; providing critical police intelligence to commanders and staff; and enabling detailed planning, targeting, enhanced decisionmaking, and support to legal actions by staff and commanders in support of policing and LE-related missions.

LAW AND ORDER OPERATIONS

2-1. PIO is most commonly associated with L&O operations. It is in the context of L&O operations, and more specifically LE and policing, that the skill sets and capabilities required for PIO are honed. *Law and order operations* encompass policing and the associated law enforcement activities to control and protect populations and resources to facilitate the existence of a lawful and orderly environment. (FM 3-39) L&O operations are the lead military police function, and it provides the foundation on which all other military police functions are framed. L&O includes policing tasks and LE tasks. *Policing* is the application of control measures in an AO to maintain law and order, safety, and other matters affecting the general welfare of the population. (FM 3-39) *Law enforcement* is those activities performed by personnel authorized by legal authority to compel compliance with, and investigate violations of, laws, directives, and punitive regulations. (FM 3-39)

2-2. PIO directly supports LE and policing operations. Commanders, PMs, and LE investigators generate IR that are required for situational understanding and decisionmaking regarding criminal investigations, disruption of criminal activity, distribution of LE assets, and mission focus. Police intelligence analysis can provide critical linkages, associations, and patterns necessary to conduct LE investigations, identify criminal networks, solve crimes, and close criminal investigations. Analyses of crime trends, patterns, and associations enable commanders, PMs, and military police staff to plan and make decisions regarding patrol distribution, resource requirements, and areas requiring increased police engagement and focus. Interagency cooperation and coordination provides critical information that can be further analyzed and fused by the military police and USACIDC staff and police intelligence analysts in support of Army LE efforts.

2-3. In support of host nation police organizations, analyses of trends, patterns, and associations in an organization can also provide insight into systemic problems internally in the police organization (such as training deficiencies or administrative issues). PIO integrated within L&O operations in support of full spectrum operations can provide critical analyses and situational understanding of civil considerations as they relate to host nation police systems, organizations, capability, and capacity. Military police and USACIDC elements provide L&O and integrated PIO support at every echelon. Information sharing among all elements operating in the AO is a critical factor in a successful police intelligence analysis and the production of relevant and timely police intelligence products. These cooperative efforts can result in the substantial exchange of threat information, enabling police intelligence analysts to produce vital police intelligence products that provide early warning to commanders, PMs, and LE investigators—allowing them to develop protection strategies to counter complex criminal threats.

CIVIL CONSIDERATIONS FOR ASSESSING POLICE SYSTEMS AND THE CRIMINAL ENVIRONMENT

2-4. Military police evaluate police-related civil considerations through an assessment of the police and criminal environment using the variables of police and prison structures, organized criminal networks, legal systems, investigations and interviews, crime-conducive conditions, and enforcement gaps and mechanisms (POLICE). Military police and the USACIDC elements identify existing host nation police organizations, to include personnel and leadership. PIO integrated within L&O operations enables the staff and police intelligence analyst to analyze and assess police structures and identify current police capability and capacity, to include the existence or lack of, a functioning legal system. Military police also conduct crime and criminal analysis to assess the criminal environment, to include the existence of organized criminal elements, crime-conducive conditions, and general levels of criminal activity. The factors of POLICE are used to determine–

- **Police and prison structures**. What police and prison structures exist? This factor may answer information requirements, such as–
  - Does a functional police or security force exist?
  - What police infrastructure is available? Is it in operational condition? What is needed?
  - Is the indigenous police force corrupt?
  - How is this police force received by the community?
  - Can the indigenous police force be relied on as an asset to assist U.S. and joint forces?
  - What equipment, communications, and other capabilities does the indigenous police force have if it is reliable? What equipment and capabilities are needed?
  - Does the police force have adequate systems in place to operate effectively (such as administrative, training, logistical, and investigative)?
  - How many prison structures exist in the AO? What are their types and capacities? Are they operational?
  - Are jurisdictional boundaries established? What is the historical reason for the establishment of jurisdictional boundaries?
- **Organized criminal elements**. Is organized criminal activity present? If so, what are the–
  - Indications of organized crime?
  - Motivation factors for the organized criminal activity—financial or facilitating insurgent activity?
  - Specific criminal activities identified?
  - Public attitudes toward organized criminal activities?
  - People, organizations, or businesses targeted by organized criminal elements?
- **Legal systems**. What is the composition of the legal system–
  - Is there a law-enforcing mechanism? If so, what is it?
  - Is there an adjudicating body?
  - Does the legal system operate based on the rule of law? If not, what is the basis?
  - Are all three elements of the criminal justice system (police, prisons, and judiciary) present, functional, and synchronized?
  - Are appropriate administrative records systems in place to support the legal system?
- **Investigations and interviews**. Are adequate criminal investigative systems functioning and enforced–
  - Do adequate investigative capabilities exist to perform police and administrative investigations (such as criminal, traffic, internal affairs, and administrative functions)?
  - Are adequate administrative and database systems in place to support investigations, to include PIO?

- How are internal and external investigations, inquiries, and assessments initiated, managed, tracked, and reported? Are records appropriately transparent to the public? Are they consistently applied?
- Are police and criminal investigative capabilities leveraged to support site exploitation and targeting?

- **Crime-conducive conditions**. What conditions exist that contribute to the initiation, development, and expansion of crime–
  - What specific resources or commodities are available and attractive to criminals?
  - What locations are vulnerable to criminals?
  - What security gaps exist that could create vulnerabilities to criminal behavior (such as systems, procedures, and physical security measures)?

- **Enforcement gaps and enforcement mechanisms**. What enforcement gaps are present and what assets are available? Are gaps present or imminent due to movement or elimination of an asset or capability? Do these enforcement mechanisms include–
  - Local security or police forces?
  - Guards?
  - Response forces (such as special response teams, civilian police special weapons units, and military and paramilitary response forces)?
  - Informal religious, ethnic, or family structures and influence?
  - Organized criminal elements?
  - Multinational or interagency organizations?
  - Informal social authorities?

POLICE DEVELOPMENT AND TRANSITION TEAMS

2-5. PIO, when properly resourced and conducted, provides an invaluable tool to U.S. Army commanders at all echelons and to the military police forces that support them. In operations where building police capacity and capability is a key measure of effectiveness, it is imperative to train and resource the developing host nation police and security forces so that they can also leverage the ability to connect people to locations and events, while at the same time recognizing trends, patterns, and associations. Military police and USACIDC personnel working in, or in support of, police development and transition teams (PDTTs) not only train host nation police and security forces to conduct police intelligence activities, but also place them in an advantageous position to gain information about the police force, criminal environment, and other information about the population in which the host nation police operate.

2-6. Military police conducting missions to build host nation police capability and capacity will likely be required to engage in the vetting, hiring, training, leading, and safeguarding of new police forces (often across a widely dispersed AO). These new police forces may be manned by some former police who may wish to return to their previous modes of operation to increase personal wealth and influence. There may also be criminal or insurgent elements that infiltrate newly forming police organizations for the same reasons or to carry out direct attacks on U.S. military and host nation police forces. The ability to conduct effective PIO will be a critical task in these situations.

Integrating Police Intelligence Activities

2-7. There is no single doctrinal template for how forces engaged in building police capacity and capability should be organized for their mission. The organization of forces will be determined by mission assignments, the current OE, and what forces are available to theater-level commanders. If PDTTs are determined to be the commander's main effort, then resources may be more robust; however, the force will always be constrained by resource availability. Regardless of resource constraints, military police conducting or supporting PDTTs are in a unique position to observe, interact, and gain significant information on the host nation police they support.

2-8. In the context of PIO, PDTTs support separate but complementing requirements. These requirements are to–

- Report passive observations and deliberately collected information to their chains of command and technical channels for analysis and integration into the operations process.
- Train and build host nation policing capability to conduct police intelligence activities in support of internal police and criminal investigative missions.

2-9. PDTTs working side by side with their host nation counterparts gain access to information regarding the personnel, systems, infrastructure, customs, and disposition of the police and the population they serve. It also enables military police to assess the criminal environment of the host nation with a level of detail and insight not typically available to U.S. Soldiers. Although building a police intelligence capability in host nation police organizations is typically not the first priority of police development and transition teams, it is important to lay the groundwork for police intelligence capability through the identification and task organization of all available resources that can support PIO in the host nation organization. When a police intelligence capability is present in host nation police organizations, U.S. military police forces will benefit from the host nation effort by virtue of their organizational oversight and information sharing.

Building Host Nation Police Intelligence Capability

2-10. Building host nation police intelligence capability and capacity requires a detailed assessment of the host nation police organization, followed by the training and mentoring of host nation police personnel by military police Soldiers and multinational and civilian LE personnel supporting police development and transition teams. As U.S. military police units conduct police development and transition activities with host nation security forces to build police capacity and capability, a careful mission analysis is required to determine the current training and status of the host nation forces. Some OEs may have intact host nation police organizations with significant existing capabilities to conduct policing and investigative activities (to include PIO) in the population. Others may have limited or no existing capability and capacity.

2-11. It is important to accurately assess these capabilities and capacities. Failure to properly identify existing capabilities can result in wasted resources and time to build what is already available. Also, if adequate capability exists, U.S. forces can alienate host nation personnel or be seen as condescending toward the host nation population. PDTTs should take care to properly assess and assist host nation police with legitimate requirements and avoid preconceived notions of host nation limitations. This action requires a significant cultural understanding, close coordination and interaction with host nation police personnel, and a robust PIO effort on the part of military police and USACIDC elements early in an operation to accurately assess police capabilities and capacities to arrive at an accurate assessment of gaps in those capabilities.

2-12. The ability of host nation police to support and conduct the full range of police intelligence activities and enabling tasks may be limited by personnel education and training, available resources, societal norms, host nation legal systems, and tactical environments. For example, in some societies, taking a photograph of a person is generally not accepted. These populations could be expected to resist being photographed or having an iris scan taken. In other areas and societies, many of the modalities of biometrics and forensic analysis may not be understood and, therefore, will not be acceptable. A history of abuse of police power in a host nation can adversely affect development of police intelligence capability. Deliberate police engagements with prospective leaders of emerging police forces are vital in establishing a hierarchy of available and planned police intelligence capabilities.

Organizing Police Intelligence Operations in Police Development and Transition Teams

2-13. PDTTs working to build a host nation police capability and capacity require a coordinated and synchronized effort across the entire AO. They are typically employed by assigning individual PDTTs to specific police stations or organizations. The teams are arrayed in a manner that maintains the integrity of military police squads, platoons, and companies. Command and control of these elements is typically retained in a functional military police battalion and brigade chain of command. Functional alignment of PDTTs in a military police chain of command ensures synchronized and consistent application of policy, operational decisions, training, uniform standards, and applications of police and criminal investigative capability across the entire AO. FM 3-39 discusses military police task organization and criteria that would warrant functional versus decentralized command and control of military police forces.

2-14. Centralized functional alignment and reporting in a functional military police battalion or brigade provides a consistent, synchronized, and comprehensive focus and allows military police staff and police intelligence analysts the ability to collate police information collected across the AO, thus enabling the analysis and identification of trends, patterns, and associations vital to understanding civil considerations in the OE as they pertain to the criminal and security environment. This enables the identification of problem areas, specific I&W, and informed decisionmaking.

2-15. Military police units maintain and facilitate communications in their assigned military chain of command. PDTT mission boundaries will often cross or be embedded in the AOs of multiple maneuver units (and possibly across host nation police or governmental boundaries). Coordination of PDTT activities crossing unit boundaries is critical to the protection of U.S. and host nation elements. Further, this coordination synchronizes the PIO efforts of PDTT elements to support the IR of maneuver commanders across multiple AOs. Military police Soldiers conducting PIO in support of PDTTs should aggressively conduct coordination with all operational elements in the area to ensure that IR are synchronized and relevant information and police intelligence is shared appropriately.

2-16. When implementing a police intelligence collection plan and subsequent staff and analysis, the experience and training of the force available must be considered. The amount of L&O and police intelligence analytical experience that military police units bring to the AO or to a PDTT mission may vary greatly. Military police commanders can enhance their organic capability through formal and informal associations, including task organization changes, cross-unit partnerships, multinational partnerships, and other programs (including the LE Professionals Program and support from civilian police officers). Reserve and National Guard military police units often have a high percentage of civilian police officers who may have years or even decades of investigative and analytical experience. Although most common in military police units, there may also be civilian police officers in other reserve component organizations who may be detailed to help with PDTT missions. Commanders should identify unique skills and capabilities in their ranks of assigned and attached reserve component Soldiers and civilian and multinational police personnel early in any mission or operation to ensure optimum employment of critical capabilities.

2-17. A strong forensic analysis capability with forensic laboratory support is required for successful host nation police intelligence activities. If not available at the commencement of PDTT support, this area should be addressed early to ensure a viable host nation capability. Military police, USACIDC, and other U.S. elements conducting PIO have access to forensic laboratories, either CONUS-based or via expeditionary forensic facilities in the theater of operations. These facilities may also support host nation requirements until a host nation capability is developed.

ADDITIONAL POLICE INTELLIGENCE CAPABILITIES SUPPORTING LAW AND ORDER OPERATIONS

2-18. PIO integrated within L&O operations and the other military police functions provides a unique capability that readily transitions from major combat operations (MCO) to stability operations and the civil security and civil support lines of operation. Police intelligence capabilities integrated within maneuver and other multifunctional headquarters can enable near-real-time actionable police intelligence for tactical commanders. Fusion cells and activities can provide relevant information and police intelligence applicable across all levels of war. (Chapter 6 provides specific information on police intelligence fusion.) LE professionals integrated within multifunctional headquarters elements and the Criminal Investigation Task Force are examples of specific PIO capabilities supporting commanders in support of full spectrum operations.

Law Enforcement Professionals

2-19. The Law Enforcement Professionals Program embeds a police intelligence capability directly into corps, division, brigade combat team, battalion, and company headquarters to assist commanders. This program provides expertise and methodology to understand, identify, target, interdict, and suppress criminal networks or threats using criminal enterprises and techniques to facilitate operations. Typically, embedded LE professionals are civilian or Army investigators with extensive background and experience in complex criminal investigations (civilian investigators are used when requirements exceed U.S. Army LE capacity). These experts are assigned in the PM section to support L&O planning and police intelligence fusion and integration and provide advice to the command on collection and targeting missions. LE professionals are managed by the Office of the Provost Marshal General and integrated by the echelon PM.

2-20. LE professionals ideally join a maneuver formation before deployment to gain a better understanding of unit tactics, techniques, and procedures and standing operating procedures (SOPs). They provide an understanding of criminal networks and tactics, techniques, and procedures to identify networks, key individuals in the network, and methods for analyzing and building evidence for targeting and/or criminal prosecution. LE professionals coordinate closely with USACIDC personnel, PM sections, military police commanders and staff, MI personnel, host nation police and security, and forensic labs. They can provide expert advice on processing incident sites and crime scenes to identify, collect, and protect valuable evidence, such as forensic and biometric data. They can also train other personnel on the proper handling and packaging of critical evidence and assist Soldiers with understanding the requirements for valid and accurate forensic analyses.

Criminal Investigation Task Force

2-21. The Department of Defense Criminal Investigation Task Force (CITF) is a strategic-level organization with a mission to develop and fuse police intelligence with MI for the purpose of building criminal cases against terrorist criminals that have attacked U.S. interests. The organization conducts complicated criminal investigations targeting terrorists and complex criminal organizations. These cases typically cross international borders and involve criminals captured as a result of military operations, requiring coordination with international police and intelligence agencies.

CITF Capability in Support of the Operational Effort

CITF agents and analysts working with a task force were preparing criminal cases against detainees. The cases supported the task force's focus on identifying those responsible for the Mosul Chow Hall bombing and eliminating the Al Qaida cell in Mosul. Analysts began to prepare link analysis diagrams of the cell and its connections. Meanwhile, CITF agents received a request from another unit to help them prepare a criminal case against a foreign fighter detained in Fallujah. While interviewing the foreign fighter, CITF agents determined that he was a Mosul cell member who had been sent to Fallujah. The foreign fighter was wounded while fighting and abandoned. He was angry with his companions for leaving him and agreed to provide information about the Fallujah cell. With his help, the task force was able to identify the cell structure, safe houses, cache locations, and other information about the Mosul cell, to include its Emir and the chief bombmaker. As a result of the investigators' ability to link the captured fighter with ongoing enemy activities, the task force began detaining members of the cell. The foreign fighter was presented to an investigative judge for the Central Criminal Courts of Iraq and provided complete information on the cell and its activities. Using link analysis diagrams, CITF agents were able to obtain confessions from other cell members, who were also presented to the investigative judge. As a result of the operation, the Emir of the cell, along with several other members, was killed during the raids. The remaining members, including the master bombmaker, were detained and presented to the investigative judge. CITF agents were able to identify insurgent videos of bombing operations that were tied to the bombmaker and the cell. This evidence was presented to the investigative judge, who charged the men who were later convicted. Sentences for the cell members, including the foreign fighter, ranged from 15 years to death.

2-22. The CITF combines USACIDC special agents (and criminal investigators from other Services), police and intelligence analysts, and attorneys into teams. These teams synchronize and fuse information and intelligence from all available sources to conduct criminal investigations that enable criminal prosecution in U.S. or host nation legal systems.

INTERNMENT AND RESETTLEMENT OPERATIONS

2-23. *Internment and resettlement* operations are conducted by military police to shelter, sustain, guard, protect, and account for populations (enemy prisoners of war/civilian internees, dislocated civilians, or U.S. military prisoners) as a result of military or civil conflict, natural or man-made disaster, or to facilitate criminal prosecution. Internment involves the detainment of a population or group that pose some level of threat to military operations. Resettlement involves the quartering of a population or group for their protection. These operations inherently control the movement and activities of their specific population for imperative reasons of security, safety, or intelligence gathering. (FM 3-39.40) PIO is integrated into I/R operations to provide information and police intelligence, enabling commanders and military police staff to maintain a safe and secure environment for detainees, DCs, and personnel supporting I/R operations.

2-24. PIO integrated within I/R operations can also provide critical information and police intelligence to MI personnel regarding associations and patterns identified through analyses of information by police intelligence analysts. This enables MI to further refine their intelligence picture, develop additional IR to support operations, and maintain a holistic COP. See FM 3-39.40 for additional information on I/R operations.

2-25. I/R operations provide a valuable source for criminal information supporting LE efforts and the identification of exploitable information supporting other full spectrum operations. Military police Soldiers, by virtue of their I/R mission, are in a position to gather information and physical evidence for exploitation by operational elements and in support of LE investigations throughout the detention process. Current (and likely future) OEs increasingly require criminal prosecution of detainees captured in the conduct of full spectrum operations. Military police personnel should be integrated into detainee processing as close to the point of capture as possible. This facilitates operational exploitation and follow-on LE investigations (as required). If military police integration at the point of capture is not possible, military police oversight is required (at a minimum) at the first detainee processing point after the point of capture (typically a detainee holding area). The integration of military police Soldiers conducting I/R and integrated PIO as close to the point of capture as feasible enables Army LE and police intelligence analysts to–

- Identify police-related information early in the operation.
- Preserve and report potential police information (to include forensic and biometric data) and criminal evidence quickly.
- Analyze collected information and produce actionable police intelligence.
- Disseminate information and police intelligence for integration into the operations process and LE investigations.

2-26. PIO provides the ability for military police Soldiers, LE investigators, and police intelligence analysts to connect persons to other individuals, organizations, objects, and events relevant to the criminal domain. These associations may be relevant to incidents inside an I/R facility; however, they may also associate the individual with persons outside the I/R facility and events that may have occurred before detention. These associations can be especially relevant during counterinsurgency operations. For example, military police Soldiers in one area may obtain evidence from a crime scene that implicates a detainee at a U.S. or host nation detention facility. This may be confirmed through detention facility biometric enrollment data. This confirmation may result in a request for additional information on the detainee, initiating a follow-on interrogation by either MI (for HUMINT interrogation) or Army LE investigators (for LE interrogation supporting a criminal investigation). Military police Soldiers in a facility may find evidence connected to another person or incident outside the facility. This information would be documented, secured, and passed through the chain of command to the appropriate supporting MI unit and/or Army LE element for additional action and investigation.

SAFETY AND SECURITY

2-27. PIO is critical to maintaining good order and discipline in detention facilities. I/R operations are inherently risky due to the high density of detainees or refugees and relatively low numbers of guard personnel supporting operations. PIO in the I/R environment supports the commanders risk management efforts (see FM 5-19). Detainees may benefit from a break down in good order and discipline in facilities and take steps to facilitate that process. To limit or prevent cooperation with U.S. authorities, detainees may attempt escapes, form organizations and associations to control the internal workings of a facility, or intimidate other detainees. Military police commanders and staff responsible for these facilities must continuously collect information and conduct thorough and ongoing analyses to identify and counter these activities and the associated risks.

2-28. In a facility, military police Soldiers will have extensive contact and visibility with detainees. The effort to maintain good order and discipline requires cooperation across functional lines. Military police commanders and staff should ensure that personnel supporting I/R operations from other functional specialties are briefed to be alert to activities, writings, or conversations that can fulfill IR for the commander and staff. Critical information can be obtained through coordination and information sharing with MI HUMINT teams. Medical personnel will treat injured and sick detainees and can provide observations regarding detainee behavior, interaction, or spontaneous statements. Engineers will perform repairs on damaged facilities and note changes in other physical characteristics. Host nation and U.S. interpreters will be in a position to hear detainee conversations, read graffiti, and screen inbound and outbound mail. All of these interactions are opportunities to gather information that could enhance a commander's understanding of the AO. A debriefing program should be established and followed to ensure that observations by personnel are documented and passed to military police staff and police intelligence analysts for evaluation and analysis.

2-29. Resettlement operations are conducted to provide safety and security for DCs. Unlike internment operations, DCs are not typically detained against their will. Resettlement facilities, however, can manifest some of the same safety and security issues inherent in internment operations. Any facility housing hundreds or thousands of individuals in a confined space is likely to experience safety and security issues. These situations may be a result of anger and frustration on the part of individuals under significant amounts of stress. These situations may also be the result of criminal elements in the population seeking to intimidate or exploit their fellow DCs. In some operations, "blacklisted" personnel may infiltrate the DC population. Regardless, the same techniques employed to identify individual criminals, counter criminal elements, and enable criminal investigations in internment facilities are useful in the context of resettlement facilities.

CRIMINAL INVESTIGATIONS

2-30. Police information and police intelligence can help Army LE investigators to develop patterns and criminal associations in a facility. This can lead to identification and documentation of criminal behavior and individual perpetrators. This information and police intelligence also enables the commander and military police staff to identify criminal groups forming in the facility and to take steps to interdict these groups before serious breaches of security occur. Information collected and police intelligence produced may also be valuable to Army LE investigators conducting criminal investigations focused on crimes within and outside the facility. PIO can link detainees in the facility to crimes, criminals, and activities outside the facility. This enables Army LE investigators and police intelligence analysts to further develop their understanding of the criminal environment, key players, and associations, thus allowing investigators to focus their efforts more effectively.

2-31. Commanders may also direct criminal investigations concerning events in a facility. These events may include a variety of serious criminal infractions, to include attacks on other detainees or U.S. personnel, contraband smuggling, and escape attempts. Care must be taken to recognize, preserve, collect, and process items with evidentiary value. Once collected, this evidence is packaged and forwarded to a supporting forensic lab for further examination and analysis.

INTELLIGENCE SUPPORT

2-32. Doctrine and legal requirements call for close cooperation between MI and military police personnel during all I/R operations, especially during detainee operations. This tenet of I/R operations ensures the maximum benefit to the commander and the mission and that U.S. forces stay within the limits of U.S. and international laws and treaties (see FM 3-39.40 for more information). Due to the extensive contact and visibility military police Soldiers and support personnel maintain with detainees, they become recipients of large amounts of information. This information is collected passively through activity observations, contraband or writing (such as notes and graffiti) discoveries, and overheard conversations. These observations are reported through the chain of command and collated by staff and police intelligence analysts. Simultaneously, this information is passed to the supporting MI personnel through intelligence channels. This sharing of information enables MI personnel to capitalize on passively collected information, further enhancing their ability to form a coherent picture of the environment. Information collected and passed through the intelligence channels is also passed through operational channels to contribute to the Army operations process.

MANEUVER AND MOBILITY SUPPORT OPERATIONS

2-33. *Maneuver and mobility support* is a military police function conducted to support and preserve the commander's freedom of movement and enhance the movement of friendly resources in all environments. (FM 3-39) Military police conducting MMS operations are arrayed across the AO. By virtue of this dispersion, they are capable of observing and collecting significant information relevant to policing and LE operations. This dispersion of military police Soldiers regularly places military police in close contact with U.S. and host nation personnel and offers substantial opportunities for police engagement and information collection. This information is collated and analyzed by military police staff and police intelligence analysts.

2-34. Throughout MMS operations, military police engage and observe the local population and environment. Military police Soldiers understand the commander's intent and the key actions required for operational success. They are also aware of the enemy and criminal threats that could have an impact on that success. By viewing, and subsequently reporting, these environmental and social conditions from a policing viewpoint, Soldiers can enhance a commander's situational awareness. Early collection of information regarding police and prison systems, organizations, and capabilities; identification of key host nation personnel; and assessments of the criminal environment enable enhanced situational understanding and shape civil security and civil control operations.

2-35. PIO integrated into MMS planning and execution enables more informed decisionmaking by commanders, military police staff, Soldiers, and leaders conducting MMS missions. Police intelligence products may identify areas of substantial criminal activity. This situational understanding enables commanders to make prudent decisions regarding the security of convoys transiting the areas or may drive military police to locate and recommend alternate routes to bypass areas of significant risk in conjunction with movement control staffs. Information and police intelligence regarding locations, capability, and disposition of host nation police and security elements can be critical to military police conducting MMS, enabling them to plan for host nation response forces and potential safe havens. It can also identify host nation police elements that may be infiltrated by criminal or insurgent elements, arming personnel with the knowledge to avoid those locations and to exercise caution when interaction is required.

2-36. Populace and resource control operations place military police Soldiers in regular contact with the populace and significant amounts of potentially valuable police information. Military police conducting these tasks may receive police information regarding persons wanted for crimes or questioning. Their continual interaction with the population can facilitate the collection of biometric and background data on persons that can later be compared against databases of other biometric data, enabling the identification and location discovery of persons of interest.

AREA SECURITY OPERATIONS

2-37. *Area security* is a form of security operation conducted to protect friendly forces, installation routes, and actions within a specific area. (FM 3-90) Military police units perform AS to protect the force and to enhance freedom of action for units to conduct assigned missions. The mobility and communications capabilities of military police units make it possible for them to detect threat elements and rapidly report these contacts. AS missions place military police elements in the position to frequently observe and make contact with the local population, facilitating police engagements and information collection. PIO integrated throughout AS mission results in significant collection opportunities and the provision of critical information to satisfy IR and increase situational understanding. Military police are typically one of the first to respond to incidents in an AO, particularly in sustainment areas. The knowledge of military police Soldiers in evidence collection and preservation at incident sites can be critical to protecting key police information for future analysis.

2-38. Military police elements observe the area around them at all times and remain aware that changes in the anticipated social order may be indicators of enemy action or coercion. Military police conducting AS operations will seek out host nation police and security elements operating in their assigned AO. This facilitates the collection of data pertaining to civil considerations, specifically focused on the variables of POLICE. Military police Soldiers will identify police locations, to include data that enables military police staff and police intelligence analysts to–

- Assess police capability and capacity.
- Conduct crime and criminal analyses.
- Recognize crime-conducive conditions.
- Identify enforcement gaps and mechanisms.

2-39. Military police patrols may also identify indications of criminal activity. This data, when reported through the chain of command, contributes to overall situational understanding and enables the staff and analyst to identify patterns and activities that indicate the existence of organized criminal activity or areas of significant criminal activity.

2-40. Police intelligence analysis allows military police staff, Soldiers, and leaders conducting AS missions to plan and execute measures to counter the effects of criminal activity on military operations. These countermeasures may include–

- Implementing vulnerability assessments.
- Developing procedures to detect terrorist actions before they occur.
- Hardening likely targets.
- Conducting offensive operations to destroy an enemy.
- Identifying high-threat areas and recommending bypass routes.

2-41. Military police units use checkpoints and roadblocks to control the movement of vehicles, personnel, and materiel and to prevent illegal actions that may aid the enemy. These control measures serve as a deterrent to terrorist activities, saboteurs, and other threats. Similar to MMS considerations, information and police intelligence regarding locations, capability, and disposition of host nation police and security elements can enhance AS operations and identify friendly capabilities and host nation police elements that may be infiltrated by criminal or insurgent elements.

Chapter 3

Integration Into the Operations Process

Commanders must understand how current and potential threats organize, equip, and employ their forces. They also need to understand the host nation police and security forces operating in the AO when nation building and stability operations are required. PIO is a military police function that supports, enhances, and contributes to a commander's situational understanding and development of a holistic COP. It consists of activities that are integrated within all military police operations. Results of PIO are continually propagated into the COP and the operations process. The operations process is the context in which military police capabilities are integrated into combined arms application. This chapter provides discussion of how PIO, integrated in all military police operations, is integrated into the Army operations process. It also provides information on PIO applications in the context of the three levels of war and support to unified action.

POLICE INTELLIGENCE OPERATIONS ACTIVITIES

3-1. PIO uses the Army intelligence process to execute activities required to generate information, products, and knowledge that will enhance the situational understanding of the police and criminal environment and guide policing activities in the OE. The intelligence process is comprised of five activities: generate knowledge, plan, prepare, collect, and produce (see FM 2-0 and figure 3-1, page 3-2).

3-2. There are three major points of differentiation between the specific application of PIO and the general application of the intelligence process. The first point is the LE and policing focus of PIO and its application of technical policing and investigative systems, technologies, and processes to analyze data and information with an objective to understand the criminal and police or security environments. This point enables focused policing operations and activities. The second point is the application of PIO by military police and USACIDC Soldiers, operating as LE, which allows for the collection of information related to criminal investigations and not restricted in the same manner as the intelligence community (non-LE) in regard to U.S. persons. Finally, PIO is not a military intelligence discipline. PIO activities are LE functions conducted in the operations section and conducted by operational elements. PIO staff and analysts coordinate and synchronize their activities and share LE information (within mission and legal constraints) with G-2 or S-2 elements.

3-3. Throughout the intelligence process (conducted in the context of PIO), Soldiers analyze, assess, and propagate information and police intelligence. These three integrating activities, performed continuously and simultaneously, occur throughout the conduct of all five base activities in the process. The process is not linear or sequential; information and police intelligence are continuously injected. Similarly, information and police intelligence are continuously pushed into the Army operations process to complement and enhance integrating processes (such as IPB, targeting, ISR synchronization [and its related integration], CRM, and KM) and to military police and USACIDC organizations to enable focused planning operations. This makes PIO fluid and demands continual analysis, assessment, and propagation of police information and intelligence as additional collected information shapes situational understanding. PIO contributes to the commander's situational understanding, enhances the COP, and adds critical police information to the intelligence process. See FM 2-0 for a detailed discussion of the intelligence process.

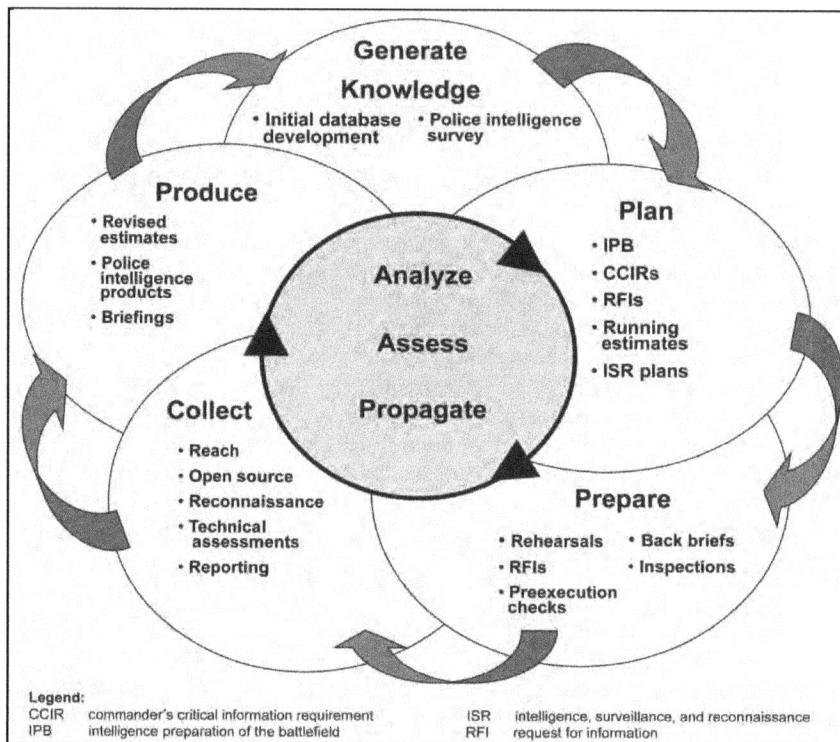

Figure 3-1. Police intelligence operations activities

3-4. PIO is conducted in support of posts, camps, stations, and throughout full spectrum operations. The process is the same regardless of the environment. Differences in execution primarily relate to the collection and sharing of police information and police intelligence to ensure compliance with U.S. laws. During LE operations on U.S military installations, the PM, through his operations staff, executes and manages PIO in support of L&O operations. USACIDC personnel conduct PIO at group and battalion levels, according to the USACIDC Criminal Intelligence Program. USACIDC elements are austere, but possess a limited ability to conduct PIO. USACIDC elements depend on the USACIDC groups and battalions for extensive PIO support.

3-5. Military police staffs and PM sections at all levels perform PIO activities to varying degrees, depending on mission requirements, personnel and capabilities available, and commander's guidance. The focus at any echelon is dependent on the specific mission, commander's intent, investigative requirements, and CCIR. At the company level, application of PIO is extremely limited, focusing on current and projected tactical missions. At the brigade level and higher, PIO focus is broader, addressing operational and strategic concerns affecting an entire AO.

3-6. In functional military police brigades and battalions, the S-3 is responsible for the day-to-day conduct of PIO and ensuring that the basic PIO activities are implemented and support the commander's intent and information requirements. This includes ensuring that PIO is fully integrated within all military police operations and synchronized with the operations process. The S-3 works closely with the S-2 to ensure this synchronization. In multifunctional organizations, the PIO process is managed by the PM section, operating as part of the G-3 or S-3. In these organizations, the PM section ensures that the PIO process is synchronized with other staff processes. The continuous flow of collected police information and intelligence enables a fused intelligence picture and provides constant input to the operations process and its integrating processes. The five activities that comprise PIO are explained in the following paragraphs.

GENERATE KNOWLEDGE

3-7.   Generating knowledge refers to actions aimed at gathering and collating information to support operations planning and execution. It is performed continuously in an effort to understand the AO in which military police and USACIDC elements will operate. Generating knowledge is driven by the commander and begins at or before receipt of a mission to build a base of relevant knowledge of the OE required for planning and conducting operations. The generating knowledge process should begin as early as possible, in some cases when only the general location or category of a mission for a projected operation is known. This process lays the foundational base and situational understanding on which future PIO is built. Knowledge generation includes information on the OE (threat, civil considerations, terrain, and weather). It also fills knowledge gaps regarding mission requirements and functional capabilities available to the unit. Knowledge sources may include in-theater and reachback capability; existing databases, open-source information, academia, and research organizations; after-action reviews; and coordination with U.S. and multinational elements with relevant information.

3-8.   The initial actions taken to generate knowledge result in the creation and population of data files directed by the commander and assessed by the staff. This data is the basis of information on which future collection and analysis are built. The military police, USACIDC, and PM staff (including police intelligence) analysts assess the OE to determine what information is required for collection, based on the mission set and known characteristics of the OE. This initial data build focuses on supporting command requirements, the IPB, and answering CCIRs and other IR. PIO typically will focus on civil considerations specifically relating to the police and criminal environment using the variables of POLICE. These variables are discussed in detail in chapter 2.

3-9.   Generating knowledge is a continuous process. Many factors can drive the requirement to update baseline knowledge, to include current operations, higher operations, results of police intelligence analysis or assessments, changes in missions, and changes in the OE. Significant changes in the OE can include many factors, such as political and/or election results, shifts in influence on a population or region (including the effects of informal groups, such as tribal, criminal, or insurgent groups), changes to police and prison infrastructure, changes to capabilities organizations and systems affecting the police and security environment, and events outside the unit's projected AO that may impact operations. During a deployment, a unit's information database becomes a source of information for follow-on units to complete the generating knowledge step. During and after deployment, the generate knowledge step also supports the collection of lessons learned data. Generating knowledge is the precursor for conducting IPB and mission analysis and is also the basis for developing the initial police intelligence survey.

PLAN

3-10. Staff planning develops the means to support the commander's concept of operations and intent. Planning in the context of PIO consists of the activities that identify relevant IR and develop the means to collect information to satisfy those requirements. Planners review the CCIR, set priorities, and provide guidance for the management of collection or interdiction assets. Consideration is given to identifying what, where, when, who, and why.

3-11. Military police and USACIDC planners preparing for PIO must rapidly access information and conduct collaboration and information sharing with other units and organizations across the OE. This planning includes reaching forward while preparing to deploy and making full use of reachback capability from the AO to ensure that planners and analysts have a clear picture of the OE before arrival and throughout operations. The situation in one AO will likely have an effect on other adjacent AOs. Knowledge of the broader operational area will provide insights for a particular AO as well.

3-12. Planning results in identified police information requirements which, in turn, may become CCIR. The commander's intent, planning guidance, and CCIR drive the planning of PIO. The CCIRs (PIR and friendly force information requirement) drive the planning of the ISR effort and establish priorities for the management of collection assets. The G-3 or S-3, the PM, and the G-2 or S-2 must work closely to ensure that the police information collection plan is synchronized and integrated with the ISR effort at all echelons (based on staff planning) to achieve the desired collection results. Military police or USACIDC assets with specific collection capabilities or knowledge to perform collection activities are also identified. PIO planning activities include–

- Participating in IPB.
- Identifying and managing police information requirements.
- Preparing the police information collection plan.
- Establishing guidelines in the commander's intent to focus collectors.
- Disseminating CCIR and police information requirements to subordinate units and collection assets.
- Providing input and continuous updates to military police running estimates.
- Identifying appropriate collection assets.
- Reviewing intelligence flow to synchronize tasks and resources.
- Evaluating collected and reported information.
- Establishing the communications and dissemination architecture.
- Providing input (in the form of a police information collection plan) and coordinating the development and revision of the intelligence synchronization plan and the ISR plan as mission requirements change.
- Establishing debriefing procedures to gather collected information (this includes debriefing patrols with no deliberate collection mission to gain information gathered during the execution of normal operations).
- Participating in crime prevention program analyses, law enforcement and/or threat working groups, fusion cells, and other applicable meetings and venues. (Chapter 6 provides discussion on working groups, fusion cells, and interagency coordination.)

Developing the Police Information Collection Plan

3-13. Prioritized information requirements are used to develop a police information collection plan. The police information collection plan is prepared based on specific police IR, commander's guidance, available collection assets, and other factors (including time and self-protection). The plan is developed to document and prioritize information requirements and assign against collection assets. Identifying and evaluating potential collection resources is critical to the collection plan. Potential collection assets should be evaluated for availability, capability, and reliability.

3-14. Information requirements are filled through a number of methods and capabilities. Collection to fulfill information requirements may result from deliberate tactical reconnaissance and surveillance (R&S) efforts, LE surveillance, active police engagement by either tactical or LE patrols, and passive observation and collection during the execution of other military police functions. They may also occur through coordination and liaison with other military units (U.S. and multinational), including civil affair and other elements conducting reconnaissance, other LE agencies, and NGOs. Military police Soldiers, USACIDC personnel, or civilian LE professionals supporting U.S. forces may also conduct technical assessments based on unique technical training, equipment, knowledge, and capabilities. Information derived from biometric identity data and forensic examinations can be used to fill information requirements and provide critical data needed to complete analyses and form relevant and accurate police intelligence.

3-15. The missions that are to be tasked to respective collectors must be determined. Information collectors can typically be tasked with more than one mission at a time. However, it is imperative that their tasks be prioritized, based on mission requirements and available time. Organic assets are generally more responsive; however, capabilities beyond the scope of organic military police or USACIDC assets may be required. Regardless, appropriate tasking orders or requests must be issued to request collection assets or capability beyond those organic to the initiating command. When issuing tasking orders or requests, the following must be specified–

- The collection objectives.
- The specific collection tasks (PIR with indicators) and where to look (named areas of interest [NAIs]).
- The start and termination times for collection or surveillance operations and the time the information is needed.
- The reporting procedures (such as to whom, how often, and on what frequency net to report).
- The location and activity of other elements operating in the AO.
- The identification and coordination for linguists or special skills personnel, such as civilian or host nation police, engineers, psychological operations personnel, civil affairs personnel, MI personnel, or reconnaissance assets.
- Other necessary information bearing on operations in the AO.

Identifying Collection Assets

3-16. The commander or PM, supported by the operations staff, selects and prepares collection assets, based on their capabilities and limitations. Military police and USACIDC Soldiers are trained collectors and highly adaptable to any collection plan. These Soldiers operate in direct contact with the local population, allowing them to identify, assess, and interact with potential sources of information. Military police personnel can also effectively collect information as a deliberate collection mission or concurrent with the conduct of other missions and functions. Information can be collected actively (through direct observation and/or engagement with target personnel) or passively (by observing and listening to the surrounding environment and personnel). These collection activities span all environments and spectrums, from routine and relatively stable environments associated with LE in support of posts, camps, and stations to the extreme instability of the MCO.

3-17. On military installations, military police and USACIDC personnel are the lead for targeting, collecting, and interdicting against a broad range of threat activities, including terrorism, organized crime, contraband trafficking, and other illegal activities. Collection of police information in this environment is conducted by military police and USACIDC assets through deliberate surveillance missions or through missions tasked to LE patrols and conducted in the course of their routine patrol or investigative activities.

3-18. In support of full spectrum operations, military police personnel may be tasked as the primary collectors of information on enemy forces operating along extended LOCs and on MSRs, or in support of a movement corridor (see FM 3-90.31). During this time, the priority of effort for military police units may be focused on MMS and AS operations. Concurrent with the requirements to collect information in support of identified IR, personnel conduct police information collection supporting PIO. This information collection, pertinent to the police and criminal environment, facilitates the transition to stability operations and the establishment and maintenance of civil security and civil control. As the dominant operation transitions from offense and defense associated with MCO to stability operations, the weighted focus for military police units typically shifts from MMS and AS to L&O and possibly I/R operations. Military police and USACIDC personnel will typically increase PIO efforts during stability operations to focus support to host nation police and internment and corrections activities. USACIDC elements will increase documentation of threat criminal activity identified during military operations in preparation for potential criminal prosecution. During stability operations, technical police collection and assessment efforts increase significantly.

3-19. Missions that may result in police information collection opportunities include –

- Deliberate collection missions–
  - Route R&S.
  - Area and zone reconnaissance.
  - LE surveillance.

- Tactical missions where concurrent deliberate or passive collection may be executed–
  - Tactical patrols (mounted and dismounted).
  - LE patrols (mounted and dismounted).
  - Cordon-and-search operations.
  - Checkpoints and roadblocks.
  - Traffic control points.
  - Entry control points.
  - Interactions with local officials and the populace.
  - Detainee operations.
  - DC operations.
  - Site exploitation.
- Routine LE and security missions–
  - LE raids.
  - Field interviews.
  - Corrections and detention operations.
  - Emergency response activities.
  - Criminal investigations.
  - Interviews and interrogations.
  - Access control operations.
  - Physical security inspections.

3-20. Staffs at battalion level and higher will also prepare a synchronization matrix. The synchronization matrix is a tool to manage collection assets across time and space (location) to ensure coverage of all priority IR and to eliminate unnecessary redundancy. The synchronization matrix will also be used to deconflict and integrate ISR with adjacent units and units operating in the same AO (to include LE agencies).

3-21. After a thorough evaluation of the availability, capability, and disposition of the potential collection resources, elements possessing the appropriate collection assets and capability are tasked according to the collection plan and associated synchronization matrix. Military police and USACIDC staff and leaders recommend which asset or assets are most suitable to perform a particular collection mission. A good collection strategy answers the following questions–

- Are organic military police or USACIDC Soldiers the best collectors for this mission?
- Are special-skilled personnel required? If so, who?
  - Are there other military police or USACIDC technical capabilities available through reachback or other support mechanisms?
  - Are other U.S military, interagency, or multinational assets available? Are they potentially better collectors?
  - Are linguists, MI, engineer, civil affairs, or other specialized assets required?
- Is specialized equipment required? If so, what kind and how many?
- Should the collection effort be conducted while Soldiers are performing other military police functions (such as MMS, AS, or L&O)?
- Can (or should) the collection be done by non-LE personnel?

3-22. An important part of collection planning includes ensuring that coordination across all stakeholders is completed before initiating the collection mission. Possible stakeholders, beyond military police and USACIDC assets, include the SJA and other LE agencies operating in the AO. This coordination will help eliminate duplication of effort, interference with an ongoing effort, or violations of legal limitations. In a deployed OE, coordination and synchronization is conducted with the G-2 or S-2, and the terrain manager must be notified of activities in their AO to ensure appropriate responses in emergencies and to reduce the likelihood of fratricide. Notification also increases the likelihood of receiving information that may be critical to the collection effort.

PREPARE

3-23. Preparation includes staff and leader activities that take place on receiving the operation order (OPORD), operation plan (OPLAN), warning order, or commander's intent to improve the unit's ability to execute tasks or missions. Preparation transitions staff, unit, and Soldier actions from the planning to the execution stage.

3-24. Preparation consists of a series of activities that help Soldiers and units improve their ability to execute an operation and create conditions that improve the probability of success. Preparation activities (such as preexecution checks, back briefs, rehearsals, and inspections) help all elements involved to understand their role, practice complicated tasks, and ensure that equipment and weapons function properly.

3-25. An element tasked with a collection mission ensures that appropriate preparation is conducted. Upon being tasked for a collection mission, leaders conduct thorough mission analysis before execution. Leaders of the tasked collection asset plan for a myriad of considerations, to include–

- The method the element will use to get to its assigned area (such as routes, passage points, and boundaries). These locations may include –
  - Friendly elements and suspected threat activity in the area, including friendly elements (such as the nearest medical facilities [to include trauma centers], friendly bases or stations, and response patrols or forces [in the event that a compromise or engagement occurs]).
  - Restricted or danger areas.
  - Call signs and frequencies.
  - Passwords and recognition signals.
  - Movement through friendly AOs.
- Procedures for departing or reentering friendly lines or AOs.
- Fire and close air support—enroute, at the mission location, and on the return.
- Casualty evacuation procedures.

COLLECT

3-26. Collection involves gathering and reporting police information to answer IR and the gathering of relevant data and raw information or existing intelligence products. The collected police information is then available for analysis and subsequent production and dissemination. The goal of any collection effort is to answer specific IR and to produce actionable intelligence. To be effective, collection efforts are generated and driven by the operations process; they must be planned, focused, and directed, based on the CCIR, police intelligence, and investigative requirements.

3-27. Development of a viable collection strategy, including management and supervision of the collection effort, is critical to successful PIO. Military police, USACIDC, or other collection assets collect information and data about criminal or other threats and police systems, infrastructure, processes, capabilities, and resources. Collection may also target and answer IR concerning environmental and geographical characteristics, cultural and ethnic norms, formal and informal authority structures, and other factors affecting policing activities and the criminal environment. A successful PIO effort results in the timely collection and reporting of relevant and accurate information. This collected information is critical to successful compilation of police intelligence databases, enabling analyses of police information, and the production of police intelligence.

3-28. The collection and managing of police information and intelligence is enabled by, and subject to, the laws, regulations, and policies described in appendix C. These documents ensure the proper conduct of PIO. In the United States and its territories, collection of police information and intelligence involving U.S. citizens is limited to LE personnel performing legitimate LE functions. Intelligence personnel are generally restricted from collecting or maintaining information or intelligence on U.S. citizens. While restrictions may be present in an OE where PIO targets individuals other than U.S. persons, the ability to collect and share police intelligence is less restrictive. Restrictions and guidance regarding the collection and maintenance of police information and intelligence may be included in the following–

- USCs.
- Executive orders (EOs).
- National Security Council intelligence directives.

- ARs.
- Status-of-forces agreements (SOFAs).
- ROE.
- Other international laws and directives.

3-29. The success of police information collection depends on skillful management and execution by personnel. When an organization with a collection asset is tasked and receives a collection plan, the commander and unit operations section perform the following–

- Review police information collection plans and identify the collection requirements.
- Implement the plan by–
  - Tasking subordinate collection elements.
  - Establishing guidelines for discretionary decisions regarding police information collection efforts.
- Update the collection plan as necessary.
- Perform police information collection efforts through–
  - Reconnaissance (such as route, zone, area reconnaissance, and technical assessment teams).
  - Surveillance.
  - Interviews and interrogations.
  - Evidence collection (to include forensic and biometric data) and evidence response teams.
  - Coordination and information sharing with adjacent units.
  - Searches of database records.
  - Examinations of statistical records.
  - Reviews of case files.
  - Reviews of administrative data.
  - Open source data. This data can include many sites that cannot be accessed through computers connected to a DOD network, such as social networking or other prohibited sites. Personnel should coordinate with the network manager for specific restrictions. For ongoing mission-essential access, approval for standalone systems connected via civilian service providers may be obtained.
  - Police engagement. This includes patrol interaction with the population; liaison with host nation authorities, military and civilian police agencies, and other organizations; and the exchange of police information with host nation authorities, military and civilian police agencies, and other organizations.

Reporting and Recording Collected Information

3-30. Established debriefing procedures to gather collected information, including debriefing patrols with no deliberate collection mission to gain information gathered during execution of normal operations, is critical to the collection process. Recording and systematically cataloging information obtained by assigned collection assets and routine patrols is critical to the PIO process and may fill important gaps in the overall COP. Police information may be recorded manually or by direct input into an electronic database. The information is compiled for assessment and analysis by the staff and assigned police intelligence analysts. If raw police information or police intelligence derived from rapid analysis of the information is identified, it is fed into the intelligence process (as applicable). Due to the restrictions placed on information gathered on U.S. citizens, police intelligence must be provided to the PM operations section or military police unit S-3 for further action when the AO is in the United States and its territories.

3-31. Recording consists of systematically cataloging the information. At a minimum, recording defines the source of the information, subject, and the time and date the information was collected. Recording information can be performed by writing it down or by entering it into a database system. Databases are discussed further in chapter 5. The information is recorded by the military police or USACIDC staff element responsible for PIO.

3-32. Some information may be of immediate time value and passed without analysis due to time sensitivity or other factors. *Exceptional information* is information that would have answered one of the commander's critical information requirements if the requirement for it had been foreseen and stated as one of the commander's critical information requirements. (FM 6-0) This exceptional information is immediately formatted and disseminated through the appropriate command, staff, and functional LE channels (PM, USACIDC, and interagency LE) for action as appropriate. When in the United States or its territories, due to the restrictions placed on information gathered on U.S. citizens, police intelligence must be maintained within military police, USACIDC, and interagency LE channels. Commanders with responsibility for LE may also be included in police intelligence dissemination when required.

Processing

3-33. Police information processing involves the evaluation of initial information to reduce raw data into manageable portions for analysis and production. Following analysis and production of police intelligence, processing involves an initial evaluation to ensure that the police intelligence is accurate, precise, and relevant. During processing, police information and subsequent police intelligence is prioritized according to current collection and production requirements. Military police and USACIDC staff responsible for managing police information and police intelligence will–

- Prioritize incoming data according to collection and production requirements.
- Organize police information and intelligence by category (such as crime, threat, or police systems and capabilities).
- Organize police information and police intelligence by a particular product or user.
- Enter the information into databases.
- Collate police information and actionable police intelligence into interim products.

PRODUCE

3-34. Production involves combining analyzed police information and intelligence from single or multiple sources into police intelligence or police intelligence products in support of known or anticipated requirements. Production also involves combining new and existing police information and intelligence to produce updated police intelligence that can be used by commanders, PMs, and other members of the staff to revise military police running estimates, apply to the military decisionmaking process (MDMP), and facilitate enhanced situational understanding. During the production phase, military police, USACIDC, or other staff members exploit information by–

- Analyzing the information to isolate significant elements.
- Evaluating the information to determine accuracy, timeliness, usability, completeness, precision, and reliability. It must also be evaluated to determine if it is relevant, predictive, and properly tailored.
- Combining the information with other relevant information and previously developed police intelligence.
- Applying the information to estimate possible outcomes.
- Presenting the information in a format that will be most useful to its user.

3-35. The military police staff deals with numerous and varied production requirements that are based on PIR and IR; diverse missions, environments, and situations; and user format requirements. Through analysis, collaboration, and reachback, military police and USACIDC units or the PM section in other units use the collective analysis and production capability of higher, lateral, and subordinate echelons to meet PIO requirements.

INTEGRATING ACTIVITIES

3-36. Throughout the intelligence process (when applied in the context of PIO), police information is analyzed, assessed, and propagated. These three continuing activities drive and shape the intelligence process, and they are integrated throughout the conduct of PIO activities.

ANALYZE

3-37. *Analysis* is the process by which collected information is evaluated and integrated with existing information to produce intelligence that describes the current—and attempts to predict the future—impact of the threat, terrain and weather, and civil considerations on operations. (Training Circular [TC] 2-33.4) The intelligence staff analyzes intelligence and information about threat capabilities, friendly vulnerabilities, and AO to determine how they will impact operations.

3-38. During police intelligence analysis, police information and raw data become police intelligence. Analysis is based on critical examinations of all available and relevant information to determine capabilities and trends and to develop predictive analysis for the police and criminal environments and specific criminal threats. The police intelligence analyst specifically analyzes police information and data and conducts predictive analysis in an effort to–

- Determine the COA that a specific criminal threat is likely to take, enabling commanders, PMs, and investigators to identify possible friendly COAs to counter the threat.
- Predict crime trends in an AO, based on extrapolation of statistical crime data, enabling adjustments to patrol and distribution to counter criminal activity.
- Determine presence, capabilities, and likely actions of organized criminal elements in the AO.
- Determine the status and capabilities of police organizations, infrastructure, and systems.
- Determine capability gaps in existing police organizations, infrastructure, and systems.
- Identify probable trends and effectiveness pertaining to police organizations, based on analyses of current and historical performance, equipment, and personnel data.
- Identify likely areas of corruption and public distrust of policing systems, based on current and historical data and information.
- Determine patterns in criminal activity and LE in the AO that can assist in identifying crime-conducive conditions.
- Determine the construct, capability, and functionality of host nation legal systems, focusing on the police and prisons.
- Determine the identity of individual criminals, criminal groups, and applicable associations.

3-39. Analysis continues throughout all PIO activities. During the analysis phase, military police staff and police intelligence analysts evaluate police information and information gained from other sources for relevancy, reliability, and timeliness. Evaluating police information includes determining whether the information is relevant to existing IR and if pieces of police information are related. Initially, information may seem irrelevant; however, it should be indexed, queried, and periodically reviewed in future analyses. When reevaluated, this fragmentary information may be fused with additional data and information received to provide an understanding not achievable when analyzed as a singular piece of data. Additionally, it must be determined whether the police information is reliable for presentation or if additional confirmation is required. Last, it must be determined if the police information and police intelligence has been collected and analyzed in time to affect operations. Chapter 5 contains additional considerations and techniques specific to police intelligence analysis.

3-40. Police information and intelligence must be integrated into the operations process and the COP to affect operations. Integrating police information and intelligence in tactical plans exploits the information and intelligence gathered, promoting the emergence of the bigger common operational picture. As police information continues to be collected, reported, recorded, and analyzed, a more holistic picture begins to emerge.

ASSESS

3-41. *Assessment* is the continuous monitoring and evaluation of the current situation and progress of an operation. (Field Manual Interim [FMI] 5-0.1) Continuous assessment plays a critical role in evaluating the information collected during the PIO process. The continuous assessment of PIO activities, available information and intelligence, and various aspects of the mission variables are critical to ensuring that the staff–

- Answers the CCIRs and IRs.
- Provides appropriate input to redirect assets in support of police intelligence collection and assessment of changing requirements.
- Provides clarification to ensure that collection asset elements understand the intent and target to achieve resolution of police IR.

PROPAGATE

3-42. Propagation of police information and intelligence includes activities involving direct dissemination, access approval, database information sharing, and COP updates. Timely and accurate dissemination of police information and police intelligence enabling effective decisionmaking is key to successful PIO.

Dissemination

3-43. Dissemination is the act of getting relevant information to the right personnel, units, or agencies; it is critical to the timely integration of police information and intelligence. Dissemination entails delivering timely, relevant, accurate, predictive, and tailored police intelligence to appropriate and authorized stakeholders. Identifying recipients, determining the product format, and selecting the means of delivery are key aspects of dissemination. Recipients of information and police intelligence generated through PIO efforts must be evaluated to ensure compliance with any legal dissemination restrictions, mission requirements, and protection considerations. Stakeholders may be any element or entity that–

- Possesses an IR that can be answered by the information or police intelligence disseminated.
- Operates in an AO that may be directly or indirectly impacted by the information or police intelligence.
- Possesses an assigned mission that may be directly or indirectly impacted by the information or police intelligence.
- Provides support to elements impacted by the information or police intelligence.

3-44. Information presentation may be in a verbal, written, interactive, or graphic format. The type of information, the time allocated, and the directives of the commander, unit, or agency requiring police information and intelligence all influence the information format. In the LE community, some standard formats and means exist for disseminating police information and police intelligence between agencies; many formats are developed locally. These dissemination conduits are typically closed to personnel and agencies outside the LE community. In the operational Army operating outside the United States or its territories, police information and intelligence may be disseminated across tactical command and control systems or appropriate military networks. These networks and systems facilitate the dissemination of answers to CCIRs.

3-45. Military police and USACIDC staff responsible for police intelligence must identify the appropriate and authorized users of police intelligence products well in advance of a mission to ensure that the right products get to the right people at the right time. Typically, in LE operations in the United States and its territories, the users are the personnel or organizations initiating the requirements and those further identified as needing the products. Identified LE-sensitive police information and intelligence are retained in LE channels. When supporting operations in an OE outside the United States and its territories, the recipients of police information and intelligence are typically more broadly defined and are not limited to LE.

3-46. Military police and USACIDC staff must also determine what method will be used to disseminate police intelligence products. Methods of dissemination may vary from such tools as military police reports and police bulletins to threat assessments and information briefs. Geospatial products may provide assistance to personnel by highlighting necessary information (see FM 3-34.230). Regardless of the method used, military police and USACIDC staff must ensure that the products are delivered to the appropriate users when, where, and in the proper form needed. Dissemination occurs at every echelon and is entered in the data stream for continued analysis, when applicable. Frequently, when police intelligence products are delivered, additional police information collection requirements are identified.

Note. Local police intelligence files may be exempt from certain disclosure requirements by AR 25-55 and the *Freedom of Information Act*. When a written extract from local police intelligence files is provided to an authorized investigative agency, the following statement must be included on the transmittal documents: THIS DOCUMENT IS PROVIDED FOR INFORMATION AND USE. COPIES OF THIS DOCUMENT, ENCLOSURES THERETO, AND INFORMATION THEREFROM, WILL NOT BE FURTHER RELEASED WITHOUT THE PRIOR APPROVAL OF THE INSTALLATION PROVOST MARSHAL.

Granting Access and Sharing Rights

3-47. Granting access to databases, information, or intelligence ensures that personnel, units, or organizations with requirements and legal authorization for access to police information and intelligence are provided the means to obtain the required information. Police information and intelligence may be stored in established LE-sensitive, classified, and unclassified databases and associated programs, networks, systems, and other Web-based collaborative environments. Every effort will be made to ensure that LE agencies operating in the AO and any multinational and U.S. military organizations have access, as appropriate and within legal and policy guidelines. Access and sharing rights are granted through applicable national agencies and according to applicable regulations, policies, and procedures for personnel accesses and clearances, individual system accreditation, specialized training for access and systems or database use, and special security procedures and enforcement.

3-48. Sharing access is primarily the result of establishing a collaborative environment for transferring police information and intelligence. Advances in database technology, combined with an explosion in information sharing and networking among police agencies, has resulted in the development and expansion of these robust information repositories. Army LE personnel continue to access the National Crime Information Center (NCIC) database, but can also turn to databases containing fugitive information from corrections systems and terrorist threat information from the United States Department of Homeland Security (DHS) and Federal Bureau of Investigation (FBI) systems. DOD proprietary automation systems, such as the Centralized Operator's Police Suite (COPS) Information Management System and the Army Criminal Investigative Information System (ACI2), greatly improve interoperability and eliminate seams that criminal and other threats might otherwise exploit. Access to local, theater, DOD, non-DOD, and commercial databases allow analysts to leverage stored knowledge on topics ranging from basic demographics to threat characteristic information. The challenge for an analyst is to gain an understanding of the structure, contents, strengths, and weaknesses of the database, regardless of the database type.

3-49. Each intelligence discipline has unique databases established and maintained by a variety of agencies. Database access is accomplished through unit or agency homepages via Secret Internet Protocol Router Network (SIPRNET) (Intelink-S) and the Joint Worldwide Intelligence Communications System (JWICS) (Intelink). The Distributed Common Ground System–Army (DCGS–A) provides a net-centric and enterprised ISR, weather, geospatial engineering, and space operations capability to organizations at all echelons. DCGS–A will be the ISR component of the modular and future force Battle Command System and the Army's primary system for ISR tasking, posting, and processing information and understanding the threat, terrain, weather, and civil considerations at all echelons. Databases are discussed in greater detail in chapter 6.

3-50. The laws governing the sharing of police information and police intelligence between the LE and intelligence communities are very specific. Generally, intelligence agencies cannot collect, gather, or store information from LE agencies. For exceptions to this requirement, see EO 12333, paragraph C-4. Appendix C contains information on sharing information between intelligence communities and other legal aspects of police intelligence collection and sharing.

Updating the Common Operational Picture

3-51. The *common operational picture* is a single display of relevant information within a commander's area of interest, tailored to the user's requirements and based on common data and information shared by more than one command. (FM 3-0) The COP is a single display of all relevant information conveyed through reports, automatic updates, and overlays common to all echelons and digitally stored in a common database. It facilitates battle command through collaborative interaction and real-time sharing of information between commanders and staffs.

3-52. To support full spectrum operations, new or updated police information and police intelligence must be regularly input into the COP to provide the most current situation. Military police unit staffs and PM sections coordinate through echelon G-3 or S-3 and G-2 or S-2 personnel to provide continuous results of PIO for inclusion in the COP.

POLICE INTELLIGENCE OPERATIONS INTEGRATION WITH THE OPERATIONS PROCESS

3-53. The *operations process* consists of the major command and control activities performed during operations: planning, preparing, executing, and continuously assessing the operation. The commander drives the operations process. (FM 3-0) The activities of the operations process are sequential, but not discrete; all overlapping and recurring activities occur as circumstances demand (see figure 5-3 in FM 3-0). Throughout the operations process, the warfighting functions are synchronized through five integrating functions: IPB, ISR surveillance and integration, targeting, CRM, and KM.

3-54. The PIO function is integrated throughout each of the other military police functions (L&O, I/R, MMS, and AS). PIO provides police information and police intelligence to military police commanders and staffs to support ongoing operations throughout the conduct of all five activities. Simultaneously, PIO continuously feeds information to the operations process through the integrating functions. Integrating police information and police intelligence products into the operations process will ensure that the criminal aspects of the threat in the AO are considered for all operations. See FM 3-0 for additional information on the operations process. Figure 3-2 provides a graphic representation of PIO support to military police operations and the operations process.

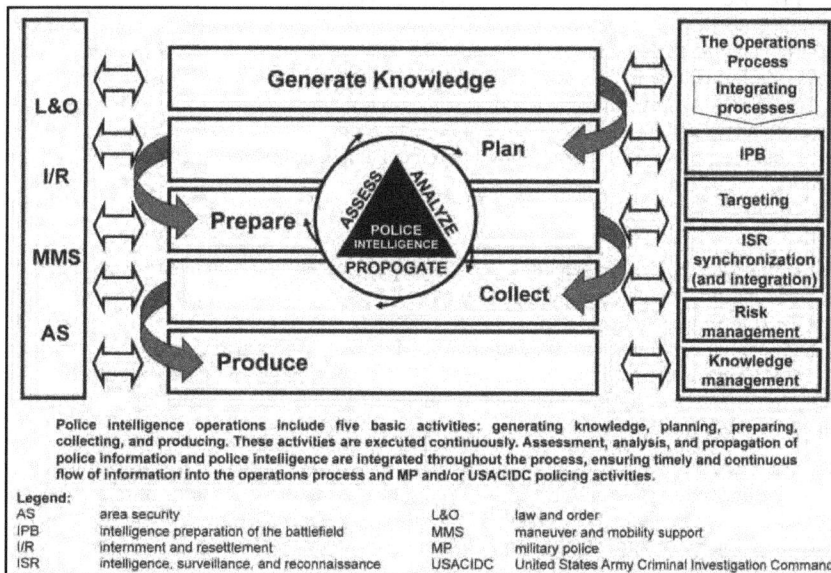

Figure 3-2. PIO support to military police operations and the operations process

3-55. The PIO function represents the military police capability to collect, analyze, and process relevant information from many sources focused on policing and LE activities. PIO activities are continuously conducted by military police and USACIDC personnel to collect, analyze, and disseminate police information and police intelligence on infrastructure, systems, populations, and individuals gathered while conducting military police operations. Information is collected and analyzed from a policing viewpoint (see FM 3-39). Information and intelligence from other operational elements are also fused with information collected by military police and USACIDC Soldiers to develop a common operational picture. Police information obtained in the execution of the remaining four military police functions (L&O, I/R, MMS, and AS) and subsequent police intelligence can help form a complete view of the OE and increase situational understanding, shaping future operations across all military police functions.

3-56. Information collected through the execution of PIO is disseminated throughout the LE community and pushed into the intelligence and operations processes. This process ensures a continuous flow of police information to promote the development of a holistic COP for commanders and staffs. PIO integration within the Army operations integrating process is addressed in the following paragraphs.

INTELLIGENCE PREPARATION OF THE BATTLEFIELD

3-57. IPB is a systematic process of analyzing and visualizing the OE in a specific geographic area for a specific mission or in anticipation of a specific mission. Although staff integration of IPB is generally led by the S-2 or G-2, all staff elements must fully participate and provide their individual areas of expertise to the effort. (See FMI 2-01.301 for more information on IPB.) Commanders and staffs develop the IPB and apply it in all phases of the operations process. They ensure that there are tactics, techniques, and procedures in place for the continual assessment, development, and dissemination of IPB products. All staff members must understand and participate in the IPB process. PIO is a reciprocating effort that both feeds, and draws from, IPB to help commanders understand their environment, mitigate vulnerabilities, and exploit opportunities. In addition to the tactical information that may be obtained through the conduct of PIO networks, the PIO function provides additional information on possible criminal threats and threats to social order that may support or drive current operations and change the friendly threat posture.

3-58. The OE is extremely complex. Military planners use several tools to help in framing and understanding the complex OEs in which military forces must operate. The eight operational variables are used to assess the OE; the six mission variables are used in mission analysis; and six additional variables are used to address civil considerations. All these tools are essential to the conduct of a complete and thorough IPB. (See FM 3-0 for information on the operational, mission, and civil considerations variables.) Military police also use the factors of POLICE (see chapter 2) to closely examine civil considerations relevant to policing and LE operations that can affect military operations and social order. The assessment of police and criminal environments provides critical civil information relating to civil security and civil control. It supports the development of information requirements, some of which may become CCIRs. These assessments shape the military police approach to other military police functions and operations in the AO. IR must be prioritized to ensure that limited collection assets are leveraged against the most critical requirements.

TARGETING

3-59. *Targeting* is the process of selecting and prioritizing targets and matching the appropriate response to them, considering operational requirements and capabilities. (JP 3-0) Targeting methods can range from lethal engagement to nonlethal weapons and informational engagements. Targeting begins in the planning process and continues throughout the operation. The Army's targeting process is described in the framework of decide, detect, deliver, and assess (D3A). This targeting methodology facilitates engagement of the right target, at the right time, and with the most appropriate assets (lethal or nonlethal), based on the commander's targeting guidance, objectives, and desired effect.

3-60. In many OEs, the threat is more criminal than conventional in nature. In these environments, it is not uncommon for enemy combatants, insurgents, and other belligerents to use or mimic established criminal enterprises and practices to move contraband, raise funds, or generally further their goals and objectives. In all OEs, criminal activity impacts the mission of Army forces and threatens Army personnel and assets. Assessing the impact of criminal activity on military operations and deconflicting that activity from other threat or environmental factors can be essential to effective targeting and mission success.

3-61. Recent developments in biometric technology, the introduction of evidence collection and examination at incident scenes, and collected material in OEs outside the United States have proven the effectiveness and relevance of PIO and its ability to provide timely, accurate, and actionable intelligence to the geographic combat commander (GCC) in an OE. The technical capabilities and knowledge of complex criminal organizations and activities leveraged by military police, USACIDC, and civilian LE professionals provide methods and reachback previously overlooked by the Army as a whole. PIO contributes to the targeting process by providing timely, relevant, and actionable police information and police intelligence regarding crime and criminal threats in the AO. Military police and USACIDC staff and police intelligence analysts must understand their role and how PIO supports the targeting process.

3-62. Military police and USACIDC staff and police intelligence analysts integrate information and police intelligence through the Army operations process and the five integrating processes, to include the targeting process. The activities that support the operations process are integrated into the targeting process during MDMP, targeting meetings, coordination with the fires cell, and other staff functions. The D3A methodology provides the structure for staffs to integrate analysis, monitor operations, and make recommendations enabling commanders to make informed targeting decisions. The process enables the commander and staff to decide which targets to engage, detect the targets, deliver (conduct the appropriate engagement operation), and assess the effects of the engagement. Table 3-1 illustrates the key activities of D3A—how military police and USACIDC staff conducting PIO integrate within the overall targeting process.

Table 3-1. Targeting methodology

D3A Activities		MP and USACIDC Staff and Police Intelligence Analyst Support to Targeting
Decide which targets to engage	Perform continuous activity based on the mission, commander's intent, concept of the operation, and planning guidance to produce or determine— <ul><li>IR.</li><li>ISR plans.</li><li>Target acquisition taskings.</li><li>High-payoff target lists.</li><li>Target selection standards.</li><li>Assessment criteria.</li><li>Relative importance of the targets.</li><li>Recommended engagement means to produce desired effects.</li><li>Expected effects of engagement.</li><li>Attack guidance matrix. (Enables the commander or leader to make a decision on who, what, when, where, and how to engage.)</li></ul>	<ul><li>Develop IR pertinent to policing and LE operations.</li><li>Develop the police information collection plan.</li><li>Ensure that police IR and collection plan are integrated and synchronized with the ISR plan.</li><li>Identify change indicators relevant to the police and criminal environment.</li><li>Identify MP, USACIDC, or other collection assets capable of collecting against specific police IR.</li><li>Nominate police-related IR as CCIRs (as required).</li><li>Nominate criminal or police-related targets as high-payoff targets (as required).</li><li>Make recommendations regarding engagement means.</li><li>Assess probable effects of recommended engagements.</li><li>Task appropriate military police or USACIDC collection elements (if applicable).</li></ul>
Detect the targets	<ul><li>Produce ISR synchronization matrix.</li><li>Dedicate collection assets to gather information.</li><li>Direct operational elements to report observations based on IR.</li><li>Develop target.</li><li>Vet target.</li><li>Determine threat/target validity.</li></ul>	<ul><li>Participate in ISR synchronization to ensure that police information collection efforts are synchronized with maneuver and other collection elements.</li><li>Monitor collection efforts.</li><li>Gather reports, evidence, and other pertinent police-related information.</li><li>Conduct debriefings of collection elements to ensure that all available police-related information is gathered and collated.</li><li>Conduct analyses of collected data to determine trends, patterns, and associations regarding crime, criminals, and associated data.</li></ul>

Table 3-1. Targeting methodology

D3A Activities		MP and USACIDC Staff and Police Intelligence Analyst Support to Targeting
		<ul><li>Identify potential targets. (criminals, crime conditions, or populations).</li><li>Develop police intelligence folders for specific cases/targets.</li><li>Recommend adjustments to the police information collection plan and policing strategies.</li><li>Identify specific targets (criminals, crime conditions, or populations) and timelines for recommended engagement.</li><li>Monitor change indicators for causal relationships (cause and effect).</li></ul>
Deliver (conduct the appropriate engagement operation)	<ul><li>Identify and task specific engagement units.</li><li>Identify engagement methods (such as ordnance and tasked information). Ensure that you consider the desired effect on the target, such as destruction, harassment, isolation, capture, persuasion, or exploitation.</li><li>Identify the engagement timeline identified and tasked.</li><li>Coordinate, synchronize, and monitor the engagement.</li></ul>	<ul><li>Task military police or USACIDC assets to conduct engagement mission (if applicable).</li><li>Identify and include in tasking order method of engagement, required timeline, and desired effect.</li><li>Obtain or develop proper information themes and messages to ensure consistency with military actions.</li><li>Monitor MP and USACIDC elements conducting target engagement and other elements engaging police-related targets.</li><li>Identify personnel and capabilities required for site exploitation.</li><li>Task MP and USACIDC elements (as required) for participation as part of the site exploitation team.</li><li>Obtain reports, evidence, witness statements, and other pertinent police-related information from the site exploitation team.</li><li>Conduct debriefings of site exploitation team participants (if available) to ensure that all available police-related information is gathered and collated.</li></ul>

Table 3-1. Targeting methodology

D3A Activities		MP and USACIDC Staff and Police Intelligence Analyst Support to Targeting
Assess the effects of the engagement	Measure and analyze results to determine: • Has the targeting objective been met? • Is additional engagement required? • Is a different engagement method required?	• Conduct assessments based on approved measures of effectiveness, measures of performance, and identified change indicators. • Determine if additional target engagement is required (on the same or new target). • Determine if the method of engagement achieved the desired effect; determine if alternative engagement methods are justified. • Recommend engagement actions and adjustments, as required. • Conduct analyses of postengagement data. • Produce police intelligence, as required. • Disseminate police information and police intelligence, as required, within mission, regulatory, and policy constraints. • Update running estimates and associated staff products.

Legend:	
CCIR	Commander's critical information requirement
D3A	decide, detect, deliver, and assess
IR	intelligence requirements
ISR	intelligence, surveillance, and reconnaissance
LE	law enforcement
MP	military police
USACIDC	United States Army Criminal Investigation Command

3-63. During stability operations, especially in a counterinsurgency environment or an AO plagued with lawlessness and extensive criminal activity, a higher level of precision may be required for targeting in and around the civilian population. The targeting methodology—find, fix, finish, exploit, analyze, and disseminate (F3EAD)—is a valuable targeting tool for precise targeting against individuals or small elements. It does not replace D3A as the primary targeting methodology but, rather, complements it when precise targeting during stability operations is required. F3EAD is best described as a process within a process that facilitates precise targeting of high-value individuals, cells, and networks.

3-64. Targeting in the Army targeting construct is typically understood as an activity executed in military operations abroad, against a foreign threat. Identification and targeting of criminal threats in the context of policing and protection of U.S. personnel and infrastructure follow the same basic methodology. PIO integrated with L&O operations in support of posts, camps, and stations is critical to understanding the criminal environment, developing linkages between criminal actors, establishing critical correlations in time and space, or identifying trends and patterns in criminal activity. All these variables are valuable in narrowing the scope of policing activities and investigations so persons of interest can be identified and interviewed, locations or material identified for examination and collection for evidentiary value, and criminal threats appropriately targeted for apprehension.

INTELLIGENCE, SURVEILLANCE, AND RECONNAISSANCE SYNCHRONIZATION

3-65. *Intelligence, surveillance, and reconnaissance* is an activity that synchronizes and integrates the planning and operation of sensors, assets, and processing of exploitation and dissemination systems in direct support of current and future operations. ISR is a combined arms operation that focuses on PIR while answering the commander's critical information requirements. (FM 3-0) Information may be collected from multiple sources, to include military police and USACIDC assets. Once the information is analyzed, the resulting data is considered intelligence.

3-66. The G-2 or S-2 generally leads ISR synchronization during full spectrum operations. PIO will provide information and analyzed police intelligence to the intelligence community for fusion with intelligence gathered from other collection assets to answer CCIRs concerning the OE. ISR operations continue throughout the operations process. In the operations process, ISR synchronization (led by the intelligence officer [an integrating process]) and ISR integration (led by the operations officer [a continuing activity]) contribute to effective ISR operations.

3-67. ISR synchronization refers to the–

- Analysis of IR and gaps.
- Evaluation of available internal and external assets for collection against IR.
- Determination of collection capability gaps.
- Recommendation of ISR assets for collecting information to satisfy the CCIR.
- Request for information for external collection support.

3-68. ISR integration refers to the task of assigning and controlling a unit's intelligence, surveillance, and reconnaissance assets (in terms of space, time, and purpose) to collect and report information as a concerted and integrated portion of operation plans and orders. ISR integration ensures assignment of the optimum collection assets through a deliberate and coordinated effort of the entire staff. The G-3 or S-3 develops tasks based on specific information requirements (developed during ISR synchronization). Specific information requirements are assigned to collection assets and units. For complex or high risk collection requirements, combined arms collection assets may be assigned. (See FM 3-0 for more information on ISR.)

3-69. In functional military police or USACIDC elements, ISR synchronization and integration are conducted as an internal operation to support the PIR and the CCIR of the echelon commander (military police and USACIDC brigades, groups, or battalions). IR specific to PIO are synchronized with other operational or tactical IR (normally by the S-2), and a collection plan is developed. When military police staff conducts an IPB, police or criminal information gaps may be encountered. These gaps may become the military police commander's police or criminal information requirements. If the gap cannot be filled with available data from the S-2 or G-2, the USACIDC, the host nation, or other agencies, the commander may task subordinate military police units or request USACIDC assistance to support the collection effort. All IR is then integrated into a consolidated synchronization matrix within the overall operational plan and assigned to collection assets by the S-3. The S-3 then tasks the appropriate unit to conduct the collection mission. If the organic military police or USACIDC unit requires outside capability, coordination and requests for support must be completed.

3-70. In multifunctional elements, PM sections work closely with the G-2 or S-2 and the G-3 or S-3 to identify IR that provide clarity and understanding specific to the police and criminal dimension that supports the commander's operational plan. IR information is developed and nominated for prioritization and assignment of collection assets. The PM section conducts an analysis and recommends the optimum collection asset work through the G-3 or S-3 to coordinate tasking orders for the appropriate subordinate element to conduct the collection mission. If collection assets outside the command are required, the PM section coordinates the request for collection assets.

3-71. Though restricted to LE personnel, the same ISR processes apply to LE operations in support of posts, camps, and stations. The PM section or USACIDC element conducts an analysis of the IR and gaps to determine available internal and external assets for collection against those requirements. These information requirements may be regarding policing activities affecting patrol distribution plans, traffic operations, crime trends, crime prevention, disruption of criminal activity, or specific individual investigations. When a capability gap exists, the PM or USACIDC SAC may request assets external to the organic elements. These gaps may be from an adjacent military police or USACIDC element or through interagency cooperation with civilian LE organizations. These assets are then tasked with specific collection requirements to close information gaps pertinent to the mission, investigation, or other data requirements.

COMPOSITE RISK MANAGEMENT

3-72. *Composite risk management* is the decisionmaking process for identifying and assessing hazards, developing and implementing risk mitigation actions to control risk across the full spectrum of Army missions, functions, operations, and activities. (FM 5-19) Information obtained through PIO also directly contributes to the risk management process through identification of potential threats and conditions that pose a risk to U.S. forces and civilians. These risks may be in the form of a credible threat of direct terrorist actions against a unit or base, the presence of criminal activity directed at U.S. assets or personnel, or identification of environments where police organizations and enforcement are either lacking or corrupt; thus lawlessness is prevalent and random crime poses a threat. (See FM 5-19 for information on CRM.)

3-73. Police information and intelligence resulting from PIO may identify threats before they manifest themselves. These threats may be conventional, criminal, or environmental. The continuous flow of information and intelligence from military police and USACIDC elements into and out of the Army operations process, to include the CRM process, can provide early identification of potential threats to personnel and equipment providing commanders and staffs time to properly assess the threat, determine the risk to their personnel and equipment, and develop and implement control measures to mitigate the threat.

KNOWLEDGE MANAGEMENT

3-74. *Knowledge management* is the art of creating, organizing, applying, and transferring knowledge to facilitate situational understanding and decisionmaking. Knowledge management supports improving organizational learning, innovation, and performance. Knowledge management processes ensure that knowledge products and services are relevant, accurate, timely, and usable to commanders and decision makers. (FM 3-0)

3-75. PIO activities produce relevant and timely information and intelligence to facilitate situational understanding and decisionmaking. The unique contribution of information pertinent to civil considerations, specifically related to the police and criminal environment in the OE, is critical to fully understanding the dynamics of criminal threats and the ability of policing organizations to combat these threats.

POLICE INTELLIGENCE OPERATIONS SPANNING THE LEVELS OF WAR

3-76. The levels of war are doctrinal perspectives that clarify the relationship between strategic objectives (ends), operational approaches (ways), and tactical actions (means). No finite limits or boundaries exist between the levels of war; they correlate to specific levels of responsibility and planning, helping to organize thought and approaches to a problem. They provide a clear distinction between headquarters and the specific responsibilities and actions performed at each level.

OPERATIONAL AND STRATEGIC LEVEL

3-77. Military police activities at the strategic level include force planning, military police-related policy and doctrine development, and the execution of operations focused primarily on the means and capabilities to generate, mount, sustain, and recover military police forces. Additionally, protection tasks, host nation police engagement and development, and I/R operations place a heavy demand on military police planning requirements. PIO is integrated seamlessly throughout all military police operations. Planning for military police operations in any of the military police functional areas inherently includes PIO considerations. Military police staff and commanders at the strategic level advise on–

- LE investigations and analyses supporting strategic level objectives.
- The ability of joint, interagency, intergovernmental organizations (IGOs), and multinational LE agencies to identify, monitor, and defeat criminal networks.
- Implementation of the rule of law.
- Service policing capabilities and interoperability.
- Detainee and DC operations.
- Protection of strategic-level infrastructure, to include seaports of debarkation (SPODs) and aerial ports of debarkation (APODs) from criminal and irregular threats.
- LOC security.
- Military police force generation priorities.
- Recommended use of specific joint policing capabilities to optimize strengths and minimize limitations.
- Airbase and airfield security.
- Base camp security and response force planning.
- Targeting against criminal actors.
- Foreign humanitarian assistance.
- ROE and the rules for the use of force.

3-78. Military police activities at the operational level focus on the impact of geography and force projection infrastructure on the GCC's operational design. Military police planners must determine the basic, yet broad, mobilization, deployment, employment, and sustainment requirements of the GCC's concept of operations. Operational planning requires military police staff to merge the OPLAN or OPORD with specific military police missions, to include PIO requirements in support of those missions and available military police forces to achieve success. Many of the military police activities listed earlier for strategic operations are also performed at the operational level. At the operational level, military police also–

- Prioritize limited assets and mitigate risks to maximize effectiveness and focus police intelligence assets on established priorities.
- Conduct operational assessments and PIO with intelligence officers to analyze the threat. They conduct master planning and plan for the protection of high-risk personnel (HRP) and facilities.
- Develop police intelligence products and services and make recommendations on protecting the force and support for the rule of law, based on analyses of police intelligence collected at all levels.

3-79. The OE in any stability operation may be filled with hardened criminals and opportunists conducting criminal activity that jeopardizes civil security and the strategic and operational plan. Many insurgent groups operate in a manner that has more in common with organized criminals—their methods, structure, and local relationships—than they have with conventional military threat forces. Aggressive military police collection and analyses of information concerning police and prison organizations, systems and capabilities, and assessment of the criminal dimension in the OE support strategic and operational lines of effort. PIO in the confines of I/R facilities is not only critical to maintaining order in the facility, but can enhance HUMINT efforts by providing passively collected information to the operations process.

TACTICAL LEVEL

3-80. Operational planning and tactical planning complement one another but have different aims. Operational planning links tactics and strategy by establishing operational objectives needed to achieve strategic objectives, sequencing events to achieve operational objectives, initiating actions, and applying resources to bring about and sustain these events. Tactical missions are complex, and planning must consider both symmetric and asymmetric threat capabilities. Tactical planning emphasizes flexibility and options. Comprehensive planning may be feasible only for the first event or phase in an operation; succeeding actions depend on enemy responses and circumstances. Regardless, the staff must plan for PIO integration and develop and continually revise relevant information requirements. These requirements can then be integrated into the conduct of military police missions. Specific military police and USACIDC capabilities are required, depending on the nature of tactical operations.

3-81. Typically, baseline military police units and USACIDC agents can accomplish PIO requirements during offensive and defensive operations. The military police Soldier and USACIDC agent must understand how operations affect security functions in the AO. PIO executed during MMS and AS missions can provide the commander with increased situational understanding and information and police intelligence critical to civil security and civil control objectives as operations transition to a stability focus. During offensive operations, military police–

- Understand the IPB, the CCIR, and the PIR and make efforts through the PIO function to support those requirements.
- Conduct deliberate PIO and L&O operations in the local population.
- Provide information on MSR conditions along LOCs to facilitate movement and protection for the force. Perform I/R operations to reduce the impact on forces. Military police coordinate the treatment of DCs with the host nation or foreign forces during I/R functions while passively collecting police information and conducting criminal investigations as required.
- Conduct MMS functions to assist the commander in facilitating the shift of forces to support the main effort and enhance overall trafficability. Military police conduct reconnaissance and assessments of the routes to support maneuver commanders in orchestrating the effort to mass, sustaining offensive momentum. Information gathered also enables the staff to determine trafficability and feasible or suitable improvements to the LOCs.
- Conduct AS operations to protect command and control nodes, such as the main CP and tactical CP. They maintain surveillance, provide early warning, and attack the enemy with supporting and organic fires, ensuring freedom of action of the force. Information collected by military police elements facilitates quick response by enabling the attack of enemy reconnaissance forces in the AO. Military police gather and develop police information during movement corridor operations.

3-82. During defensive operations, military police–

- Understand the IPB, the CCIR, and the PIR and make efforts through the PIO function to support those requirements.
- Conduct PIO and L&O operations in the local population.
- Consider the type and size of the AO, LOC security, and threat and plan for internment operations and resettlement operations, considering the effect on the movement of friendly forces. Perform necessary I/R operations resulting from previous offensive or ongoing stability operations to reduce the impact on other friendly forces. Military police coordinate the treatment of DCs with the host nation, interagency, and NGOs, as appropriate.
- Conduct MMS operations to aid a force to maneuver and mass. Military police must anticipate transitions from the defense to the offense and assist the forward movement of reserves or reaction forces. Deliberate police engagement and PIO targeting the local population can provide critical police information regarding threat conditions and the local environment, enabling commanders to make appropriate decisions.
- Conduct AS operations to deny information to enemy reconnaissance elements seeking the location of the defending force. Military police conduct aggressive R&S to deny enemy access to critical logistical and sustainment facilities. They support movement corridors established in high-threat areas. Military police elements position assets to control key terrain or improve the defensive capability of bases and base clusters and gather critical information in support of integrated PIO.

3-83. During stability operations, the demand for increased specificity in technical capability may be required. This is especially true during extensive nation building when ongoing support to host nation police and prison systems is required. Support to policing and penal institutions (which may include training, development, or mentorship) is a critical capability to enable the maneuver commander at the tactical level during stability operations. Military police facilitate the ability to discern and identify patterns and plan specific strategies that are based on the criminal threat, providing specific threat information in the form of police intelligence. Stability operations may be supported through all five military police functions. However, support to stability operations may be primarily focused on L&O and I/R operations. PIO, as an integrated military police function, is executed continuously throughout all military police operations. This includes potentially establishing, using, and transferring host nation PIO information. Specific missions during stability operations may include the following–

- Establishing a strategic LE stationing plan.
- Executing theater LE operations.
- Establishing, operating, and transferring police stations to trained and skilled host nation police.
- Establishing regional police academies.
- Controlling the movement of civilians and providing relief to human suffering.
- Establishing and training regional or urban police patrol operations (such as traffic control management and emergency first-responder operations).
- Establishing and training special police operations (such as special reaction teams, emergency response, protective services, riot control, and functional patrols).
- Establishing and training criminal investigative capabilities.
- Establishing indigenous highway patrols.
- Establishing indigenous police information systems (such as administrative, logistics, training, and operations).
- Establishing vehicle registration systems.
- Conducting information management liaison operations for all required echelons.
- Establishing host nation police reports, forms, databases, and management protocols.
- Recommending the procurement of material to create police infrastructure, communications equipment, and uniform sets.
- Establishing strategic detainee and penal system templates.
- Executing theater detainee operations.
- Establishing, operating, and transferring theater-level internment facilities to host nation control.
- Establishing regional detainee and penal academies.
- Transferring or adjudicating criminal detainees.
- Establishing juvenile detainee operations.
- Training special teams (such as special reaction teams, forced cell moves, escorts, and riot control teams).
- Conducting counterinsurgency-related detection efforts.
- Conducting multilevel information management liaison operations.
- Establishing rehabilitative and reconciliation programs to facilitate the return of detainees to society.
- Providing detainee and penal police transition teams.
- Recommending procurement of internment infrastructure (such as utilities, communications equipment, and uniforms).
- Establishing indigenous detainee automation and information systems (administration, logistics, operations, and training).
- Establishing standard detainee reports, forms, databases, and management protocols.
- Establishing and supporting resettlement facilities in support of civil-military operations.

UNIFIED ACTION

3-84. *Unified action* is the synchronization, coordination, and/or integration of the activities of governmental and nongovernmental entities with military operations to achieve unity of effort. (JP 1-0) Unified action includes coordination and/or integration of the activities and actions of other government agencies and multinational military and nonmilitary organizations. See FM 3-0 for more information on unified action.

3-85. Successful PIO requires unified action. The joint nature of U.S. military operations requires close coordination among the Services. Military police and USACIDC personnel conducting PIO regularly coordinate with their counterparts from the other Services to pass and receive information and police intelligence and to leverage inherent capabilities. Integration and synchronization of police intelligence activities may occur in-theater or out of theater. For example, extensive forensics analytical capability supporting PIO at the tactical and operational levels may occur in-theater by modular deployed forensics assets or through laboratory capabilities outside the theater of operations. Combined efforts between U.S. LE elements, multinational, and host nation military and civilian police agencies in collecting, analyzing, and sharing police information and intelligence are conducted throughout the AO to enable successful civil security and civil control efforts and transition to host nation control. At the strategic level, the CITF provides integrated and synchronized investigative and analytical support to elements in multiple AOs.

3-86. *Multinational operations* is a collective term to describe military actions conducted by forces of two or more nations, usually undertaken within the structure of a coalition or alliance. (JP 3-16) Military police and USACIDC staffs coordinate and share information and police intelligence (as necessary and applicable) with multinational forces supporting the overall operation. Many multinational military police organizations provide extensive policing capabilities and experiences, to include analytical capabilities and insights that are not resident in the U.S. military. Proactive liaison with these elements not only ensures unified action but complements and enhances U.S. capabilities. See FM 3-0 for more information on multinational operations.

3-87. *Interagency coordination* occurs within the context of Department of Defense involvement, the coordination that occurs between elements of the Department of Defense, and engaged U.S. government agencies for the purpose of achieving an objective. (JP 3-0) Military police conducting PIO share information and police intelligence with other U.S. government agencies operating in the AO. This decreases the likelihood that information gaps pertinent to policing and LE operations cause unintended consequences that could jeopardize the operations of either the agency or U.S. military organizations. Interagency cooperation in sharing police intelligence also fuses the capabilities of the separate agencies to enhance police intelligence and overall situational understanding. Commanders and PMs typically establish liaison and information-sharing networks with civilian organizations directly impacting military police operations to facilitate integration of civilian agency, military police, and U.S. military capabilities.

3-88. Unified action also involves synchronizing joint or multinational military operations with activities of indigenous populations and institutions, IGOs, and NGOs. Indigenous populations and institutions, IGOs, and NGOs may be a significant source of valuable police information, although this information will typically be collected informally and passively in the course of normal operations.

This page intentionally left blank.

Chapter 4

Sources of Police Information

Military police collect police information from a growing variety of sources in their AO. Information is obtained through military police reconnaissance, surveillance, threat, and technical assessments; access to LE and intelligence databases and reachback sources; and police engagement opportunities with the local population, informants, government officials, NGOs, and other military units and LE organizations. Information collection occurs in all OEs and is focused on IR tied to the CCIR or to specific missions being performed. These sources of police information are essential to developing a clearer picture of the networks, trends, patterns, and associations that are critical to combating threat forces and criminal elements, while identifying and mitigating organizational, system, and infrastructure shortfalls affecting policing operations.

INFORMATION REQUIREMENTS

4-1. Collection includes the activities required to gather and report police information to answer IR. Collection may involve gathering new relevant data and raw information or exploiting existing police intelligence products. IR drive the collection effort of military police and USACIDC elements. Effective collection efforts are generated and driven by the operations process. They are planned, focused, and directed, based on the CCIR, threat assessments, police intelligence, and investigative requirements. Whether on a CONUS installation, at an operating base preparing for MCO, or in a remote village during stability operations, success comes from integrating information gathered during military police collection and assessment activities and conducting analysis and fusion with other sources of information to answer IR.

4-2. Commanders designate the most important, time-sensitive items of intelligence they need to collect and protect as CCIR; PIO anticipates and responds to the CCIR. As discussed in chapter 3, the intelligence community, LE, or other staff sections and subordinate units may nominate PIR. Police intelligence analysts monitor the PIR and subordinate IR for information of value in determining enemy and criminal COAs.

4-3. Requirements related to civil considerations concerning police and prison systems, policing activities, and criminal environments are of specific interest to military police and USACIDC commanders and staff and police intelligence analysts. PIR of interest to police intelligence analysts may include the identification of previously unknown criminal or terrorist organizations. Methods and routes for the concealment and movement of contraband (such as weapons, money, personnel, or drugs) may also be of particular importance. Capability and capacity of host nation police and prison systems and infrastructure, determination and impact of criminal activity in the AO, and the functionality of the criminal justice system are also of specific concern and focus for military police and USACIDC personnel.

4-4. At times, received PIR or IR data may be specific enough to be recognized as having immediate value. Other times, PIR will simply fill in a piece of a puzzle. It is important to monitor both current and previous PIR and IR reporting. Older information that was not originally recognized as being of value may increase in importance as other new information is gained through information sources or ongoing investigations.

COLLECTION OF POLICE INFORMATION

4-5. Collection is a continuous activity. Military police commanders, staff, and USACIDC personnel identify gaps in existing police information and develop IR. In turn, a police information collection plan is developed and targets are nominated for collection against the IR requirement. This collection may be completed by many means, including–

- Military police patrols.
- Police engagement.
- Military police reconnaissance, surveillance, and assessments.
- Criminal investigations.
- Interviews and LE investigations.
- Collected evidence (including biometric data and forensic evidence).
- Data mining, database queries, and use of reachback centers.

4-6. Reliability of the information collected should always be scrutinized to check its viability and credibility. See chapter 6 for more information on assessing reliability. This is especially critical when dealing with individuals providing information, regardless of the OE.

4-7. Military police should be aware of underlying motivations that may drive persons providing information. While conducting LE in support of posts, camps, and stations, persons may be motivated to pass information to military police due to a sense of duty or justice; the military culture is based on values that encourage a sense of duty, honor, and doing what is right. This is beneficial when policing military communities. Others may come forward because they may be complicit in criminal activity and are cooperating in hopes of receiving leniency. Some may seek to obtain revenge against an individual who has done something (whether real or perceived) to slight, hurt, or anger them. These are but a fraction of the possible factors that may motivate members of a population to come forward to LE personnel with information.

4-8. There is likewise a myriad of motivators that may compel members of the indigenous population to interact and share information with military police operating in support of full spectrum operations. Many of the same motivations in paragraph 4-7 apply. Additionally, when military police interact with the population, individual sources may be influenced by feelings of support for overall U.S. goals. This support may stem from being victims of a brutal government regime that has been eliminated or subdued or victims of disasters or ethnic strife. In either of these examples, victims may see the United States as a liberating force. Some may hope for money or support. Motivations of self-interest, such as fear of criminal, terrorist, or insurgent elements, may cause victims to seek out U.S. or other multinational forces. In all environments and circumstances, military police (commanders, staffs, and police intelligence analysts) must be cognizant of the potential motivations behind individuals providing information and their track record of reliability in reporting information on the enemy or criminal threat.

METHODS AND SOURCES OF INFORMATION

4-9. PIO activities are integrated within each military police function. During the execution of L&O, MMS, and AS, military police patrols are arrayed across the AO to perform a myriad of policing, protection, and other missions. The ability of military police commanders to disperse assets across the AO allows for a significant number of specialized sensors and collectors to gather information required to fulfill CCIR, IR, and other investigative requirements. In most OEs, military police patrols are continuously moving in and among the population. This places military police patrols in a unique position to both passively observe the population and to actively engage the population to gain general information or to satisfy specific IR. This continuous presence helps military police build a rapport with the populace in general and with specific persons that may be in a position to provide valuable information.

ACTIVE AND PASSIVE COLLECTION

4-10. Police information can be gathered as a result of passive or active (deliberate) collection efforts during the course of normal tactical or LE patrols and activities. These patrols and activities can be conducted during L&O, I/R, MMS, or AS operations. Passive collection is the compiling of data or information while engaged in routine tactical missions or LE activities; during passive collection, the military police Soldier or patrol is not on a dedicated reconnaissance, assessment, or collection mission. Passive collection occurs every time military police Soldiers and other Army LE engage with or observe the people or environment in which they operate. Examples of passive collection include establishing contact with the local population to support rapport; maintaining efforts to clarify and verify information already obtained through observations or other means; or simply observing activity, lack of activity, or other variations from the normal.

4-11. Active or deliberate collection occurs when military police or other Army LE elements are directed to obtain specific information about an area or target. These requests may be tied to a commander's PIR or PM's IR regarding the AO or directly tied to specific police investigations. This IR information will generally be briefed to military police Soldiers and Army LE as part of their patrol or mission briefing prior to mission execution. Post mission debriefs are a critical factor to ensuring that information gathered by military police and Army LE elements is collected by the appropriate staff elements for timely dissemination and analysis. Appendix A provides further information on PIO briefing and debriefing requirements.

MILITARY POLICE PATROLS

4-12. Military police patrols are typically arrayed across the AO during the conduct of their assigned missions supporting L&O, I/R, MMS, and AS missions. The dispersion of military police patrols, whether single team, LE unit, or larger squad or platoon-size elements, makes them effective collection assets. Skills of observation and evaluation are inherent in police training; this training further enhances the capabilities of military police patrols to contribute to the collection effort in support of PIO and other requirements. Military police Soldiers regularly observe and interact with the people and environment in which they are operating. This regular contact and interaction with the population and environment make military police patrols effective in both passive and active collection operations. By default, passive collection occurs regularly in the course of routine tactical and LE patrols and activities, based on their proximity to the populace and infrastructure and the ability to observe and interact with those elements. Through this passive collection, military police patrols may fulfill general IR applicable to the entire AO, or they may discover information that has not been specifically requested, but has recognized value.

4-13. Military police patrols may be directed to conduct a deliberate collection mission to obtain specific information about an area or target. These requests are typically tied to a commander's PIR in a deployed OE or to a PM's IR in support of posts, camps, and stations. Deliberate collection may also be tied to requirements for specific police investigations. Information and guidance pertaining to the specific IR is provided during formal mission or patrol briefings before mission execution. Deliberate preparation specifically for the mission is required. Collected information is provided to commanders and staff, along with details revealing the circumstances of the discovery, through standard patrol reports and/or debriefings. Post-mission patrol reports and mission debriefs are critical to ensuring information is gathered and provided to the staff for timely evaluation, dissemination, and analysis.

POLICE ENGAGEMENT

4-14. Police engagement is a cornerstone to successful long-term police operations. Successful police organizations interact with and gain support from the majority of the population they serve. This holds true for both civilian and military forces in any OE and is reflected in the military police motto: *Assist, Protect, Defend.* Police engagement occurs—formally and informally—any time military police and USACIDC personnel interact with area residents, host nation police and security forces, media personnel, and any of the numerous other avenues that allow personnel to gain and share information about threat and criminal activity in an AO. Data (information) obtained through police engagements must be collected, analyzed, and distributed in a timely fashion to be of maximum value to commanders, Soldiers, and the mission.

4-15. Police engagement is a specific type of information engagement; it occurs between police personnel, organizations, or populations to establish trust and maintain social order and the rule of law. Military police and USACIDC personnel engage local, host nation, and multinational police partners; police agencies; civil leaders; and local populations to obtain critical information that can influence military operations or destabilize an AO. The goal of police engagement is to develop a routine and reliable network through which police information can flow to military police and USACIDC personnel and into the operations process. Based on the tactical situation and designated IR, police engagement can be formal or informal.

4-16. Police engagement is an activity with two distinct purposes. It is used to inform the populace or other agencies and organizations of specific data points and themes in an effort to persuade the population to cooperate with civil and military authorities; mitigate potential or occurring discontent or animosity; provide advanced notification of program, policy, or procedural changes to mitigate potential problems; or gain support and develop a sense of community involvement. Police engagement is also a means to interact with and gain valuable information from the population or other agencies and organizations. It is enhanced by regular contact and the subsequent development of trust.

4-17. Formal police engagement is generally conducted as part of deliberate information engagement strategies to gain support or information or to convey a message. This function requires preparation, coordination, and proper reporting after a police engagement activity. Through formal police engagements, military police and USACIDC personnel interact with and influence a wide range of personnel and organizations, to include indigenous or multinational police, civil leadership, governmental agencies, and NGOs. It is essential that information and data exchanged are accurate and consistent with the informational themes and operations they represent.

4-18. Informal police engagement is widespread and less directive in nature; however, it is no less important to the overall success of the mission. Every interaction between military police Soldiers and personnel outside of their military police unit has the potential to be an informal police engagement. This level of engagement can occur dozens of times in a single shift. It is not constrained by location, prior coordination, or resources. By building a rapport with the community, military police Soldiers establish avenues to obtain police information.

4-19. Commanders set the priorities and strategic goals for police engagement and resource police engagement activities. Individual military police Soldiers and teams interacting with the population conduct the bulk of police engagement missions. During formal and informal police engagement, military police leaders and Soldiers maintain a deliberate focus and commitment to identifying criminal actors, crime-conducive conditions, and other criminal or policing factors that could destabilize an area or threaten the short- or long-term mission success. Police engagement should be reported through established reporting methods at the conclusion of the mission. This can be done through verbal back briefs, written patrol reports, automated databases, or other reporting mediums. The information can then be evaluated for further dissemination, analysis, and action, as required. If valuable information is identified, an informal police engagement can quickly transition to a deliberate collection effort. Chapter 6 discusses the production and dissemination of police information and intelligence.

Community Leaders

4-20. Community leaders can be a valuable source of information specific to their areas of influence. They will typically have historic knowledge of persons and activities in their cities, towns, neighborhoods, or bases. While all information received should be confirmed and vetted, community leaders can provide military police, USACIDC personnel, and police intelligence analysts with valuable information regarding the criminal history in their area (such as activities, persons, and groups), the arrival of new persons or the emergence of groups, and activities and observations that are "out of the norm." These leaders can also provide insight into the disposition of the population reference police in the area (such as animosity, levels of trust, and perceptions).

4-21. Community leaders in another culture may require time and effort by military police and USACIDC personnel to build a level of trust that will facilitate open sharing of information. Care must be exercised to ensure that interactions with local leaders are initiated at the appropriate level. Failure to do so may result in individuals feeling slighted or developing an inflated sense and perception of importance among other community members. These assessments should be made early in an operation to determine the appropriate level of engagement. Community leaders may include–

- City or town government officials.
- Installation or base commanders and staff.
- School officials.
- Neighborhood mayors and watch leaders.
- Religious and tribal leaders.
- Informal leaders.

Initial Complaints and Contacts

4-22. Military police and USACIDC personnel can gain a significant amount of information from initial complaints or calls for response due to specific emergencies or incidents. The initial contact with complainants or individuals at the scene of an incident (such as witnesses, victims, or potential perpetrators) can result in valuable pieces of information that may not be available with the passage of time. These circumstances provide witnesses, victims, and perhaps contact with potential perpetrators that have recent memory of an event or a valuable observation. It is important that this information is captured and documented as quickly, thoroughly, and accurately as possible. The passage of time will result in faded memories; modified recollections based on external inputs; internal rationalizations and thought patterns; and intentional or unintentional corroboration between witnesses, victims, and perpetrators. Accurate and timely information is critical to the development of accurate assessments by the military police, USACIDC staff, and police intelligence analysts.

Interagency Coordination

4-23. Military police and USACIDC personnel regularly interact with representatives of local, state, and federal LE agencies. In a deployed OE, this interaction may also expand to OGAs, such as the Department of State, multinational partners, and host nation governmental organizations. NGOs may also be present in an AO, depending on the type of operation and the security environment. The development of appropriate relationships with these entities can provide a wealth of valuable information to military police and USACIDC operations. See chapter 6 for more information regarding interagency coordination. Interagency coordination may include–

- Host nation police.
- Civilian LE agencies (local, state, federal).
- Multinational police forces.
- U.S. governmental agencies (such as the Department of State or DHS).
- NGOs (such as the Red Cross or Doctors Without Borders).

MILITARY POLICE RECONNAISSANCE, SURVEILLANCE, AND ASSESSMENT

4-24. Military police reconnaissance and assessment capabilities cover a wide span. These task capabilities range from tactical reconnaissance requiring relatively little technical capability to technically specific assessments requiring military police or USACIDC elements with specialized technical training and experience. Tactical reconnaissance missions by military police Soldiers still benefit from the basic LE training that separates military police Soldiers from non-military police Soldiers. Military police and USACIDC Soldiers with specific technical capabilities may augment baseline military police patrols or be employed as part of a multifunctional reconnaissance or assessment team. Capabilities in military police and USACIDC units that facilitate the conduct or support of reconnaissance and assessment include–

- Area, zone, and route reconnaissance.
- Detention requirement assessments.
- Police and prison infrastructure assessments.
- Police and prison capability and capacity assessments.

- Investigative capability assessments.
- Police and/or legal system assessments.
- Criminal activity threat assessments.
- Personal security vulnerability assessments.
- Terrorism threat assessments.
- Forensic capability assessments.

4-25. Commanders and staffs must fully understand the capabilities and limitations of available military police assets. This prevents the tasking of a collection asset that does not possess the requisite equipment, training, or expertise to successfully complete the mission. Some reconnaissance and assessment requirements require the collection of technical information with capabilities not present in baseline military police elements. Military police reconnaissance efforts may be focused on technical assessments of police and criminal environments, infrastructure, systems, persons, or specific incidents. These assessments may be in support of L&O or I/R missions that further support civil security and civil control efforts. See FM 3-39 for a full listing of military police and USACIDC elements and additional information on their specific technical capabilities. Military police technical expertise may also be integrated with other types of reconnaissance capabilities to achieve a more holistic reconnaissance effort. Teaming or task organization during infrastructure reconnaissance is an example of this (see FM 3-34.170).

4-26. Military police reconnaissance and assessment efforts are critical to gaining information and subsequently developing police intelligence required to enhance situational understanding; plan, execute, and assess missions supporting civil security and civil control lines of operation; and compile critical information and evidence required for establishing cases for criminal prosecutions (if necessary). Military police reconnaissance efforts conducted early in an operation are instrumental in establishing the baseline knowledge and understanding required for shaping stability or civil support operations and success in attaining U.S. objectives to assist the host nation or civilian LE in establishing a criminal justice system and governance under the rule of law. Many of these R&S missions are focused on civil considerations outlined in the framework of POLICE. Military police elements may conduct reconnaissance and assessments to collect information on existing host nation police and prison organizations, facilities, and other infrastructure required for policing and prison operations and to determine the presence of criminal, terrorist, or irregular threats in the AO. While conducting route, area, and zone reconnaissance and security missions, military police patrols collect and report information specific to MSR trafficability, threat presence, key terrain, and other mission variables. Military police patrols also collect information regarding the security environment, locations of host nation police stations, locations of host nation prison facilities, and general population disposition. Military police reconnaissance patrols are capable of satisfying multiple commander CCIRs for AO and IR specific to policing and criminal environments.

4-27. In any OE, military police may be tasked to conduct surveillance on specific populations, locations, or facilities to satisfy CCIR that have been identified and disseminated through the operations process. Military police units may conduct surveillance and countersurveillance to gain information to help guard against unexpected threat attacks in the AO or to gain information critical to understanding, planning, and executing missions supporting civil security and civil control. When surveillance is required in populated areas, military police Soldiers may be a more acceptable asset due to the perception of military police as an LE organization rather than a combat element. Military police may conduct initial surveillance of host nation police and prison facilities to assess security and threats before engaging host nation police or security personnel or to assess the feasibility of a facility for future use by host nation and military police elements.

4-28. Military police and USACIDC personnel may be required to conduct surveillance focused on observing specific criminal or threat targets and gathering required information. LE surveillance may be required to confirm suspected criminal activity, establish association of a suspected criminal in terms of time and place, and confirm association between persons, groups, or entities. Surveillance may be physical observation of a person or location, visual surveillance by remote video equipment, or audio surveillance via a myriad of technologies employed to intercept audio evidence. LE surveillance is typically associated with specific criminal investigations. However, LE surveillance may also be performed to conduct assessments, such as traffic studies, physical security assessments, or other security and protection requirements.

CRIMINAL INVESTIGATIONS

4-29. *Military criminal investigations* are official inquiries into crimes involving the military community. A criminal investigation is the process of searching, collecting, preparing, identifying, and presenting evidence to prove the truth or falsity of an issue of law. (FM 3-19.13) Criminal investigations involve activities to collect pertinent information related to a criminal or suspected criminal activity. These activities are focused on determination if in fact a crime has been committed, to identify any perpetrators, and collect and organize evidence for the purpose of enabling successful prosecution.

4-30. Military police Soldiers investigate a wide range of crimes, incidents, and accidents in environments where military personnel, assets, and interests are found. These investigations range from simple investigations completed quickly by Soldiers on routine patrols to extremely complicated fraud investigations spanning several years. Investigations may result from information gathered and police intelligence developed during operations that point to a person, network, or location that could be associated with threat forces. At other times, investigations may result from known criminal events or incidents.

4-31. All military police Soldiers are trained to conduct initial investigations. Specially trained military police investigators and USACIDC special agents conduct most formal criminal investigations in the Army. These investigators are trained in technical investigation techniques, to include evidence identification, processing, and preservation critical to successful criminal investigations. USACIDC typically maintains purview over all criminal cases as outlined in AR 195-2. Military police Soldiers investigate incidents by identifying, collecting, and preserving potential evidence; observing physical characteristics of locations and items; and conducting interviews with witnesses, victims, suspects, and technical experts.

4-32. Police intelligence analysts support investigators through the collection, collation, and analysis of investigative information from case files that involve allegations and testimony from witnesses, suspects, and victims. Information drawn from these case files can benefit from the inherent analytical framework and scrutiny performed by investigators. Information can also be derived through testimonial evidence or from quality information that has been vetted through the rigor of the criminal investigative process and can result in timely and relevant information and police intelligence in support of criminal investigators. Information gained via criminal investigative files can result in an accelerated generation of police intelligence. In complex cases involving criminal networks or criminal activity crossing jurisdictional boundaries, analysis can be a laborious and time-consuming process.

4-33. Typically, police information and police intelligence associated with criminal investigations is LE-sensitive and remains within LE channels. Depending on the environment and mission, this police intelligence may be directly integrated into the operations process to enhance situational awareness in the Army at large. PIO can provide significant, relevant, and timely police intelligence derived from U.S. and host nation criminal investigative efforts focused on active criminal, terrorist, and irregular threats against U.S. and host nation assets and interests (see FM 3-19.13 for in-depth discussion LE investigations).

INTERVIEWS AND LAW ENFORCEMENT INTERROGATIONS

4-34. Although physical evidence, records, and recordings can often provide critical bits of information about an incident, there is almost always significant benefit in asking questions of persons who have some knowledge of an incident (including preparation and aftermath activity). There are three categories of question-and-answer sessions: interviews, LE interrogations, and tactical interrogations. Interviews are conducted with persons who may or may not have information important to an incident and are, by general definition, not confrontational. Interviews are used by LE personnel during the initial-response phase to determine facts regarding an incident. They are also conducted by military police or USACIDC personnel in an effort to gain background or corroborative information. LE interrogations are conducted by military police investigators, USACIDC special agents, or host nation security forces with individuals suspected of a crime in which some type of prosecutorial outcome is expected. LE interrogations are generally more confrontational than interviews. Tactical interrogations are conducted by MI Soldiers when the status of a person and the circumstances of the incident indicate that the matter will not likely be part of a criminal prosecution.

> *Note.* LE interrogations are separate from intelligence interrogations. Intelligence interrogations are covered by FM 2-22.3. LE interrogations are covered by AR 190-30 and AR 195-2.

Law Enforcement Interviews

4-35. There are four main categories of interview processes that investigators use to learn more about crimes, attacks, and incidents (FM 3-19.13 provides information on LE interviews). These categories include–

- **Canvass.** Canvass interviews offer the opportunity to talk to large numbers of people quickly to determine if they are aware of the incident and have information that may prove useful to the investigation. Canvass interviews may be done immediately after an incident as a way of determining who saw or heard anything that might be important to an investigation and to obtain necessary contact information.
- **Victim.** Victim interviews are question-and-answer sessions with victims of crimes or incidents. The interviewer will often work to establish rapport with the victim by expressing sympathy or understanding as a way of eliciting their support. It is imperative that investigators remain objective at all times during victim interviews.
- **Witness and subject or suspect.**
  - Witness interviews seek to obtain information from people who saw, heard, or know information of value about an incident. Many of the same factors that make victim interviews unreliable are also present during witness interviews.
  - Suspect and subject interviews are conducted with persons that are suspected of having committed a crime or caused an incident or with individuals who are actually charged with a criminal offense. All of the factors for obtaining accurate reports from witnesses and victims apply in interviews with suspects; however, the suspect's fear may be magnified.

Law Enforcement Interrogations

4-36. The difference between a suspect interview and an LE interrogation is the level of certainty the investigator has regarding the guilt of the subject and the ability the subject has to leave at will. An interview is generally unstructured and takes place in a variety of locations, such as residences, workplaces, or police stations. It is conducted in a dialogue format in which investigators are seeking answers to typically open-ended questions, and the guilt or innocence of the person being interviewed is generally unknown.

4-37. An interrogation is planned and structured. It is generally conducted in a controlled environment, free from interruption or distraction, is monologue-based, and progresses with the subject under threat of detention if he attempts to end the interrogation. Based on these factors, the investigator must be reasonably certain of the suspect's guilt before initiating an interrogation. FM 3-19.13 contains more information regarding interviews and LE interrogations.

EVIDENCE

4-38. Evidence encompasses a wide array of physical objects, testimony, electronic data, and analyses; it is a key source of police information. Evidence consists of objects, material, or data that can provide proof or a high probability of proof that an incident, association, or pattern will lead to a conclusion or judgment. The thoughts, intuition, and opinions of an analyst or investigator are not evidence; however, they can be critical in forming a conclusion or judgment. Effective evidence collection requires planning, preparation, execution, and training. Evidence collection teams can be selected ahead of time to focus training and resources. Digital cameras, rubber gloves, paper bags, boxes, tape, and marking supplies are all tools required to properly collect evidence. Evidence collection should be performed as a deliberate and methodical process, unless the tactical situation requires a hasty collection effort. Evidence should also be handled by as few personnel as possible to avoid contamination and risk of breaking the legal chain of custody.

4-39. Chain-of-custody documentation is critical for evidence to be used in criminal proceedings. Chain of custody extends from the moment of collection, through final disposition, and must document every transfer of custody in between. Chain of custody should always be maintained and documented to ensure validity of the evidence in a criminal trial. Even if criminal proceedings are not anticipated due to the tactical situation, individuals may be detained and criminal prosecution sought at a later date. Following proper evidence procedures, including chain-of-custody documentation, ensures that collected evidence can be used in criminal proceedings.

4-40. The most recognizable evidence consists of physical items that are related to crimes or incidents, including firearms, illegal drugs, and blood-spattered clothing. Although these items all have obvious evidentiary value, their value is increased when placed in the hands of police intelligence and forensic analysts. For example, when properly handled and analyzed, weapons confiscated at the scene of an attack on U.S. forces may provide—through the discovery of fingerprints or deoxyribonucleic acid (DNA) evidence—information on the individuals who last handled the firearms. The barrel and firing pin of a weapon may be an exact match to a weapon used in previous attacks against U.S. or multinational partners. The evaluation of drugs and associated materials may also provide fingerprints or DNA evidence; a chemical analysis may even specify the region the drug was grown in or how it was processed.

4-41. The tremendous growth in electronic devices, including cell phones, digital cameras, laptop computers, and global positioning systems (GPSs) has also expanded the types of evidence that can be collected. Photographs, video and audio recordings, recording equipment, and computers (to include other portable data storage such as diskettes, thumb drives, memory cards, and media players) can provide a wealth of information about a criminal or terrorist organization, including identities, training techniques, weapons capabilities, targets, and locations. Photographic evidence may come from U.S. or host nation security forces, including manned or unmanned aircraft.

4-42. Written or printed (hard copy) documents are a valuable source of police information. Fingerprints and DNA can be lifted from sheets of paper or envelopes. The type of paper or print used may provide clues as to the system used or the age of the document. Word choices and spelling may provide clues as to a person's background and education. A handwriting analysis may give investigators another means of identifying a specific individual. Lists kept near the computer may be valuable as they may contain passwords, Web site addresses, access codes, e-mail addresses, and aliases. This category of evidence also includes identity papers, including passports, visas, licenses, property ownership, and shipping documents. An analysis of written and printed documentation may identify locations that an individual has visited, suppliers used, funding sources, and associates (see FM 3-19.13 for more information on evidence collection).

4-43. The use of forensic evidence and biometric identification through numerous modalities, such as fingerprints, DNA, and iris scans; firearms and toolmark analyses, and forensic examinations has significantly increased the ability of investigators and police intelligence analysts to add clarity and certainty to their understanding of events and the involvement of individuals in those events. Forensic and biometric capability requires–

- Military police personnel, LE investigators, and trained Soldiers who can recognize, preserve, and collect potential forensic evidence.
- Forensic laboratory examiners who can extract usable information from the collected evidence.
- Biometric collection and storage capability and manipulation software for comparison and analysis of biometric samples.

4-44. Biometric and forensic identification tools and capabilities can be significant assets to distinguish friendly and threat forces and in establishing identity dominance in the AO. These tools are also critical in criminal investigations to identify an individual, establish a person's presence at a specific location in relation to time and space, establish a suspect's physical contact with material related to an investigation, or identify indicators of deception. Military police and USACIDC organizations extensively employ the use of biometric and forensic capabilities while conducting LE in support of posts, camps, and stations or full spectrum operations.

Biometric Data

4-45. *A biometric* is a measurable physical characteristic or personal behavioral trait used to recognize the identity or verify the claimed identity of an individual. (JP 2-0) *Biometrics* is the process of recognizing an individual based on measurable anatomical, physiological, and behavioral characteristics. (JP 2-0) Biometrics applications measure these biological characteristics or personal behavioral traits and compile the data in databases for future comparison.

4-46. These characteristics and traits can be useful for tracking individuals, making positive identifications, establishing security procedures, or using as tools to detect deception based on measurable biological responses to stimulus. Biometric data can be used for protection and security efforts and as evidence in investigations and criminal prosecutions. The following two major types of biometric data are useful to police and intelligence collectors–

- **Identification data.** This data includes biological information, such as fingerprints, voiceprints, facial scans, retinal scans, and DNA. This data is used to match an individual to a source database. Police assets can verify the identity of a specific individual from a target population during screening or search the database to establish the identity of an unknown individual.

- **Data that indicates source truthfulness.** Biometric devices, such as the polygraph, are useful in determining a subject's truthfulness. This device is useful to criminal investigators, but has limited use across the Army and in routine military police operations or intelligence due to training and certification requirements and the level of expertise needed to accurately use the equipment and interpret the data. USACIDC and the United States Army Intelligence and Security Command maintain the only polygraph capability in the Army. The Commanding General, USACIDC, in coordination with the Army Deputy Chief of Staff for Operations and Plans, exercises overall Army Staff responsibility for the DA Polygraph Program and for providing policy guidance with respect to using the polygraph in criminal investigations. The Army Deputy Chief of Staff for Intelligence provides policy guidance for use of the polygraph in intelligence and counterintelligence applications (see AR 195-6).

4-47. Military police and USACIDC staff and investigators or police intelligence analysts can leverage biometric data to develop trends, patterns, and associations between individuals. Biometric data that results in identifications, confirmation of an individual's presence at specific times and locations, and determinations of truthfulness or deception can be extremely useful in building singular associations to linking groups, cells, or organizations.

Forensic Evidence

4-48. Forensics is the deliberate collection and methodical analysis of evidence that establishes facts that can be used to identify connections between persons, objects, or data. It is most commonly associated with evidence collected at crime scenes or incident sites, but also includes methodologies for analysis of computers and networks, accounting, psychiatry, and other specialized fields. Forensics is typically employed to support legal proceedings that lead to criminal prosecution. Additionally, forensics is used during analysis and subsequent targeting in support of full spectrum operations. The USACIDC supports Army forensics requirements through the USACIL. The USACIL facility is stationary due to the nature of the equipment required and other operational requirements.

4-49. Operational requirements for forward-deployed forensic capability have resulted in the development, deployment, and operation of mobile forensics laboratories in the supported AO. The USACIDC provides limited deployable forensics labs to support commanders conducting full spectrum operations as far forward as possible. This expeditionary capability enables timely forensic analyses across a broad range of forensic capabilities, to include latent fingerprints, toolmarks, firearms, and DNA. USACIDC laboratory capabilities may be operated in conjunction with forensic laboratory capabilities resident in our sister Services, capitalizing on complementary capabilities to support the operational commander.

4-50. Forensic analysis expands the ability of police intelligence analysts to establish trends, patterns, and associations by providing scientific documentation of relationships between persons, objects, or data. Criminals, terrorists, or other threat elements tend to operate in predictable ways. The challenge is identifying the patterns. The analyses and comparisons of fragments left at the scenes of improvised explosive device (IED) bombings or sites in an AO can identify similarities in the materials used, the construct of the trigger device, and other variables. This can lead to the development of patterns in which events can be associated with the same bombmaker. Information derived from analyses of the materials used, to include the identification of chemical characteristics, can enable police intelligence analysts to develop associations leading to specific suppliers of those materials. All these efforts can lead investigators to the resolution of criminal investigations and operational commanders to develop targeting strategies, as appropriate.

4-51. Proper handling of material from crime scenes or incident sites is critical to the success of forensic examination by forensic scientists and technicians. Military police are trained to properly identify, preserve, and collect material, whether in the context of crime scene processing, collecting, or through protecting material at an incident or sensitive site. Operational requirements have resulted in all Soldiers being trained on the basics of evidence collection and preservation in the context of incident sites in an operational AO.

INFORMANTS AND LAW ENFORCEMENT SOURCES

4-52. In some circumstances, investigators may attempt to gain recurring access and insight into the workings of a criminal or terrorist network. At other times, they will seek similar access to an organization that may knowingly or unknowingly provide support to criminals or terrorists. Army LE personnel frequently obtain information from informants or LE sources. Informants or LE sources may be insiders who, for a variety of reasons, are willing to provide such information. At times, these persons may be anonymous and available only once or twice. At other times, they will be known to the investigator and may be willing to provide additional information, including information they obtain specifically at the request of an investigator or analyst.

4-53. Informants are informal contacts that are willing to provide information to LE personnel; there is no formal relationship established between an informant and LE personnel. They can be repetitive sources of information or may provide information only once. LE sources are managed formally and include strict controls to protect the source and control contact and information flow. Army LE sources are registered and managed by USACIDC source managers.

Note. Personnel involved with selecting, recruiting, and managing a registered source will normally coordinate and deconflict their sources with other source managers operating in the AO. This coordination occurs between USACIDC source managers and the supporting HUMINT and counterintelligence sections. TC 2-22.303 states that at each echelon, the HUMINT and counterintelligence section coordinate with nonintelligence activities (such as LE) and with non-DOD agencies See TC 2-22.303 for more information on MI source operations. Army LE sources are governed by AR 195-2.

4-54. Individuals may be motivated to serve as informants or LE sources for a variety of reasons. They may be motivated by money, either through the assumed protection of their assets or through payments from investigators. Other informants or LE sources may cooperate with U.S. and LE authorities to prevent prosecution or attack or to direct prosecution or attacks against their rivals. Still others are motivated by feelings of patriotism, justice, or simply because they support U.S. ideals. Some informants and LE sources will be motivated by feelings or revenge against the organization they are reporting against. It is important for police investigators and police intelligence analysts and staff to understand these motives. This understanding may provide insight into biases and potential areas of informant or LE source unreliability that may make information suspect or, at minimum, warrant more deliberate corroboration.

INTERNMENT AND RESETTLEMENT OPERATIONS

4-55. Detained or imprisoned individuals frequently are sources of information pertaining to other investigations and trials due to their direct or indirect connections with crime or criminal activity or personnel internal or external to the detention facility. Only trained interrogators or investigators are authorized to interrogate or interview detained or imprisoned individuals. HUMINT interrogations are not LE-related collection activities and, therefore, are executed only by trained intelligence personnel. Military police Soldiers are prohibited from conducting or participating in HUMINT interrogations of detainees. Trained police personnel, usually military police investigators or USACIDC special agents, may interview or conduct LE interrogations of individuals for specific LE investigation purposes.

4-56. Military police guard personnel continuously employ passive collection techniques to gather information about the population of U.S. military corrections facilities and I/R facilities in support of full spectrum operations. This passive collection stems from observing the activities, routines, and interactions of prisoners, detainees, or DCs in resettlement facilities. Military police personnel conducting I/R operations use both observation and listening techniques to gain and maintain situational awareness critical to protection of the cadre and population in the facility. This passive collection requires attention to detail and significant and continuous attention on the part of the military police Soldier. Information collected by guard personnel is passed through their chain of command to the echelon G-2 or S-2 using established debriefing procedures.

4-57. Information collected in an I/R environment assists the staff in determining potential security issues. Criminal groups may organize and exert their influence or act out in violent manners, often targeting I/R facility cadre or other persons in the population. These associations can be critical to LE investigators as they develop criminal cases for crimes committed external and internal to a facility. Regular debriefings of the cadre and guard personnel operating in close proximity to the population in the facility can provide the military police staff and police intelligence analyst the pieces of information necessary to develop and identify the formation of disruptive trends, patterns, and associations in the facility.

4-58. Persons in a facility may also provide information relevant to criminal or threat activity outside the facility. This information should be immediately reported to the military police staff for dissemination to the appropriate external element for action. In the context of corrections operations, this will typically be SJA and Army LE investigators. In an I/R facility in a deployed OE, the appropriate external element will be the command chain and the S-2 or G-2. The external element may also require additional HUMINT or LE interviews or interrogations. FM 3-39.40 contains additional information concerning I/R operations and associated PIO.

OPEN SOURCE AND PUBLIC INFORMATION

4-59. Open source and public information can provide a significant amount of information that may be useful to police intelligence analysts. Trends, patterns, and associations can be determined from open sources, such as newspapers, press releases, and other publications. With the proliferation of data in the public domain over the internet, police intelligence analysts can find significant information for integration and fusion with existing police information and intelligence. Individuals, groups, and organizations regularly populate public sites, providing valuable information about their associations, organizations, motivations, and other aspects of their operations and activities.

CONTRACTORS

4-60. A *contractor* is a person or business that provides products or services for monetary compensation. A contractor furnishes supplies and services or performs work at a certain price or rate based on the terms of a contract. (FM 3-100.21) Contractor support in the modern OE has expanded significantly. Contracted support often includes traditional goods and services support, but may include interpreter communications, infrastructure, security, and other technical support.

4-61. Integration of contractor information as an element of unified action falls into two categories: passively collected information provided by contractors and contracted personnel directly integrated into operations to fill capability gaps. Military police and USACIDC Soldiers may gain valuable information from contractors. Contractors perform functions throughout an AO and may witness events firsthand or through interaction with host nation, U.S. military, multinational, IGO, or NGO personnel. Military police and USACIDC Soldiers should not overlook contractors as a possible source of information. Policing capabilities may be contracted and integrated into U.S. military operations to enhance existing capabilities; however, these actions are typically short-term solutions.

REPORTING COLLECTED INFORMATION

4-62. Information collected is of no use unless it is provided to the appropriate personnel in a timely manner. Following any collection activity, reports must be compiled for the staff, investigator, or commander requiring the information. The location of physical evidence must also be preserved and reported to maintain chain-of-custody requirements and to allow timely reexaminations of other evidence. Appropriate data should be provided to police intelligence analysts supporting LE and investigative operations. Collection efforts in support of military police operations during full spectrum operations— whether military police reconnaissance, technical assessment, police engagement activities, or data mining—must be documented and provided to the military police or USACIDC staff and police intelligence analysts for further assessment and analysis.

4-63. Immediate assessment of collected information may lead to the identification that the information has answered an IR or a PIR. When identified, information should be reported to the appropriate staff, commander, investigator, or PM. Investigators, staff, and analysts must monitor the CCIR of their higher, subordinate, and adjacent units to support this immediate recognition of CCIR. Time-sensitive information identified as exceptional should be immediately reported through the appropriate staff and command channels for action. (See FM 6-0.)

4-64. While it is important to produce police intelligence, it is extremely important to share not only police intelligence but also raw information, when appropriate. The value of raw information should not be overlooked; an item of information that is not of particular value to one investigation may be important to an adjacent LE organization, unit, or a replacement unit at a later date. Terrorists and criminal enterprises have robust information-sharing capabilities. Tactics used successfully in one location may be used elsewhere in a matter of hours or days. Information sharing allows staff and analysts to see a broader spectrum of conflict. However, police information or intelligence may be so important that its existence cannot be immediately shared. In some instances, it may be possible to develop a synopsis of information that conceals the method, technique, or source. When sharing such synopsized information, it is also important to provide contact information to allow the receiving element to ask further questions and possibly receive additional information.

4-65. If there is no operational requirement to withhold information, it should be disseminated to U.S. forces or other local LE organizations as quickly as possible. Information dissemination may be in a verbal, written, interactive, or graphic format and may be pushed directly to a cooperating organization (see chapter 6 for a more in-depth discussion of PIO dissemination).

4-66. Before the release of police information and police intelligence, it is important to ensure that the release is according to U.S. laws. It is generally more restrictive to share information on U.S. persons. Additionally, individuals detained outside of U.S. territories during military operations typically have fewer protections than those detained in U.S. territories and possessions during LE activities. It is important to coordinate with SJA or higher headquarters regarding legal restrictions on the release of information.

This page intentionally left blank.

Chapter 5

Analysis

PIO is conducted across the spectrum of conflict. The ability of military police and USACIDC Soldiers to provide timely and relevant information is enhanced through the integration of PIO across all military police operations. The results gained from the collection and analysis of police information and the subsequent production of actionable police intelligence drives military police operations. PIO produces police information and police intelligence, enabling LE agencies to proactively identify criminal threats and their capabilities. Military police personnel, enabled by dedicated analyses of police information and production by military police and USACIDC staff and police intelligence analysts, provide proactive policing activities and support the interdiction and prosecution of criminals and terrorists who threaten U.S. citizens. Police intelligence products produced through analyses of police information can also greatly enhance a commander's situational understanding supporting all elements of full spectrum operations. Critical thinking and predictive analysis techniques applied by trained police intelligence analysts support the formation of a holistic COP and continuously feed the operations process and its supporting integrating processes: IPB, targeting, ISR synchronization (and the associated integration), CRM, and KM.

RESPONSIBILITIES

5-1. The commander, PM, and LE investigators play a critical role in the analysis process. They determine IR needed to plan and execute an operation. The commander provides guidance to the staff to ensure that the analysis effort is integrated with other capabilities of the command (biometrics, forensics, and exploitation) and that it is focused on critical requirements and priorities. The commander approves or modifies the recommended PIR.

5-2. Stakeholders (commanders, PMs, and LE investigators) in the analysis of police information must deconflict their priorities to ensure that their limited analysis assets are synchronized and focused in a manner that best supports operational and investigative requirements. Military police and USACIDC staff and police intelligence analysts must understand the priorities of commanders, PMs, and investigators so decisions regarding analysis priorities are consistent with stakeholder requirements.

5-3. PMs responsible for LE in support of posts, camps, and stations and military police or USACIDC commanders are responsible for PIO in their assigned AOs. PIO is an operational function; the S-3, G-3, or PM operations officer is typically responsible for planning and directing PIO. An integral element of PIO is the analysis of police information enabling the subsequent production of police intelligence. The operations element responsible for PIO will typically have a trained Soldier or DA civilian police intelligence analyst assigned. An analyst's skill set includes–

- Technical expertise.
- Knowledge of targets.
- Analytical-technique expertise and experience.
- Search and organizational abilities.
- Inductive reasoning and data-synthesizing abilities.
- Report-writing and briefing abilities.

5-4. The CCIAC at USAMPS is the approved course to train police intelligence analysts for military police and USACIDC units. In support of full spectrum operations outside the United States or its territories, military police and USACIDC staffs conducting PIO coordinate closely with the S-2 or G-2 to ensure that PIO is synchronized and integrated in the intelligence process. In support of posts, camps, and stations, police information and intelligence typically remain in LE channels due to legal restrictions placed on intelligence collection on U.S. citizens. See appendix C for more information on legal authorities pertaining to PIO.

5-5. PIO conducted in support of installations, posts, camps, and stations in the United States and its territories must be conducted within legal and policy restrictions regarding the collection and maintenance of information on persons in the United States. In these OEs, LE personnel may collect information and maintain police information and police intelligence on specific individuals and groups, if a military nexus exists (an offense that has been committed or evidence that exists indicating that a crime may be committed that has a military connection). Intelligence personnel are typically restricted from collecting or storing information or intelligence on U.S. persons. In OCONUS operations dealing with non-U.S. persons, the restrictions on collecting and maintaining information and intelligence are typically less restrictive.

5-6. In support of full spectrum operations, police information and intelligence fed into the operations process is fused with other information and intelligence. Police information and intelligence is integrated within the overall COP to enable commanders to take effective actions against threat forces. Police intelligence analysts, MI analysts and, in selected cases, other LE and intelligence agency analysts provide mutual support to each other. Close coordination and interaction between these elements enhance the effectiveness of PIO. Analysts at all echelons exchange requirements, information, and intelligence products horizontally and vertically throughout the system (see chapter 3 for more detailed discussion of PIO as part of the operations process).

5-7. Regardless of the environment, police intelligence analysts analyze information and produce intelligence data with the objective of supporting commanders, PMs, and investigators. The ultimate goal for police intelligence analysts and staff performing police intelligence activities is to develop actionable intelligence. The trained police intelligence analyst provides the following capabilities to the unit commander, PM, or LE investigator–

- Development of initial background data and knowledge relative to police operations and the criminal environment for a specific AO or police investigation.
- Compilation and integration of collected police information for subsequent analysis and dissemination.
- Information and police intelligence on crime and criminal trends, patterns, associations, and other police-related statistics and information that increase understanding of–
  - Offenders, groups, and criminal networks.
  - Funding sources of criminals.
  - Activities of specific individuals and groups (supporter, financier, corrupt official, supplier, trafficker, smuggler, recruiter, or other categorization).
  - Geographic relationships of crime and criminals.
  - Human terrain from the perspective of policing and the criminal domain.

- Identification of police information gaps and recommendations of IR and collection strategies.
- Identification of systemic issues in police organizations.
- Predictive analyses of crime and criminal activity.
- Recommendations regarding policing and investigative strategies to address crime and criminal threat trends.
- Liaison and information exchange with other military police, LE, civilian, and military elements operating in the AO.
- Analysis and police intelligence products tailored to the specific missions or audiences.
- Support to the targeting process, which includes–
  - Producing actionable police intelligence.
  - Recommending targeting strategies.
- Support to LE and LE investigators in case developments–
  - Identification of background information.
  - Identification of gaps in information and police intelligence relevant to specific investigations.
  - Recommendations for additional LE and investigation efforts.

ANALYSIS OF POLICE INFORMATION

5-8.   The purpose of police intelligence analysis is to answer PIR and other supporting IR and produce police intelligence in support of LE missions and Army operations. Analysis in the context of PIO is conducted from a policing and LE investigative viewpoint and is focused on policing activities, systems, capabilities, and the criminal dimension in the OE.

5-9.   Analysis is one of three continuing activities in the intelligence process (and likewise in PIO) that involve integrating, evaluating, analyzing, and interpreting information from single or multiple sources into a finished product (police intelligence). Police intelligence products must include the needs of the commander, PM, or investigator and be timely, accurate, usable, complete, precise, reliable, relevant, predictive, and tailored.

5-10. Analysis enables the development and recognition of patterns and relationships. Tools and techniques for analysis provide methods to manage or manipulate those relationships and patterns to draw relevant and accurate conclusions. More simply, analysis is a structured process through which collected information is compared to all other available and relevant information to–

- Develop theories and form and test hypotheses to prove or disprove accuracy.
- Differentiate between the actual problem and the symptoms of the problem.
- Enable the analyst to draw conclusions.
- Develop threat COAs.

5-11. Analysis requires manipulating and organizing data into categories that facilitate further study. Patterns, connections, anomalies, and information gaps are assessed during the analysis of police information. The initial hypothesis and data comparison is accomplished by performing the following steps–

- Observe similarities or regularities.
- Ask what is significant.
- Categorize relationships.
- Ascertain the meaning of relationships or lack of correlation.
- Identify RFIs and the need for additional SME analyses.
- Make recommendations for additional collections, to include locations and time constraints, for the ISR matrix.

5-12. There are many categories of analyses used to organize and guide the analytic process. Analysis is a very broad term without consistent nomenclature, especially across analytical disciplines. Military police and USACIDC personnel apply a policing and investigative focus in the use of analytic methods. Examples of categories and techniques particularly relevant to police intelligence analyses are discussed in the following paragraphs.

AREAS OF ANALYTICAL FOCUS

5-13. Military police and USACIDC personnel analyze, synthesize, and develop analytical products based on available information. All analytical techniques use cognitive thought and require analysts to deduce, induce, and infer while working toward conclusions that answer specific IR. Depending on specific requirements and missions, categorizing the effort helps to focus the analyst's efforts toward specific data, considerations, and results. The following paragraphs discuss several analytical focus areas.

COMMUNICATION ANALYSIS

5-14. Communication analysis, formerly referred to as toll analysis, depicts telephone records, including the analytical review of records reflecting communications (such as telephones, e-mails, pagers, and text messaging) among entities that may be reflective of criminal associations or activity. It may result in identification of the steps required to continue or expand the investigation or study.

5-15. While communication analyses have long been a key element in the context of LE investigations, advances in technology have elevated the importance, capability, and scope in regard to tracking communications activities of individuals and organizations during investigations. Communications analysis can enable an analyst to document incoming and outgoing calls, locations of phones, date and time of calls, duration of calls, and other communications data. This facilitates identification of communication patterns and associations relative to specific communications equipment.

CRIME AND CRIMINAL TARGET ANALYSIS

5-16. Crime and criminal target analysis enables the staff and analysts to identify potential criminal targets and crime-conducive conditions, including assessments of vulnerability and relative importance or priority for targeting. A key aspect to performing a crime and criminal target analysis is the determination of the effect desired and the optimal method of targeting.

5-17. Military police and USACIDC personnel use crime and criminal target analysis to identify criminal targets and crime-conducive conditions and to make recommendations on appropriate engagement methods. Targeting could range from police (information) engagements to the application of nonlethal and lethal force, depending on mission and operational variables. Crime and criminal target analysis will be discussed in greater detail later in this chapter.

CRIME AND CRIMINAL THREAT ANALYSIS

5-18. Crime and criminal threat analysis is a continuous process of compiling and examining all available information concerning potential criminal threat activities. Criminal and terrorist threat groups or individuals may target U.S. military organizations, elements, installations, or personnel. A criminal threat analysis reviews the factors of a threat group's operational capability, intentions, and activity and the OE in which friendly forces operate. Threat analysis is an essential step in identifying and describing the threat posed by specific group(s) and/or individual(s).

5-19. Criminal threat analysis techniques are regularly applied to antiterrorism, physical security, and conventional criminal activities. Irregular forces operating in an AO against U.S. interests may use criminal and terrorist tactics, techniques, and procedures that also make them viable targets for friendly threat analysis. Threat analysis and assessments are discussed in greater detail later in this chapter. Crime and criminal analysis supports the production of the crime prevention survey (CPS) and other threat assessments. Specific aspects of crime and criminal threat analysis are discussed later in this chapter.

CRIME PATTERN ANALYSIS

5-20. Pattern analysis is the process of identifying patterns of activity, association, and events. A basic premise is followed when using this technique: activities, associations, and events occur in identifiable and characteristic patterns. Crime pattern analysis looks at the components of crimes to discern similarities in the areas of time, geography, personnel, victims, and modus operandi. Crime pattern analysis can be critically important when facing a threat in which doctrine or the mode of operation is undeveloped or unknown but is necessary to create a viable threat model. Crime pattern analysis is particularly applicable in LE and investigative applications and against irregular forces during full spectrum operations. Crime pattern analysis is discussed in greater detail later in this chapter. Crime pattern analysis can be employed using several different analytical methods. These tools include–

- Crime and criminal trend analysis.
- Pattern analysis.
- Link, association, and network analysis.
- Flowcharting.
- Time, event, and theme line charting.

FUNCTIONAL ANALYSIS

5-21. Functional analysis is focused on assessing a threat disposition and action for a particular type of operation. Functional analysis is based on the concept that certain operations or tasks are explicitly unique; certain actions or functions must be implicitly performed to accomplish those operations or tasks. The functional analysis provides a framework for understanding how specific threats make use of their capabilities. Functional analysis is applicable regardless of how the threat is characterized. Specific knowledge and training enable analysts to apply the functional analysis process, which effectively addresses specific types of threats (see TC 2-33.4 for additional information on the functional analysis). Functional analysis typically consists of the following steps–

- Determine the threat objective.
- Determine the functions to be performed to accomplish the identified threat objective.
- Determine the capabilities available to perform each function.
- Graphically depict the threat use of each capability.

5-22. In the context of the functional analysis, military police staff and police intelligence analysts also conduct a criminal threat risk analysis. The purpose of the criminal threat risk analysis is to determine the relative risk that a specific criminal threat poses to military forces, assets, or the population in general. A heightened criminal threat probability typically drives a more rapid and focused action on the part of military police, investigators, and other police agencies working in concert.

FINANCIAL CRIME ANALYSIS

5-23. The purpose of a financial crime analysis is to determine the extent to which a person, group, or organization is receiving or benefiting from money obtained from nonlegitimate sources. Financial crime analysis is applicable to many criminal investigations, including organized crime, drug trafficking, human trafficking, and property crime, particularly those involving crimes where money is a motivating factor. This type of analysis focuses on financial and bank records, the development of financial profiles (through net worth analyses, identifications of sources, and applications of funds), and business records. Examples of crimes in which financial crime analysis is relevant include–

- Fraud.
  - Insurance fraud.
  - Contract fraud.
- Bribery.
- Embezzlement.
- Theft.
  - Deception.
  - Product substitution.
- Racketeering.
- Other economic crimes.

TERRAIN AND GEOGRAPHIC DISTRIBUTION ANALYSIS (CRIME MAPPING)

5-24. Terrain analysis is conducted to understand the effects of terrain on operations. A terrain analysis in policing operations has the same primary objective as conventional operations: to reduce the commander's operational uncertainties as they relate to terrain. Terrain analysis is used most heavily in the context of specific police activities, such as special reaction team (SRT) operations, protective services, and large-scale crime scene or search operations. Terrain analysis is also critical in the context of physical security applications and in antiterrorism and other protection operations. Typically, the factors of observation and fields of fire, avenues of approach, key terrain, obstacles and movement, and cover and concealment are used in terrain analysis efforts; however, the application of each aspect is significantly different from conventional operations, due to the policing and protection focus. Geospatial products may enhance terrain analysis and geographic distribution analysis (see FM 3-34.230).

5-25. Geographic distribution analysis seeks to identify and map the occurrence of a specific activity or incident over a particular geographic area and emphasizes the use of graphics to depict the activity and emerging patterns. This further enables the analyst to identify hot spots and facilitates geographic profiling to predict potential occurrences. Geographic distribution analysis can also display locations of connected series of crimes, enabling determination of probable areas of bases of operation, offender residences, or other key locations.

5-26. Geographic distribution analysis tools vary from incident "pin mapping" using a physical map and colored pins, stickers, or other methods to identify specific occurrences in an effort to recognize a pattern, to leveraging geographic information system (GIS) software technology. GIS software may be used by police intelligence analysts to conduct geographic distribution analysis, allowing the use of layered graphics, blending geographic data and descriptive information to map places, events, and criminal incidents for analysis to identify patterns and associations. GIS is discussed further later in this chapter.

POLICE INFRASTRUCTURE AND CIVIL CONSIDERATIONS ANALYSIS

5-27. Infrastructure analysis generally focuses on two types of civil information: basic infrastructure data and the actions of local populations. Performing analyses of infrastructure and populations is especially important when conducting stability or civil support operations, to include operations in support of police and prisons, the establishment of the rule of law, and antiterrorism operations. The defining elements of areas, structures, capabilities, organizations, people, and events are used by the Army to guide the assessment of the six characteristics or variables affecting the tactical variable of civil considerations. TC 2-33.4 contains additional information on the analysis of infrastructure and civil considerations.

5-28. Military police have developed the memory aid POLICE to guide the assessment of civil consideration focused on police activities and systems and the criminal dimension. In the context of PIO, the overall goal of infrastructure analysis is the identification and analysis of issues that impact police and prison infrastructure and the population. This identification enables commanders to identify criminal threats, potential disruptive events, and LE operations. POLICE is discussed in chapter 2 of this manual.

POLICE OPERATIONS ANALYSIS

5-29. Operations analysis refers to the study of activities necessary for the day-to-day functions of a specified organization. It is a management tool used to identify problem areas and improve operations. In PIO, these activities cover a range of possible activities: patrol and resource allocation, administrative functions, logistical support, training, investigations, and other critical policing activities. Operations analysis can be focused internally or externally. Military police may conduct an operations analysis to assess and improve their own operations. In the context of PIO, military police conduct assessments of host nation policing and prison capabilities. This mission is typically conducted during, but is not limited to, stability operations.

PREDICTIVE ANALYSIS

5-30. Predictive analysis employs multiple analytical techniques to analyze current and historical information and intelligence to predict future activities, behaviors, trends, or events. It captures statistical and historical data and, through analyses of previous and current associations, uses patterns and trends to enable the analyst to predict potential incidents or activities. Predictive analysis is not guessing; it is based on reasoning, deliberate analysis, and appropriate analytical tools and methodologies. It may focus on specific criminal or disruptive individuals, groups, or organizations to determine their capabilities, vulnerabilities, intent, and probable COAs. Predictive analysis can also be valuable in identifying crime trends and extrapolating future patterns. The value in predictive analysis lies in enabling commanders and PMs to make informed decisions regarding threat mitigation and interdiction. It also enables them to make adjustments in task organization and asset distribution to counter negative or disruptive trends.

ANALYTICAL TOOLS AND TECHNIQUES TO IDENTIFY TRENDS, PATTERNS, AND ASSOCIATIONS (CRIME PATTERN ANALYSIS)

5-31. There are many tools and techniques available to staffs and police intelligence analysts to focus efforts and maximize the effectiveness of analyses. These tools and techniques are used to recognize trends, patterns, and associations. These techniques are not used as singular methods but, rather, are sometimes concurrent and often consecutive activities that complement and enhance each other. Qualitative and quantitative data are used in these techniques. Qualitative data refers to nonnumerical data. This type of data lends itself to content analysis and the identification of historical trends, patterns, and associations. Quantitative data is typically numerical, and analyses of quantitative data are typically statistical in nature.

5-32. Military police and USACIDC staff and police intelligence analysts use these tools and techniques to fuse or disparate information in police intelligence products. They are also used to help in developing crime trends and patterns and performing predictive analysis. These tools and techniques help military police and USACIDC personnel determine what crimes or events are taking place, where they will be located, what time they will occur and, oftentimes, what future activities may occur. When coupled with S-2 or G-2 efforts supporting full spectrum operations, these tools may link crimes to threat group activities that may impact the common operational picture, IPB, and CCIR. Throughout the analysis of police information and the production of police intelligence, relevant information and intelligence is provided to the operations and integrating processes. See chapter 3 for information on PIO integration into the operations process.

ESTABLISHING TRENDS (TREND ANALYSIS)

5-33. Trend analysis refers to the gathering, sorting, prioritizing, and plotting of historical information. It provides analysts and supported commanders, PMs, and investigators a view of how events, elements, and conditions have affected police operations and criminal dimensions in the past. Statistical analysis allows an analyst to extrapolate data to predict future actions or occurrences. This historical perspective provides continuous insights for developing coherent possible and/or probable COAs for the criminal threat and the ability to predict specific occurrences. The results of trend analysis are sometimes referred to as statistical intelligence. In the context of PIO, statistical intelligence refers to data collected from police reports, raw data files, and other historical data assembled into useable maps (or other geospatial products), charts, and graphs. This information is used to indicate past crimes and trends, patterns, or associations. This information must be maintained and updated to be effective.

5-34. Police intelligence resulting from trend analysis is the baseline that analysts and units should use as a statistical point of reference for future analyses. Trends can be depicted in many different formats, to include graphs, maps (or other geospatial products), and narrative summaries. Ideally, trend analysis products should be depicted visually and in a report format. A trend analysis is extremely useful for–

- Specific occurrences.
  - Traffic accidents.
  - Driving while intoxicated and other alcohol-related incidents.
  - Juvenile crimes.
  - Assaults (including simple, aggravated, and domestic incidents).
  - Sex crimes.
  - Suicide.
  - Drug offenses.
  - Homicide.
  - Larcenies.
  - Gang activities.
  - Security-related incidents (perimeter breaches, unauthorized entry, exclusion area violations).
- Offenses by specific persons (persons with a criminal history).
- Locations and times of specific offenses.
- Complaints against the police.
- Number and type of citations.
  - DD Form 1408 (Armed Forces Traffic Ticket).
  - Other locally used forms.
- Calls for assistance.
- Response times.
- Special-event attendance statistics.
- Traffic flow.
  - Specific intersections or roadways.
  - Entry control points and traffic control points.
  - Traffic peaks (including daily, seasonal, holiday, and special events).

5-35. Comparisons of the recorded historical police and criminal events and associated trends derived through statistical trend analysis can provide clues to criminal and threat capabilities, modes of operation, and activities in relation to time and location. Police intelligence derived from trend analysis enables the redistribution of police assets to address specific policing problems. Trend analysis can also determine organizational problem areas and facilitate organizational adjustments or changes to improve operations.

IDENTIFYING PATTERNS (PATTERN ANALYSIS)

5-36. Pattern analysis helps an analyst identify indicators of threat activity. A pattern analysis is based on the premise that activities conducted by individuals, groups, or organizations tend to be replicated in identifiable ways. A thorough analysis of seemingly random events can result in the identification of certain characteristic patterns. Pattern recognition defines the ability of an analyst to detect and impose patterns on random events, allowing for the separation of relevant information from irrelevant information. Pattern recognition can enable an analyst to make assumptions and predictions based on previous historical patterns of activity. In the context of PIO, pattern analysis looks for links between crimes and other incidents to reveal similarities and differences that can be used to help predict and prevent future criminal, disruptive, or other threat activities.

5-37. There are numerous tools and techniques that can be used to display data and establish patterns for analyses. These tools and techniques include–

- **Association and activities matrices.** These tools are used to determine associations between persons and activities, organizations, events, addresses, or other variables. Association matrices establish the existence of known or suspected connections between individuals. An association matrix may be reflected as an array of numbers or symbols in which information is stored in columns and rows. Figure 5-1 provides an example of a basic association matrix. Activities matrices do not develop associations between people.
- **Incident maps and overlays.** This tool sometimes referred to as a coordinate's register, documents cumulative events that have occurred in the AO. This technique focuses on where specific events occur. Incident maps and overlays are a critical tool in geographic distribution analysis. GIS tools can be helpful in producing incident maps with overlay data. Figure 5-2, page 5-10, provides an example of a basic incident map.
- **Pattern analyses plotting.** This tool focuses on identifying patterns based on the time and date of occurrences.

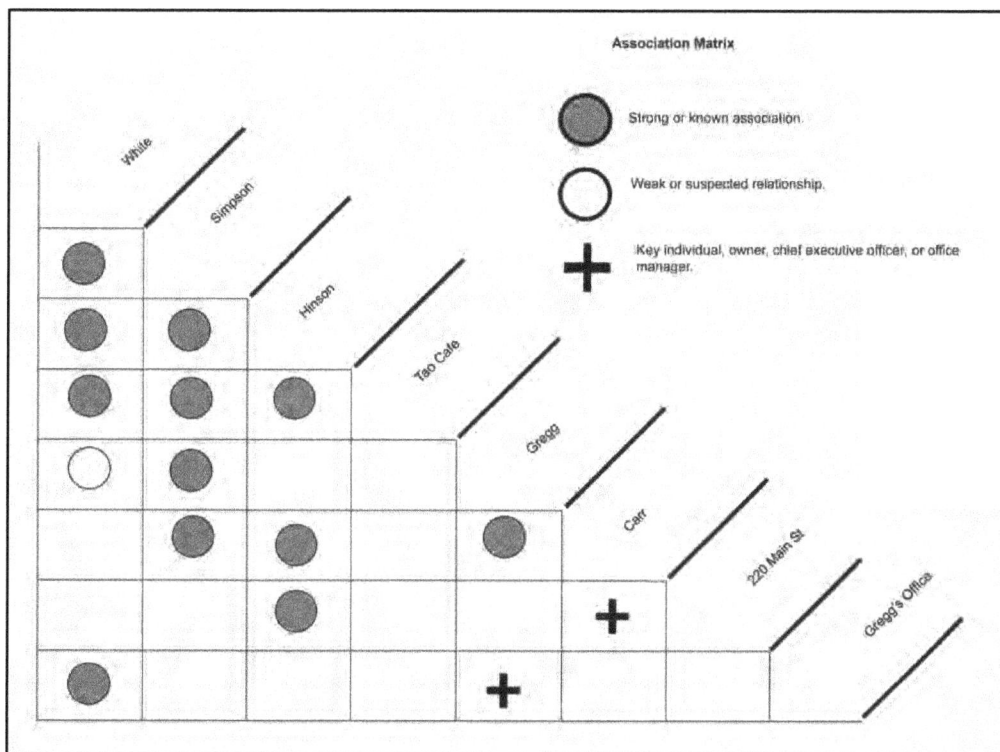

Figure 5-1. Example of an association matrix

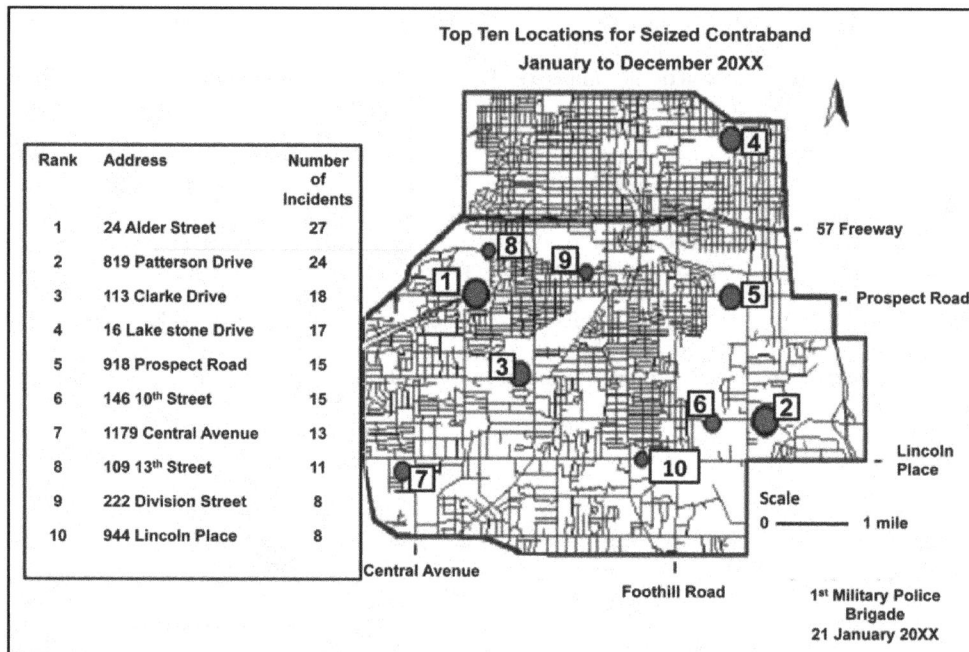

Figure 5-2. Example of an incident map

IDENTIFYING LINKAGES AND ASSOCIATIONS (LINK AND NETWORK ANALYSIS)

5-38. Link analysis is a technique used to graphically depict relationships or associations between two or more entities of interest. These relationships or associations may be between persons, contacts, associations, events, activities, locations, organizations, or networks. Link analysis is sometimes referred to as association or network analysis. Police intelligence analysts use link analyses to find and filter data that will locate people; identify ownership of assets; and determine who is involved, how they are involved, and the significance of their association. Link analysis can be especially valuable to active, complex investigations. It provides avenues for further investigation by highlighting associations with known or unknown suspects. Link analysis is normally tailored to a specific investigation; therefore, dissemination is generally restricted to other LE or military personnel acting as part of the same investigation.

5-39. The main reason for using link analysis is to provide a visual depiction of the activities and relationships relevant to the investigation or operation being conducted. The visual depiction of the network gives meaning to data absent from a visual depiction because it would be too confusing to comprehend. Link analysis is a good analytical tool for generating inferences based on what is known about the current relationships of the known individuals being targeted. The network charting tool can depict the ever-changing alliances and relationships relevant to the investigation or operation.

5-40. The results of link analysis are typically depicted on a chart, matrix, link diagram, or other graphic medium (to include geospatial products). An effective link analysis should depict the existence and strength of relationships between two or more entities of interest: individuals, organizations, businesses, locations, property, or others. Figure 5-3 provides an example of standard link analysis symbology, while figure 5-4, page 5-12, shows an example of a link diagram. TC 2-33.4 provides additional information on link analysis and other analytical tools. A link analysis assists an analyst with–

- **Determining the focus of the analysis.** The focus may be on an individual, organization, business, location, or other entity. The analysis will attempt to answer if–
  - Possible associations or relationships exist among the entities of interest.
  - Patterns or trends are apparent.
  - Information can be inferred from the gathered data.

- **Gathering or assembling information.** The collection of information in Army LE operations in the United States or its territories must have a military nexus and support an LE activity. These restrictions may not apply when supporting full spectrum operations outside of the United States or its territories, depending on the phase of the operation and SOFA in the host nation. This information may include–
  - Field interview cards or reports.
  - Pawnshop databases.
  - Vehicle records.
  - Traffic citation reports.
  - Patrol reports.
  - Initial investigative reports and statements.
  - Crime scene or incident narratives, photographs, and sketches.
  - Communication and computer records.
  - Collected evidence and lab analyses (including biometric data and forensic evidence).
  - NCIC data, be-on-the-lookout alerts, calls for service, or other police data.
  - Case files.
  - Surveillance reports.
  - Financial reports.
  - Public records.
  - Local or regional databases.
  - Other agency reports.
  - Intelligence reports (such as open source intelligence, HUMINT, electronic intelligence, and imagery intelligence).
- **Determining the type of diagram or matrix to be used.**
- **Preparing a rough draft.** This graphic may depict associations, such as weak or unconfirmed, strong or confirmed, or significant member of an entity or group.
- **Finalizing a link analysis graphic and depicting associations.**

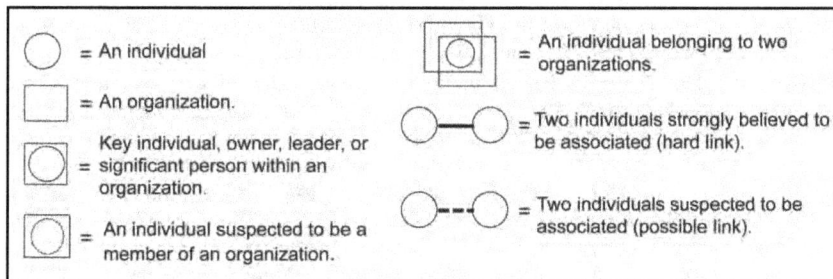

Figure 5-3. Example of standard link analysis symbology

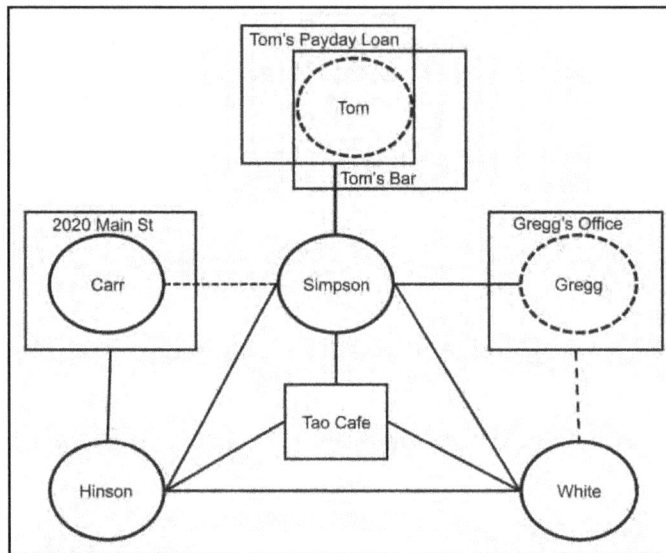

Figure 5-4. Example of a link diagram

FLOWCHARTING

5-41. Flowcharting is a series of analytical techniques that describes and isolates the distribution pattern of a criminal organization, their mode of operation, and the chronology of crime-related activities. Flowcharting allows an analyst to isolate associations and patterns identified through previous analysis techniques to depict a specific person, organization, entity association, or activity without the extraneous information that may have been present in earlier analysis techniques. The flowchart may also show gaps in time that need to be accounted for. When combined with ventures and link analysis charts, a flow chart can assist personnel in understanding relationships and where all of the involved associates fit in to the scheme of the criminal or terrorist enterprise. Some flowcharting techniques include–

- **Activity.** This technique depicts the key activities and modes of operation of an individual, organization, or group. Activity flow analysis is used to view criminal actions and identify modus operandi to determine likely suspects. Most criminals will leave unique indicators when committing a crime. These indicators are specific details, common to the specific criminal or organization, and may include details regarding types of weapons, notes, vehicles, targets, or number of people involved.
- **Time event and theme line charts.** These tools establish chronological records of activities or related events. The charts may reflect activities of individuals or groups and depict large-scale patterns of activity. Figure 5-5 shows an example standard symbology used in time event charts, while figure 5-6 shows a basic example of a time event chart.
- **Commodity.** This technique displays a graphic representation of the movement of materials or products (such as weapons, materials, drugs, money, goods, or services) in a criminal or other network, enabling an analyst to discern an organization's hierarchy.

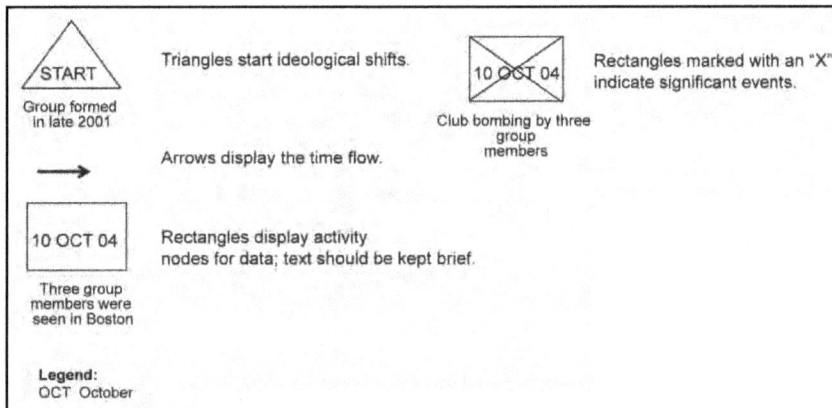

Figure 5-5. Example of standard time event symbology

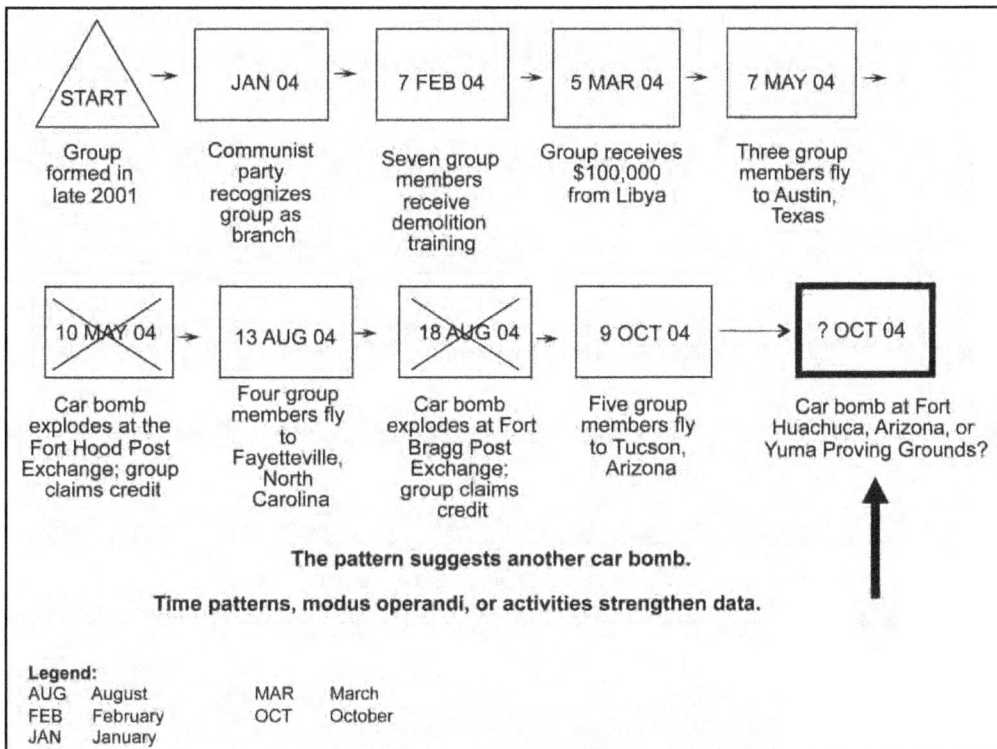

Figure 5-6. Example of a time event chart

COMPILING STATISTICAL DATA

5-42. Statistical data can be drawn from diverse sources and depicted in numerous manners. Statistical data can be very useful in determining frequencies, trends, and distributions; however, the data also has limitations. Analysts and users must be aware of the limitations and resist the desire to infer more than the presented data can accurately portray. Statistical data may be presented in charts displaying–

- Frequencies—through the use of bar, pie, and Pareto charts.
- Trends—through the use of bar and line charts.
- Distributions—through the use of GIS, trend lines, or other formats.

5-43. Data requires different types of statistical tools to present effective information in a clear and understandable manner. For example, if a requirement calls for an analyst to depict the number of reported incidents by the host nation public of contraband markets or movement of contraband material within a specific AO, attributable data or data that can be counted or put into a particular category would be required. The staff or analyst may depict these statistics on a frequency chart. A frequency chart may also be used to identify traffic accidents, fatalities, or injuries and pinpoint specific offenses (such as aggravated assaults, sexual assaults, larcenies, and juvenile offenses). However, if an analyst wanted to portray how long this activity has been occurring, he may want to depict the data on a trend chart, such as a line graph. Any data presented in graphic form should also be tabulated so that the information is readily available to back up the chart and show how data was tabulated. Supporting geospatial products may enhance the presentation.

POLICE INTELLIGENCE COLLECTION FOLDERS

5-44. Extensive working files should be created and maintained on persons, groups, or organizations that are the subject of LE investigations in support of posts, camps, and stations or are targeted by the U.S. military and its partners in support of full spectrum operations. Collection folders contain background information, analysis, spot reports, bulletins, or any other information required by an analyst to develop an understanding of the problem at hand and to compile the requisite data necessary to conduct the analysis and production of police intelligence products. These collection folders are created to establish and maintain graphic and documentary reference material and record analyses. These folders should be maintained separately from LE investigative files; access to the folders should be controlled. The baseline content of police intelligence analysis record holdings should include–

- Names.
- Locations.
- Indicators of the threat of criminal behavior.
- Signs and symbols of the threat.
- Effects of the threat.
- Identification of sources and where the specified information can most likely be obtained.

5-45. Critical information associated with a given threat includes (at a minimum)–

- Patterns.
- Modi operandi.
- Equipment or supplies used in the commission of a crime or terrorist act and how those items were used.
- Known and suspected associations.
- AOs.

5-46. Many ideological threat groups place great emphasis and importance on symbolism. This is also true of the gang culture in the United States. Unique characteristics related to specific threat groups should be included in the working files, to include–

- Important dates.
- Times.
- Symbolism.
- Modi operandi.
- Signatures.

CRIME AND CRIMINAL THREAT ANALYSIS

5-47. Compiling, examining, and reexamining all available information concerning potential threat activities is a continuous process. Threat analysis is conducted by intelligence and LE organizations to determine and monitor current and potential threats. It is an integral element in the production of a threat assessment. Threat assessments must be current to be relevant.

5-48. Intelligence and criminal information, threat information, and asset vulnerabilities are all considered when conducting a threat analysis. Intelligence and criminal information provide data on the goals, methods of operation, techniques, strategies, tactics, and targets of individuals and groups. Threat information can lead to the identification of criminals and criminal groups. A threat analysis must be a continuous activity to account for inevitable changes in the OE. As vulnerabilities are reduced in some areas, they may increase in others. Threat elements assess their targets in relation to one another. An increase in the security posture of one asset may increase the attractiveness of another asset as a target, even though the asset has not reduced its security. Changes in mission, tasks, and personnel also may have an impact on the status of the current threat analysis.

5-49. Criminal and terrorist threat groups or individuals may target DOD organizations, elements, installations, or personnel. A threat analysis reviews the factors of a threat group's operational capabilities, intentions, and activities and the OE in which friendly and threat forces operate. Threat analysis is an essential step in identifying and describing the threat posed by specific groups and/or individuals. Threat analysis is most typically associated with terrorist activity, but the same techniques are applied to conventional criminal activities.

5-50. A threat assessment integrates a threat analysis with criticality and vulnerability assessments that are required for prioritization of assets by commanders and PMs to counter threat activities and associated risks. Vulnerability and criticality information helps the analyst to identify security weaknesses and potential high-risk targets. Several factors are considered during a threat analysis to determine the level of threat posed against specific U.S. interests (such as material, structure, organization, installation, unit, or population). Threats may be direct threats against specific targets or interests or indirect threats that can disrupt operations. Threat analyses and threat assessments enable commanders and PMs to prioritize their efforts and assets to counter criminal, terrorist, or irregular threats posing the greatest risks to critical and vulnerable assets. The factors considered in a threat analysis address the following areas–

- **Existence.** Existence refers to the determination that a threat group is known to be present, assessed to be present, or able to gain access to the AO. The existence of a threat is not dependent on the actual intent or history of threat activity against U.S. interests.
- **Capability.** Capability refers to the determination that a specified threat is known to have acquired, believed to have acquired, or has demonstrated a specific capability.
- **Intent.** Intent refers to a stated desire by threat elements or an actual credible history of threat actions against U.S. interests.
- **History.** History refers to a demonstrated pattern of past activity.
- **Targeting.** Targeting refers to the assessment or additional assessment of threats. It applies if there are known plans, preparations, or activities that indicate a threat of attacks on U.S. interests.
- **Security environment.** Security environment refers to assessing political and security considerations impacting threat capability. This may include–
  - Host nation security cooperation.

■ U.S. and friendly multinational presence. Some considerations include the type and size of the presence and the location, duration, and perception of the local population and threat elements.

■ Geopolitical factors, such as war, instability, economic turmoil, status of local government, or environmental stress.

5-51. Based on the factors of existence, capability, intent, history, targeting, and security environment, the criminal or terrorist threat can be assigned a level of probability and credibility. The probability of criminal or terrorist action against U.S. interests is established as –

● High.
   ■ Threat elements are operationally active.
   ■ There is potential for significant attacks.
   ■ The OE favors the criminal or terrorist element.

● Significant.
   ■ Criminal or terrorist elements are present in the AO.
   ■ There is operational activity.
   ■ The elements possess the capability to conduct significant attacks.
   ■ The OE does not favor U.S., host nation, or criminal and terrorist elements.

● Moderate.
   ■ Criminal or terrorist elements are present in the AO.
   ■ There are no current indications of threat activity.
   ■ The environment favors U.S. or host nation elements.

● Low.
   ■ There are no indications of a threat presence.
   ■ No threatening activity is present in the AO.

5-52. Information and information sources used during analyses should be evaluated for reliability and credibility. Staffs and analysts conducting PIO must conduct continuous evaluations to ensure that information used in their analyses do not lead to false assumptions and conclusions due to problems with the initial source or the information itself. Military police and USACIDC staffs and police intelligence analysts use a source reliability scale to establish the level of reliability of an information source (see table 5-1). Information is further evaluated for credibility using the information credibility scale at table 5-2.

Table 5-1. Source reliability scale

Rating	Reliability Criteria
A = Reliable	No doubt of authenticity, trustworthiness, or competency; history of complete reliability.
B = Usually reliable	Minor doubt about authenticity, trustworthiness, or competency; history of valid information most of the time.
C = Fairly reliable	Doubt of authenticity and trustworthiness; history of reliability information some of the time.
D = Not usually reliable	Significant doubt about authenticity, trustworthiness, and competency; history of occasional reliability.
E = Unreliable	Lacking in authenticity, trustworthiness, and competency; history of unreliable information.
F = Cannot be judged	No basis exists for evaluating the reliability of the source.

Table 5-2. Information credibility scale

Rating	Credibility Criteria
1 = Confirmed	Confirmed by other sources and logical in itself.
2 = Probably true	Not yet confirmed, but is logical in itself.
3 = Possibly true	Not yet confirmed, but seems more likely than not; logical and agrees with other information.
4 = Doubtful	Not confirmed; possible but not logical; no other information is available.
5 = Improbable	Unconfirmed; not logical in itself; contradicted by other information.
6 = Unable to judge	No basis exists to evaluate the information.

5-53. An integral part of a threat assessment is the criticality and vulnerability assessment. The purpose of criticality and vulnerability assessments is to identify the importance and relative susceptibility of unit, base, or installation assets to criminal or terrorist actions. The process also helps the staff in prioritizing identified assets for command protection efforts. Assets may include personnel, equipment, stockpiles, buildings, recreation areas, communication, or transportation systems that are deemed critical. Criticality of an asset typically considers the–

- Value of an asset to a mission or population.
  - **Importance.** Importance measures the value of the area or asset located in the area, taking into consideration the function, inherent nature, and monetary value.
  - **Effect.** Effect measures the ramification of a criminal or terrorist incident in the area, taking into consideration psychological, economic, sociological, and military impacts.
  - **Recoverability.** Recoverability measures the time required to restore function to an area (if the asset is disabled or destroyed), taking into consideration the availability of resources, parts, expertise and manpower, and available redundant assets or systems.
- Ability to replace an asset or function.
  - **Mission functionality.** Mission functionality identifies key positions, special facilities, specialized equipment, and other assets required to fulfill assigned missions.
  - **Substitutability.** Substitutability identifies if there are suitable substitutes available for personnel, facilities, or materiel; if missions can be performed using substitutes; and if the substitutes will produce less-than-successful missions.
  - **Reparability.** Reparability identifies whether an injured or damaged DOD asset can be repaired and rendered operable, how much time will be required for repairs, how much the repairs will cost, and if the repairs will degrade asset performance (or if the mission can be accomplished in the asset's degraded condition).

TOOLS FOR ANALYZING AND ASSESSING CRITICALITY AND VULNERABILITY

5-54. There are numerous tools available to military police, USACIDC, or PM staffs to assess the criticality and vulnerability of a particular asset. Each of these tools has unique inherent strengths and weaknesses. Most of the tools used were developed as targeting tools and are used to analyze and assess the criticality and vulnerability of specific targets. Their use is based on the premise that, by conducting analyses and assessments of assets as potential targets, the relative criticality and vulnerabilities may become apparent. The value in these types of assessments is that it is likely that threat elements use similar analysis tools to assess their targets. For military police and USACIDC staffs using these tools, the results can be used to develop protection strategies and defeat threat tactics.

5-55. The use of multifunctional teams is typically the optimum approach when conducting vulnerability assessments. These teams may include expertise in engineering, signal and communications, network automations, medical, special operations, and legal operations, along with the security and LE expertise resident in the military police and USACIDC force structure. This multifunctional approach ensures a comprehensive assessment across a wide spectrum of technical specialties and ensures a holistic and layered approach.

Mission, Symbolism, History, Accessability, Recognizability, Poplulation, and Proximity

5-56. One of these assessment tools used to determine the criticality and vulnerability of U.S. interests examines seven variables: mission, symbolism, history, accessibility, recognizability, population, and proximity (MSHARPP). MSHARPP is a targeting tool geared toward assessing personnel vulnerabilities but can also be used for facilities, units, or other assets. A matrix is built according to the example shown in table 5-3. The assessed items are listed in the left-hand column; the MSHARPP variables are listed across the top. Each asset is assigned a number (ranging from 1 through 5) that corresponds to the applicable MSHARPP variable. The number 5 represents the greatest vulnerability or likelihood of attack; the number 1 represents the lowest vulnerability. The respective numerical values are totaled to provide a relative value as a target or the overall level of vulnerability. See DOD 0-20012.H for an in-depth discussion of the use of MSHARPP.

Table 5-3. Example of an MSHARPP matrix

Target	M	S	H	A	R	P	P	Total	Threat Weapon
Headquarters building	5	4	5	1	3	4	1	23	4,000-pound, vehicle-borne improvised explosive device
Troop barracks	2	4	5	4	4	4	2	25	220-pound, vehicle-borne improvised explosive device
Communications center	5	4	2	3	5	3	1	23	4,000-pound, vehicle-borne improvised explosive device
Emergency operations center	3	3	2	4	4	4	2	22	50-pound satchel charge
Fuel storage facility	4	3	1	5	5	1	3	22	Small-arms ammunition and mortars
Airfield	5	5	3	2	5	5	4	29	Mortars and rocket-propelled grenades
Ammunition supply point	5	5	1	1	5	3	1	21	Small-arms ammunition and mortars
Water purification facility	5	2	3	5	5	0	4	24	Chemical, biological, and radiological contamination

Criticality, Accessibility, Recuperability, Vulnerability, Effect, and Recognizability

5-57. Another assessment tool used to determine the criticality and vulnerability of U.S. interests examines the six variables of criticality, accessibility, recuperability, vulnerability, effect, and recognizability (CARVER). The CARVER matrix was developed for target selection by U.S. Special Forces to target enemy infrastructure. This tool focuses on the enemy's viewpoint to enable an analyst or assessment team to determine the hardness or softness of assets in criminal or terrorist actions. Using the CARVER method a matrix is developed for each asset. The assets are evaluated against a criteria list. The criteria can be tailored and the relative values manipulated, based on mission or operational needs (as long as consistency is maintained throughout the matrix). An example of a CARVER criteria matrix is depicted in table 5-4. The CARVER matrix is developed much like the MSHARPP matrix, with the assets listed in the left-hand column and the variables listed across the top (see the Carver matrix example at table 5-5, page 5-20).

Table 5-4. Example of a CARVER criteria matrix

Criteria	Relative Value
Criticality:	**Rating**
Immediate output halt or 100 percent curtailment. Target cannot function without asset.	10
Halt less than one day or 75 percent curtailment in output, production, or service.	8
Halt less than one week or 50 percent curtailment in output, production, or service.	6
Halt in more than one week and less than 25 percent curtailment in output, production, or service.	4
No significant effect.	1
Accessibility:	
Standoff weapons can be deployed.	10
Inside perimeter fence, but outdoors.	8
Inside of a building, but on a ground floor.	6
Inside a building, but on the second floor or in basement. Climbing or lowering is required.	4
Not accessible or only accessible with extreme difficulty.	1
Recuperability:	
Replacement, repair, or substitution requires 1 month or more.	10
Replacement, repair, or substitution requires 1 week to 1 month.	8
Replacement, repair, or substitution requires 72 hours to 1 week.	6
Replacement, repair, or substitution requires 24 to 72 hours.	4
Same day replacement, repair, or substitution.	1
Vulnerability:	
Vulnerable to long-range target designation, small arms, or charges (weighing 5 pounds or less).	10
Vulnerable to light antiarmor weapons fire or charges (weighing 5 to 10 pounds).	8
Vulnerable to medium antiarmor weapons fire, bulk charges (weighing 10 to 30 pounds), or carefully placed smaller charges.	6
Vulnerable to heavy antiarmor weapons fire, bulk charges (weighing 30 to 50 pounds), or special weapons.	4
Invulnerable to all but the most extreme targeting measures.	1
Effect (on the population):	
Overwhelming positive effects, but no significant negative effects.	10
Moderately positive effects and few significant negative effects.	8
No significant effects and remains neutral.	6
Moderate negative effects and few significant positive effects.	4
Overwhelming negative effects and no significant positive effects.	1
Recognizability:	
Clearly recognizable under all conditions and from a distance and requires little or no personnel training for recognition.	10
Easily recognizable at small-arms range and requires little personnel training for recognition.	8
Difficult to recognize at night during inclement weather or might be confused with other targets or target components. Some personnel training required for recognition.	6
Difficult to recognize at night or in inclement weather (even in small-arms range). The target can easily be confused with other targets or components and requires extensive personnel training for recognition.	4
The target cannot be recognized under any conditions, except by experts.	1

Table 5-5. Example of CARVER matrix

Potential targets	C	A	R	V	E	R	Totals
Commissary	5	7	10	8	8	10	48
Headquarters	1	4	10	8	6	6	35
Communications center	10	10	6	8	3	4	41

Economic Crime and Logistic Security Threat Analysis

5-58. The Army crime prevention program consists of the following two critical elements: economic crime threat assessment (ECTA) and logistics security threat assessment (LSTA). USACIDC elements typically focus on these threat areas. These two assessments are a basic analysis of posts, camps, and stations or forward-deployed bases and focus on ascertaining economic crime potential and vulnerabilities. The USACIDC criminal intelligence analyst and military police intelligence analyst in the AO should communicate with each other and collaborate on significant items in the ECTA and LSTA. This collaboration will result in proactive police intelligence analysis in the AO. The following outlines describe the critical elements–

- ECTAs are an assessment of the overall economic posture of an installation or activity in a USACIDC field element AO. ECTA is an important element of the USACIDC crime prevention program. ECTA is critical to maintaining a proactive effort and relating to both economic crime and logistical security operations.
- LSTAs assess logistical systems, modes of transportation, or APODs and SPODs for criminal threat vulnerabilities and terrorist threats directed at logistic pipelines, the security of U.S. government assets, and the safety of DOD personnel. LSTAs can serve as a substantial internal and external operational planning tool.

CRIME AND CRIMINAL TARGET ANALYSIS

5-59. Targeting methodology is designed to facilitate the engagement of the right target, at the right time, and with the most appropriate assets to achieve effects consistent with the commander's intent. Persons, groups, infrastructure, and activities can be targeted by many means, both lethal and nonlethal. PIO supports the targeting process, enabling selection and prioritization of crime and criminal targets and subsequent selection of the appropriate response to them, taking into account operational requirements and capabilities. Targeting entails the analysis of adversary situations relative to the mission objectives (see chapter 3). Crime and criminal target analysis enables staff and police intelligence analysts to identify potential targets, including assessments of their vulnerability and relative importance. A key objective of crime and criminal targeting analysis is the determination of timing and synchronization in the context of operations, prioritization of targets to be engaged, the desired effect, and the optimal method of targeting.

5-60. The police intelligence analyst creates police intelligence through evaluations and analyses of collected data. Collected data comes from many sources and methods. These methods range from military police reconnaissance and assessment operations in a tactical environment to covert operations conducted by USACIDC drug suppression teams, with a myriad of in-between activities. Relevant and actionable information and intelligence can be exploited to gain an advantage over the threat.

5-61. Evaluation, analysis and exploitation may occur simultaneously. New information may be obtained; recognized as relevant, credible, and time-sensitive; and be disseminated quickly to maximize exploitation. Further analysis continues to ensure fusion with other information and intelligence while staff and commanders simultaneously use the targeting process to actively exploit the data. For example, information from a reliable source may indicate that an enemy element is about to launch a major attack or that a criminal element is imminently threatening U.S. interests. In this case, the report that an attack is imminent is disseminated as soon after receipt as possible.

5-62. Police intelligence resulting from crime and criminal target analyses conducted during PIO and fused into the operations process and COP can provide valuable information to commanders and staffs to enable effective targeting. Results of police intelligence analyses may contribute to the development of tactical threat targets for commanders in an expeditionary OE and target criminals and criminal threat systems that threaten the commander's mission or the safety and security of installations, personnel, and resources. It provides information to the commander and PM, with a related situational understanding of the capabilities and challenges associated with operating within the rule of law in a given AO. This is extremely important in expeditionary environment transitioning from major combat and instability to supporting a host nation in establishing a criminal justice system under the rule of law. As the environment transitions, due process requirements will increase and targeting activities will require a higher level of specificity and probable cause to justify warrants or other legal mechanisms to authorize targeting on individuals and organizations.

5-63. The ultimate goal of a crime and criminal target analysis as it relates to PIO is to identify criminal and threat persons, groups, or organizations; identify historic and current crime trends and predict future trends and activities that enable targeting decisions; develop investigative leads through the identification of trends, patterns, and associations; and make target recommendations. Crime and criminal target analyses and subsequent support to operations occur in all environments. PIO supports the targeting process through–

- Target identification.
    - Using the criminal information gathered and stored in the data files to identify threats (crimes, criminals, and other threat elements and activities) and locations of threat activity.
    - Identifying the organizations involved in the threat activity. This may be criminal enterprises affecting U.S. interests or irregular threat groups (such as terrorists, insurgents, or groups engaging in criminal activity that disrupt or endanger U.S. operations, including threats from corrupt officials or infiltrators internal to host nation organizations).
- Analyses of police, criminal, and threat data. Data analysis can determine trends, patterns, and associations that might otherwise go unnoticed. Analysis enables ongoing crime and crime trend tracking in support of force protection and antiterrorism programs.
    - At locations in the U.S. and its territories, these analyses aid PMs and investigators in focusing their resources at the appropriate places and times to deter or interdict criminal and disruptive activity.
    - In support of full spectrum operations, military police and USACIDC personnel use this police intelligence to guide their actions and to enhance the commander's COP. This can be done as a U.S. operation or in concert with the host nation or multinational forces, depending on the mission and operational variables.
- Corroboration of source and informant information. Due to their dispersion and presence, military police and USACIDC personnel are well equipped to obtain corroborating information for otherwise unsubstantiated source data.
    - During LE operations conducted in the U.S. and its territories, this corroboration can be accomplished through data mining, witness interviews, surveillance, or other source contacts (see FM 19-10).
    - Similar techniques can also be applied in support of full spectrum operations to corroborate witness statements or evidence obtained at an incident site. This corroborated information can then be used in the legal system for prosecution or acted on by the appropriate GCC for military action, depending on mission and operational variables.
- Information sharing and support to active police investigations.
    - Ongoing investigations can be solved using information that is collected and documented by LE officers, regardless of the agency. One LE officer may have an informant who knows the perpetrator of a burglary that another officer is investigating. Aggressive and proactive analyses and information sharing can contribute to the resolution of specific investigations or criminal activity across organizational lines.

■ In OCONUS OEs, this support can assist commanders and their staffs by identifying key threat players, organizations, or cells that may be operating across or in unit boundaries or AOs. Police intelligence may identify weapons caches, facilities for the production of IEDs, or personnel involved in threat activities that are being conducted in another AO. The fusion of ongoing police information and intelligence into the operations process and the COP may provide critical information to commanders and staffs to enable effective targeting.

● Analyses of threat information. The analysis function is the hub of PIO. Analysis converts information into actionable police intelligence and contributes to other intelligence products.

■ In LE terms, the data or information collected is analyzed to develop additional leads in ongoing investigations, provide hypotheses about who committed a crime or how they committed it, predict future crime patterns, and assess the threat a crime group or activity might pose to a jurisdiction.

■ In full spectrum operations, police intelligence resulting from an analysis of threat information enhances the operations process and aids in the maintenance of a holistic COP. Police intelligence may identify threat, operational, or logistical networks; individual operators or sympathizers; and low-level criminals that can disrupt U.S. operations, including threats from corrupt officials or infiltrators internal to host nation organizations. Police intelligence is injected into the targeting process for assessment and exploitation.

ADDITIONAL ANALYSIS CONSIDERATIONS AND TECHNIQUES

5-64. There are numerous tools available to the military police and USACIDC staff and police intelligence analysts. Likewise, there are also pitfalls that can hinder the objectives and accurate and timely assessments of valuable police information. The following paragraphs discuss some of these analytical techniques pitfalls.

EVALUATION CRITERIA

5-65. The police intelligence analyst must be able to weigh data use and decide what data is credible. Five aspects determine the value of police information. These aspects include–

● **Validity.** Is the information actually a correct representative of what it is believed to signify? Do not produce police intelligence before validity is confirmed.

● **Relevance.** Is the information actually relevant to the mission or investigation? Is the data a logical connection to the priority of effort?

● **Timeliness.** Is the information or intelligence tied to a specific event or decision point or required in a hard time frame? New information is processed as it is received, but the staff must be aware of time considerations.

● **Corroboration.** Ideally, two independent sources are used to corroborate data. Failure to corroborate information can produce a flawed product. Normally, uncorroborated information is suspect and of limited usefulness. However, uncorroborated information may be useful when balanced against contextual and historical factors. An example may be information received from a confidential source that has a history of reliable and credible reporting. See source reliability and information credibility scales at table 5-1, page 5-16, and table 5-2, page 5-17.

● **Legality.** Information that is not legally obtained will risk tainting all work and expended resources. An analyst must ensure that all information is obtained in legal guidelines.

SCANNING, ANALYSIS, RESPONSE, AND ASSESSMENT

5-66. Scanning, analysis, response, and assessment (SARA) is a problem-solving approach developed and used in the LE community. In simple terms, once a problem is identified and its characteristics are analyzed, a response is developed and deployed to combat the problem. After a determined time period, the response is evaluated. The following text shows a brief discussion of each aspect of the SARA model–

- **Scanning.** Scanning is the first problem-solving step. Scanning involves the identification of a cluster of similar, related, or recurring incidents identified in the course of a preliminary review of information. It enables the analyst to select and focus on specific crime or disorder problems from among many disparate items of information.

- **Analysis.** Analysis is the use of all available sources of information to determine why a problem is occurring, who is responsible, who is affected, where the problem is located, when it occurred, and what form it takes.

- **Response.** Response is the execution of a tailored set of actions that address the most important findings of the analysis phase.

- **Assessment.** Assessment is the measurement of the impact of responses on a targeted problem. Assessment uses information collected from multiple sources, both before and after the responses have been implemented.

DATABASE AND AUTOMATION REQUIREMENTS

5-67. The increased proliferation of digital and computer technology have greatly increased the amount of information that must be assessed by commanders, PMs, their staffs and investigators. Concurrently, the expansion and use of automated systems for data storage and manipulation has become a reality and a necessity to effectively manage the volume and types of data that are available. Databases serve as repositories for raw police information and analyzed police intelligence products. This data may be maintained by a local installation, a combat unit, or a major Army or DOD command. Databases can be used during active investigations and as final storage locations for complete information on closed investigations and reports. It is imperative that investigators become familiar with the full host of available databases for both data entry and retrieval.

5-68. Advances in database technology, combined with an explosion in information sharing and networking among police agencies, has resulted in the development and expansion of these robust information repositories. Army LE personnel continue to access the NCIC database, but can also turn to databases containing fugitive information from corrections systems and terrorist threat information from HLS and FBI systems. DOD proprietary automation systems, such as COPS and ACI2 greatly improve interoperability and eliminate seams that criminal and other threats might otherwise exploit.

5-69. Access to local, theater, DOD, non-DOD, and commercial databases allows analysts to leverage stored knowledge on topics ranging from basic demographics to threat characteristics. A validated Defense Intelligence Agency customer number (acquired by the intelligence directorate of an echelon intelligence staff section [J-2], G-2, or S-2), in combination with SIPRNET and JWICS connectivity, can establish access to most online databases. The challenge for an analyst is to gain an understanding of the structure, contents, strengths, and weaknesses of the database regardless of the database type. Additionally, the procedures are often difficult for extracting portions or downloading and transferring data to unit automated information systems. Each intelligence discipline has unique databases established and maintained by a variety of agencies. Database access is typically accomplished through unit or agency homepages via SIPRNET and JWICS.

5-70. Automation increases the capability to correlate large volumes of information from many sources and assist in the analysis process. Interpretation of the information requires an analyst to develop search and file parameters. Analysis continues to be a human function—cognitive functions that manifest in reflective thinking. Information is converted into police intelligence products through a structured series of actions that, although set out sequentially, may also take place concurrently. Production includes the integration, evaluation, analysis, and interpretation of information in response to known or anticipated intelligence product requirements.

ARMY CRIMINAL INVESTIGATION INFORMATION SYSTEM

5-71. ACI2 supports Army criminal investigation operations, is accredited for unclassified LE-sensitive operations, and uses private, network-based software applications. USACIDC personnel have local office and global access to most data in ACI2. Scheduled reports and ad hoc queries provide powerful data mining capabilities. ACI2 supports numerous USACIDC operations and reports that include–

- Reports of investigation.
- Forensic laboratory reports.
- Crime prevention surveys.
- Criminal activity threat assessments.
- Criminal intelligence reports.
- Logistical security threat assessments.
- Economic crime threat assessments.
- Port vulnerability assessments.
- Terrorist information and threat reports.
- Regional criminal intelligence summaries.
- Registered source reports.
- Criminal alert notices.
- Drug suppression surveys.

5-72. These software programs help analysts and investigators by revealing the structure and content of a body of information by storing, organizing, and analyzing intelligence and presenting it in easily understood graphic format. Civilian LE partners cannot access many DOD proprietary automation systems, such as COPS and ACI2. By using these commercial products in concert with appropriate information release policies, we can bridge information gaps between Army and civilian LE. Common crime analysis databases automation, templates, and data formats improve interoperability and eliminate seams for criminals and other threat forces to exploit.

CENTRALIZED OPERATIONS POLICE SUITE

5-73. A significant tool used by the PM today is COPS—an information management system supporting worldwide military police operations. It combines all facets of LE reporting. The current applications found in COPS are the Vehicle Registration System, Military Police Reporting System, Army Correctional Information System, Detainee Reporting System, and a self-registration feature. COPS applications include daily activity LE (blotter) reports, military police reports, and other automated entries. It is accredited for unclassified LE-sensitive operations and uses a virtual private network and Web-based operations.

5-74. Typically, COPS provides military police access to automated police records from a centralized database. It allows users, with appropriate permissions, to conduct queries expeditiously from a centralized database. Name queries return limited criminal arrest history data from Army-wide military police records. A major component of the COPS database is the ability to provide real time information. This centralized database also eliminates natural borders and barriers that normally hamper the LE community. The capabilities afforded by the COPS allows for a quick compilation of statistics, based on the query input.

5-75. The COPS is capable of supplying a significant amount of statistical data to police intelligence analysts and PM staffs. This data can be manipulated to identify trends, patterns, and associations that enable PMs and their staffs to effectively allocate resources, address specific crime problems or other areas of concern, and forecast future requirements.

DISTRIBUTED COMMON GROUND SYSTEM–ARMY

5-76. DCGS–A is the Army's ISR ground processing system for SIGINT, imagery intelligence, measurement and signature intelligence, and HUMINT sensors, along with providing weather and terrain analysis. DCGS–A provides Web-based communications and interactive analytical capability. The platform, with integrated analytical tools, allows analysts to participate and collaborate in the development of products geared to mission planning, targeting, and information analysis at all echelons. DCGS–A integrates existing and new ISR system hardware and software to produce a common, net-centric, modular, scalable, multisecurity, multi-intelligence, and interoperable ISR architecture. DCGS–A provides the ability to access to data, from tactical to national sensors, across the intelligence enterprise and facilitates reach with collaboration capabilities for deployed elements. DCGS–A enables the rapid input of analytical products, increasing responsiveness to the needs of commanders and staffs.

5-77. DCGS–A facilitates the rapid conduct of operations and synchronization of all warfighting functions. This enables commanders to operate in the threat's decision cycle and shape the environment for successful follow-on operations. The DCGS–A provides the following capabilities–

- Receives and processes select ISR sensor data.
- Facilitates control of selected Army sensor systems.
- Facilitates ISR synchronization and ISR integration.
- Facilitates fusion of information from multiple sensors.
- Enables distribution of friendly, threat, and environmental (weather and terrain) data.

ADDITIONAL ANALYTICAL AND DATABASE CONSIDERATIONS

5-78. There are many commercial database and analytical applications that are useful for police intelligence analysis and data management. Some of these applications may be costly and require a significant up-front training investment; these will typically be used by dedicated police intelligence analysts. Others may be more readily available as standard database applications that can be used for more low-level analysis and statistical manipulation; these applications may also be used by dedicated police intelligence analyst but are also readily and easily available to the staff in general.

Automated Databases

5-79. A database is a tool for collecting and organizing information. A database can store information about people, types of events, or just about anything. Many databases start as a list in a wordprocessing program or spreadsheet. Without databases, information is difficult or impossible to retrieve quickly, especially under adverse conditions. Depending on the capability of the individual database software, databases can support many complex analytical functions and requirements. Military police staff and police intelligence analysts may use databases to–

- Deconflict and synchronize collection missions.
- Track requests for information (RFIs).
- Track IR.
- Prepare reports and assessments.
- Track threat and friendly events or situations.
- Develop targeting recommendations and priorities.

5-80. Many analytical software applications are compatible with various databases. This enables databases to interact with other tools to support predictive analysis, prepare graphic analytical products, and provide situational awareness to the unit commander. These databases can–

- Support time event charts, association matrices, link analysis, and other analytical tools.
- Allow operators, staff, and analysts to–
    - Compartment (protect) source-sensitive, operational database segments; files; records; and fields.
    - Create, update, and maintain databases from locally generated information.
    - Import complete or partial databases from larger or peer databases.
    - Export complete or partial databases to peer or larger databases.
    - Share database information with personnel possessing appropriate access authorization, such as peers, subordinates, or higher commanders.
- Allow data queries for decisionmaking and operational and analytical support.
- Interact with analytical programs able to correlate data and facilitate information retrieval from data repositories.
- Allow for information retrieval functions, such as browsing, Boolean functions, key word searches, concepts, and similar functions.

Automated Analytical Tools

5-81. Automation of analytical tools, such as time event charts, association matrices, activity matrices, and link analysis diagrams can significantly enhance the predictive analysis capability and pace of production. Automation enables rapid access to information. When properly evaluated, this allows critical analysis of a greater pool of information, which produces a more accurate and timely product.

5-82. Automated analysis software includes computer-assisted analytical programs that reduce the time required for analysis. These programs help the analyst in developing predictions and identifying information gaps to support targeting and collection. Automation and Web-based tools allow an analyst to–

- Track, integrate, and catalogue information and reports.
- Expedite data retrieval, data organization, content analysis, and visualization.
- Share analyses and information with other units and analytical elements, as appropriate.
- Take advantage of Web-based collaborations.
- Provide analytical results and view operations in real time.
- Share resources, such as models, queries, visualizations, map overlays, and tool outputs through a common interface.
- Apply clustering (a nonlinear search that compiles the results based on search parameters) and rapid spatial graphical and geographic visualization tools to determine the meaning of large informational streams.
- Rapidly discover links, patterns, relationships, and trends in text to use in predictive analyses.
- Capture analytical conclusions and automatically transfer them to intelligence databases and systems.

Note. There are strict legal and regulatory constraints on the storing of information on U.S. persons. The supporting SJA should be consulted to ensure that data storage is in compliance with applicable laws and regulations.

Geographic Information Systems

5-83. There are several automated GIS to help military police staff and police intelligence analysts with organizing, analyzing, and producing geographic data and products. A GIS can provide a graphic depiction of data as it relates to the geography of a specific area. GIS software uses database data to display maps and data, as required by the system operator. These tools are useful and have the capability of providing layered, three-dimensional images of specific areas of interest. Typically, data will be imported from an existing database or input manually into the GIS. Data should be continuously updated to ensure that current and accurate data is available. Once loaded, the analyst can manipulate the data to produce specific analytical products, as required.

5-84. GIS tools enable the analyst to layer informational data on top of terrain to provide a more accurate picture of the AO or a specific target. These capabilities are most useful in analyses of dense urban areas. These systems are used to track and analyze specific criminal activity and associated structures and locations, allowing the development and identification of patterns and linkages that might otherwise go unnoticed. GIS can also be used as a platform to portray the effects of terrain on operations. For example, in a crisis response scenario, GIS can provide a three-dimensional image of a target building for rapid analysis and decisionmaking where an LE raid or SRT mission is planned.

Chapter 6

Production and Dissemination

Police intelligence operations support Army LE and Army operations by producing relevant and actionable police intelligence products that support those activities and operations. The goal of PIO is achieved when police information is collected, analyzed, produced, and disseminated to military police and USACIDC units, maneuver commanders, other Service forces, host nation security forces, or the local population. Close coordination with police intelligence analysts ensures that products are tailored to meet specific requirements. The military police staff and police intelligence analysts must be proficient in packaging relevant police intelligence into usable products that are clear, concise, and targeted to the needs of the stakeholder. Police intelligence products may range from simple, free-formatted alerts to complex briefings and assessments. This chapter provides a brief description of some of the more common products that may be produced by the military police or USACIDC staff and their associated analysts.

POLICE INTELLIGENCE OPERATIONS

6-1. Police intelligence products answer IR and CCIRs and enable commanders and LE investigators to make informed decisions. These products may assist Army or civilian LE personnel in capturing a wanted felon, gaining information to assist in an investigation, or closing an investigation. When police intelligence products are fused with other police intelligence, they can greatly enhance the effectiveness of LE investigations and police operations. When supporting full spectrum operations, police intelligence can provide critical understanding to commanders regarding police and prison organizations, systems, structures, and the criminal environment in the AO. When fused with Army operational intelligence, police intelligence can greatly enhance the commanders COP.

6-2. Police intelligence products will generally contain both basic information and analyzed intelligence. It is important to keep the intended recipient and purpose at the forefront during the planning and production phases. Failure to do so may result in the production of multiple documents, each with a specific audience and purpose. Regardless of the format employed, producers of police intelligence products must take extreme care to ensure the accuracy of the products and the protection of classified or sensitive information. Information or police intelligence that must be retained in LE channels to protect information, sources, or ongoing investigations is characterized as law enforcement sensitive. The term law enforcement sensitive is used to classify information or intelligence that is obtained for, processed through, or managed by law enforcement organizations. It is essential that these data are restricted to law enforcement channels, unless otherwise directed by competent authority.

6-3. Distribution restrictions must be understood by both the producers and the recipients of disseminated police information or police intelligence. At times, products may contain data drawn from multiple unclassified sources. These police intelligence products may–

- Remain unclassified.
- Receive a distribution caveat of "Law Enforcement Sensitive" or "Sensitive but Unclassified."
- Receive a classified restriction when the results of analyses warrant.

6-4. Classification of a document or data may be required to protect an informant or LE source, a monitoring capability, a tactics, techniques, and procedures for gathering police information, or other classification criteria. It may be possible to prevent the creation a classified product simply by protecting the manner in which the information was collected or processed. In the event that a product requires classification, immediate actions should be taken to ensure that the classified data or document is properly stored to prevent unauthorized access or compromise information or intelligence. Coordination with the local offices responsible for computer network defense and security issues should be maintained to ensure that security requirements are maintained.

PRODUCTION OF POLICE INTELLIGENCE PRODUCTS

6-5. *Intelligence production* includes analyzing information and intelligence and presenting intelligence products, conclusions, or projections regarding the OE and enemy forces in a format that enables the commander to achieve situational understanding. (see FM 2-0) Police intelligence products produced by police intelligence analysts, military police, and USACIDC staff and LE investigators should enable the stakeholder (the commander, PM, or LE investigator) to gain greater understanding of the OE and enable operational objectives. Police intelligence products and reports should provide commanders, PMs, and LE investigators with useful tools to augment a holistic assessment of the security and criminal environment across the AO. Effective police intelligence products have several characteristics. These characteristics include–

- **Distinct.** The product can support or enhance other intelligence products but should provide analysis that stands on its own merit.
- **Tailored.** The product should be tailored to specific commander, PM, or LE investigator mission, objectives, and AO.
- **Actionable.** The product provides commanders, PMs, and LE investigators with situational understanding to support effective decisionmaking.
- **Accessible.** To the greatest extent possible in mission, legal, and policy constraints on information sharing, products must be accessible to stakeholders requiring the information (such as commanders, PMs, LE investigators, staffs, other LE agencies, governmental organizations, and host nation agencies).
- **Timely.** The products support the commander, PM, or LE investigator objectives and intent for operations or effects.

6-6. Police intelligence products produced by military police and USACIDC staff and police intelligence analysts are sometimes in standardized formats to ensure consistency in reporting and content. Most products are dependent on the target audience; the mission; and the specifics of the event, material, person, or organization that is the subject of the product. At the tactical level, the level of detail and type of intelligence required is much different than at the operational or strategic level. The staff and analyst must fully understand the information, IR, and specific needs of the target audience, and provide a product that enables decisionmaking appropriate to the level of the recipient.

6-7. The following sections include examples of various police intelligence products. These examples are baseline products; they will change with command and host nation requirements, technological advances, and legal restrictions. Formats may vary greatly; however, the accuracy, timeliness, and relevancy of the product is critical to the targeted audience.

BE-ON-THE-LOOKOUT ALERTS

6-8. Be-on-the-lookout (BOLO) alerts are routinely sent out by Army and civilian LE agencies. BOLO alerts are used to provide information to, and request assistance from, military and civilian LE organizations, military units, and, at times, the general public about specific individuals, vehicles, events, or equipment. These alerts are typically used when the subject matter is time-sensitive and a heightened awareness by all available personnel is requested to facilitate the appropriate action. BOLO alerts may be distributed in a printed format, over appropriate information networks, or transmitted over radio nets, depending on the breadth of distribution, time sensitivity, or other mission and environmental factors.

6-9. BOLO alerts may be general or very specific, but they should contain, when possible, enough information to prevent numerous "false positive" reports and should provide reporting and disposition instructions. These instructions should include any known dangers associated with the subject of the BOLO alert. For example, a BOLO alert for a grey BMW automobile to all military police units operating in Germany or an orange and white taxi in Iraq would be ineffective and would likely result in an extremely high number of "sightings." This type of general information might also be ignored by military police personnel for the same reason. Additional information about the driver, body damage to the vehicle, or other specific details would reduce the false positives and increase the value of what is reported. In some instances, the amount of known information is limited to one or more identifying data points. This is common in expeditionary environments where a list of names may be the only data available or immediately following a crime or incident when only rough descriptions of suspects or few witnesses are available. Figure 6-1 and figure 6-2, page 6-4, show examples of BOLO alerts.

For Immediate Release
20 March 20XX, Washington D.C.
Federal Bureau of Investigation (FBI) National Press Office
(Subject Name) Poster

Insert Photo

FBI SEEKING PUBLIC'S ASSISTANCE IN LOCATING INDIVIDUAL SUSPECTED OF PLANNING TERRORIST ACTIVITIES.

The FBI has issued a be-on-the-lookout (BOLO) alert for (subject) in connection with possible threats against the United States. In the BOLO alert, the FBI expresses interest in locating and questioning (subject) and asks all law enforcement personnel to notify the FBI immediately if he is located. Subject's current whereabouts are unknown.

Subject is possibly involved with al-Qaeda terrorist activities and, if true, poses a serious threat to U.S. citizens worldwide.

Subject is 27 years old and was born in Saudi Arabia. He is approximately 132 pounds (but he may be heavier today), 5'3" to 5'5" tall, has a Mediterranean complexion, black hair, black eyes, and occasionally grows a beard. A photograph of this individual is available on the FBI's Web site, at <http:www.fbi.gov>.

Subject carries a Guyana passport; however, he may attempt to enter the United States with a Saudi, Trinidad, or Canadian passport. Subject is also know by the following aliases:

Alias #1, Alias #2, Alias #3, Alias #4

Legend:
BOLO   be-on-the-lookout
D.C.   District of Columbia
FBI   Federal Bureau of Investigation
U.S.   United States

Figure 6-1. Example of an FBI BOLO alert

UNCLASSIFIED For Official Use Only Be-on-the-Lookout List		
Date	Individual/Vehicle	Threat Summary
4 Sep XX	1970s Chevrolet Impala, White, host nation Plate 283AC2	Used in transporting explosive materials for IED production and targeting U.S. and host nation police forces.
5 Sep XX	Late model Mercedes panel truck, dark blue with white bumpers, host nation Plate 853DJC	Possible transport vehicle used for transiting contraband weapons, stolen merchandise, and funds used in support of organized criminal networks operating in the AO. Has also reportedly used different plates, including GE65ART and UK19873.
15 Sep XX	John Doe	Individual wanted for questioning by host nation and U.S. military police personnel in connection with the murder on 4 Sep XX of a host nation police chief with possible connections to at least three additional assassinations of host nation police officials. This individual has been previously detained and subsequently released; biometric data is enrolled in Biometrics Automated Toolset and Handheld Interagency Identity Detection Equipment in the AO.
UNCLASSIFIED For Official Use Only		
Legend: AO area of operations IED improvised explosive device Sep September U.S. United States		

Figure 6-2. Example of a BOLO alert

CRIMINAL INTELLIGENCE BULLETINS

6-10. Criminal intelligence bulletins are documents produced by USACIDC and disseminated internally to USACIDC and Army LE. These bulletins are forwarded to all USACIDC field elements by the USACIDC chain of command and shared with other Army LE to alert them of conditions, techniques, or situations that could be significant factors in present or future investigations or CPSs. Local units, organizations, and entities may be provided pertinent information affecting their organizations via a crime prevention flyer (see paragraph 6-13).

CRIME PREVENTION SURVEYS

6-11. CPSs are conducted, within resource and mission constraints, by USACIDC to support commanders in the context of the Army Crime Prevention Program. The survey is a formally recorded review and analysis of existing conditions in a specified facility, activity, or area for the purpose of detecting crime, identifying conditions or procedures conducive to criminal activity, and minimizing or eliminating the opportunity to commit a criminal offense or engage in criminal activity; it is the result of a crime and criminal threat assessment and analysis. It seeks to determine the nature, extent, and underlying causes of crime and provides the commander with information for use in the crime prevention program (see AR 10-87 and AR 195-2).

6-12. A CPS may be initiated by USACIDC or at the request of the supported commander. USACIDC conducts CPSs and crime and criminal activity threat assessments of facilities, activities, events, and areas that are under Army control or that directly affect the Army community. The USACIDC may also conduct CPSs of other DOD facilities and activities when requested (if resources are available). The CPS will identify situations that are not procedural deficiencies but could, if left unchecked, result in the loss of Army assets through negligence, systemic weakness, or failures and erosion of established internal controls. The CPS is provided to the local commander responsible for the AO in question, typically commanders of posts, camps, stations, or other mature bases. A CPS identifies–

- Criminal activity in a specific location.
- Regulatory deficiencies.
- Economic threats to installations or activities.
- Domestic and international terrorist threats.
- Likely theft, diversion, sabotage, or destruction of U.S. government property or assets.
- Vulnerability of Army automated systems.

CRIME PREVENTION FLYERS

6-13. The crime prevention flyer is an external document prepared by USACIDC or PM office personnel for local agencies and entities. It is produced and disseminated to notify organizations of identified conditions that could result in another criminal incident or future loss of government funds, property, or personnel. The flyer is formatted for external distribution, with the intent to share pertinent information and facilitate cooperation and assistance in crime prevention activities. Figure 6-3, page 6-6, displays an example crime prevention flyer.

ECONOMIC CRIME THREAT ASSESSMENT AND LOGISTICAL SECURITY THREAT ANALYSIS REPORTS

6-14. The ECTA is a USACIDC assessment of the overall economic posture of an installation or activity. The ECTA process is one of the most important aspects of the USACIDC crime prevention program. ECTAs provide valuable information and police intelligence to enable the effective employment of limited USACIDCs and other LE assets. ECTAs are an important element for a proactive effort that relates to both economic crimes and logistical security operations.

6-15. LSTAs are produced by USACIDC special agents looking specifically at key logistics bases and infrastructure. The LSTA is prepared to assess logistical systems, modes of transportation, or APODs and SPODs for criminal threat vulnerabilities and terrorist threats targeting the integrity of the logistical LOCs, the security of U.S. government assets, and the safety of DOD personnel. LSTAs can serve as a substantial internal and external operational planning tool. Distribution is normally restricted to the commander of the facility, supporting LE and security elements, and higher headquarters. Due to the specifics of the report, LSTAs are normally classified.

Office Symbol   12 November 20XX

MEMORANDUM FOR Commander, 10th Sustainment Command, Port of Entry, Remotistan.
SUBJECT: Crime Prevention Flyer, Regarding: Larceny of Government Property.

1. PURPOSE: This Crime Prevention Flyer addresses the larceny reported on 21 October 20XX, and the immediate actions recommended to deter future criminal activity and loss of property.

2. BACKGROUND: Investigators have expended a significant amount of resources investigating the stated crime that occurred on 21 October 20XX. Due to conditions outlined below, the investigation has produced negative results. Losses to date have been valued at about $8,200. During the conduct of the investigation, several conditions were discovered that produce conditions conducive to criminal activity. The majority of these conditions are basic physical security deficiencies. Actions that correct the identified deficiencies can contribute to making the 10th Sustainment Command and associated warehouse areas a "hard target" for thieves and deter future break-ins. The investigation into this incident is not complete; however, the items shown below are of time-sensitive interest:

   a. The rear door to the unit warehouse did not have a security cover over the area of the door frame where the locking mechanism was located. This facilitated insertion of a pry bar to force open the door.

   b. The rear floodlights were burned out or missing. Operational floodlights would illuminate the rear entry, forcing potential criminals to operate in an illuminated area rather than in darkness.

   c. A security camera was present and functional, but not serviced (taping medium was full); therefore, the security cameras were rendered useless. Interviews revealed that the camera has not been used during the assignment of any current Soldiers or civilians.

   d. The gate at the rear entrance to the warehouse area was not secured properly, and security checks on that area were not conducted.

3. RECOMMENDATIONS: Standard physical security measures, according to AR 190-53, should be followed. These measures include—

   a. Ensuring that security lights are operational.

   b. Ensuring that security camera tapes or disks are changed in a timely manner and the camera system is employed.

   c. Modifying the rear door of the warehouse to ensure that a security cover is in place.

   d. Securing the rear gate entrance to the warehouse area and adding security checks to existing standing operating procedures.

4. The point of contact for additional information is the undersigned, at (310) 543-0820.

                                        John Q. Agent
                                        Special Agent in Charge

Figure 6-3. Example of a crime prevention flyer

FORENSIC ANALYSIS REPORTS

6-16. Forensic analysis reports are produced at labs that conduct forensic examinations of evidence and potential evidence. These reports are usually produced according to the standards of the lab conducting the analysis. When supporting LE investigations, the reports will usually have controlled distribution in LE and judicial channels. Although technical in nature, the reports may contain summaries that provide the basic data information in a more readable format. LE investigators reviewing forensic reports should contact serving labs directly for clarification of evidence or for explanation or to correlate results of other investigative findings.

INDICATIONS AND WARNING

6-17. *Indications and warning* are those intelligence activities intended to detect and report time-sensitive intelligence information on foreign developments that could involve a threat to the United States or multinational military, political, or economic interests or to U.S. citizens abroad. It includes forewarning of hostile actions or intentions against the United States, its activities, overseas forces, or allied and/or coalition nations. (JP 2-0) The G-2 or S-2 has primary staff responsible for producing I&W intelligence; however, all functional elements contribute to I&W through awareness of the CCIR and by reporting related information. PIO is planned and executed by the S-3 in functional units and the PM staff in multifunctional units; I&W related to PIO will be produced by the S-3 or PM staff and coordinated with the S-2 or G-2, as required.

6-18. Military police and USACIDC elements, by virtue of their mission and their dispersion across the AO, are often the first to see indications of an imminent threat. When this information is reported through normal reporting channels, it is disseminated rapidly to alert affected organizations, units, and adjacent LE agencies. Military police produce I&W to provide police information or analyzed intelligence for timely notification that a possible criminal threat or attack on U.S. interests has been identified and is imminent.

6-19. The nature of a threat indicator will generally dictate both the distribution list and the method used. Speed and a positive acknowledgement of both the information provided and the sensitivity of the information may be critical. At a minimum, military police, other security forces, the S-2, and the commander are normally notified of incoming I&W. As with other police intelligence products, a decision must be made about how much information to release and whether sources of information must be protected in the warning.

LINK ANALYSIS CHARTS, MAPS, AND GRAPHS

6-20. Link analysis charts, maps, and graphs provide a visual link between persons, organizations, locations, crimes, and evidence. These products may be automated through the use of commercially available programs or produced by hand using maps, overlays, matrices, or graphs. Link analysis charts, maps, and graphs are typically used extensively by LE investigators conducting criminal investigations. Link analysis products can also be designed and produced specifically for the legal community involved in judicial proceedings to assist with understanding the connection between known criminals, criminal activities, and other persons suspected of involvement in a crime or criminal enterprise. Chapter 5 provides a discussion on link analysis and examples of link analysis charts.

6-21. Some commanders and PMs may require presentations of the entire link analysis chart; however, the complexity of these products limits their use for personnel not intimately familiar with the events and subjects portrayed. Oftentimes, the staff or analyst that constructed the data may need to build a separate briefing or other presentation for the commander or PM that provides a synopsis of key linkages.

PERSONAL SECURITY VULNERABILITY ASSESSMENTS

6-22. Personal security vulnerability assessments (PSVAs) are conducted and produced by USACIDC special agents on HRP, based on their duty position, the level of threat, and geographic location (when directed by the Secretary of the Army or the Chief of Staff of the Army). They are conducted to enhance the personal security posture of HRP. At a minimum, a PSVA will include a review of procedures and measures employed at the HRP's quarters, workplace, and travel between the two locations. The PSVA scrutinizes all aspects of the physical security of the principal's office, residence, and mode of travel. A review and analysis of the principal's routine habits and his social and personal commitments are conducted. These activities are performed to determine where the principal would be most vulnerable and to reduce the likelihood of becoming a target of an individual or group.

6-23. All supporting documentation, such as blueprints, schematic drawings, still photographs, videos, and written documents, will be available for review or as attachments to the final PSVA report. The final report is typically made available to the HRP for review. Due to the nature of these reports, distribution is normally severely restricted and is provided only to the individual covered in the assessment, their immediate staff and security team, and USACIDC headquarters. A copy of the final report is kept in the HRP's file; a second copy is provided to the USACIDC Crime Records Center, Fort Belvoir, Virginia. The conduct of PSVAs is directed in AR 10-87, AR 190-58, and AR 525-13.

6-24. The PSVA final report includes–

- The date the HRP briefing was held.
- A list of persons who received the exit briefing.
- The reaction of HRP receiving the briefing.
- A list of noted problem areas and recommended solutions.
- Security recommendations.

POLICE AND PRISON INFRASTRUCTURE, CAPABILITY, AND CAPACITY ASSESSMENTS

6-25. Civil consideration is an important element in military staff analysis, assessment, and planning. Specific to military police are those civil considerations directly related to police, crime, and criminals in the form of infrastructure, capability, and capacity assessments. Military police staff and police intelligence analysts must convert this information and the resulting police intelligence into products usable by commanders, PMs, their staffs, and LE investigators conducting investigations in the AO. The acronym POLICE (discussed in chapter 2) provides a format for gathering and organizing police information.

6-26. Police and prison infrastructure, capability, and capacity assessments follow no standardized format. Product format is driven by many factors, including the–

- Target audience.
- Specific mission.
- Phase of the mission.
- Environmental conditions and status of police and prison organizations and operations.
- Severity and sophistication of criminal activity.

6-27. Police assessments typically contain data about the ability of police forces to conduct their missions, including patrolling and traffic regulation enforcement, dispatch and internal communications, sustainment of police organizations, and criminal investigations. Prison assessments may initially focus on the number of guards and beds available and security concerns affecting operations in the facility; however, over time they may focus on threat organizations operating in the facility, detainee and prisoner rehabilitative efforts, and the process for release of detainees and prisoners. These assessments provide police intelligence regarding a wide range of functional areas necessary for effective police organizations, to include–

- Personnel, such as the numbers of police and prison personnel, management structure, pay systems, internal investigations and discipline, presence of corruption (political, nepotistic, and financial).
- Security, such as the vetting of police personnel, control and security of police information, security concerns in the organization (both internal to the police or prison organization and from external factors).
- Operations, such as the organizational structure, span of control, centralized versus decentralized command of police and prison forces, and criminal training standards for police and prison personnel.
- Logistics, such as supply systems, vehicle and equipment maintenance, funding for maintenance and supplies, and sources of funding.
- Communications, such as general communications capability, availability of secure communications, and sufficient communications equipment for all police and prison personnel.

POLICE INTELLIGENCE ADVISORIES

6-28. Police intelligence advisories (PIAs) are produced to transmit information related to criminal activity in the AO of other Army LE organizations. The document can be used to relay information and police intelligence on crime patterns, methods of operation, organized crime networks, technology used by criminal threat elements, and IR and concerns involving criminal organizations and activities. Figure 6-4, page 6-10, shows an example police intelligence advisory.

6-29. Police intelligence advisories produced by USACIDC are referred to as criminal intelligence reports but follow the same format as the police intelligence advisory. Other LE organizations may have slightly different titles and format variations. The report is an informative document prepared for another USACIDC or military police element and includes the following information–

- Heading.
- Date prepared.
- Preparing office.
- Sequence number.
- Title.
- Offense or additional types of information.
- Synopsis.
- Signature blocks.
- Warning and distribution statements.

POLICE INTELLIGENCE ADVISORY

Date Prepared: 1 January 20XX

Preparing Office: 11th Military Police (MP) Detachment, Forward Operating Base (FOB) Bulldog, Remotistan.

Sequence Number: 444-09-MPR992, First Police Intelligence Advisory (PIA)

1. Subject 1.; Specialist; 555-44-6666; male; white; 6'2"; 180 pounds; brown hair; brown eyes; 345th Messkit Company, Fort Sunny, California (formerly the 123d Maintenance Battalion, FOB Bulldog, Remotistan).
2. Subject 2; Specialist; 535-33-8888; female; white; 5'4"; 110 pounds; blonde hair; blue eyes; 123d Maintenance Battalion, FOB Bulldog, Remotistan.
3. Subject 3; Sergeant; 395-65-0909, male; white; 5'8"; 143 pounds; blonde hair; brown eyes; 123d Maintenance Battalion, FOB Bulldog, Remotistan.

Offense: Wrongful appropriation/larceny of government property.

Reference is made to this office's military police report (MPR) 0443-09-MPR992.

Source of Information: The information contained in this PIA was developed during the referenced MPR and is considered reliable.

Narrative: At about 2300 hours on 1 May of this year, the 11th MP Detachment, Military Police Investigations Section, FOB Bulldog, Remotistan, while conducting an investigation of possible larceny of government property in the 123d Maintenance Battalion supply room, discovered evidence linking Subject 2 and Subject 3 to stolen government property. The stolen property includes bayonets, commercially procured personal hydration units, and laser sights. During subsequent interviews, Subject 2 admitted that, in addition to being a friend to Subject 3 and Subject 1, she conspired with them to take government property with intent to mail the items back to the United States for resale by Subject 1. Several stolen items were later found in the possession of Subject 3 and recovered. Courts martial actions are being taken against Subject 2 and Subject 3. Subject 1 has been allegedly quoted by his roommate (not considered a suspect) as saying that he had a "sweet business deal waiting for him stateside." The supporting staff judge advocate has reported there is insufficient evidence to take action against Subject 1. This is a terminal report; no further reports are contemplated pending receipt of additional police intelligence.

Warning Statement: This document is intended for law enforcement personnel, intelligence analysts, military personnel, and other officials with a need to know. Further dissemination of this report should be limited to a minimum, consistent with the purpose for which the record has been furnished (such as the effective enforcement of civil and criminal law). Additional releases require prior approval from the originator.

Report prepared by: Report approved by:
Name   Major John Surname
Military Police Investigator   Military Police Operations

Distribution:
Provost Marshal, FOB Bulldog, Remotistan
Commander, 345th Messkit Company, Fort Sunny, California
Provost Marshal, Fort Sunny, California

FOR OFFICIAL USE ONLY

LAW ENFORCEMENT SENSITIVE
Legend:
FOB   forward operating base
MP   military police
MPR   military police report
PIA   police intelligence advisory

Figure 6-4. Example of a PIA

POLICE INTELLIGENCE ALERT NOTICES

6-30. The police intelligence alert notice is a document prepared by Army LE elements. It expedites the reporting of perishable, time-sensitive, and crime-related information. A police intelligence alert notice is prepared and disseminated to attack the offender's capability of victimizing others and to alert persons, organizations, or entities identified as high-risk for criminal activity (logistics bases, units operating within the threat AO, or other high payoff targets, such as hospitals, financial organizations, or supply depots) in an effort to prevent them from being victimized by an identified threat. See figure 6-5 for an example police intelligence alert notice.

POLICE INTELLIGENCE ALERT NOTICE
TERRORIST ACTIVITY (MANUFACTURE AND EMPLACEMENT OF IMPROVISED EXPLOSIVE DEVICES)

Date Prepared: 1 January 20XX

Preparing Office: 50th Military Police Brigade, Hostile Province, Remotistan.

Source: Information was obtained from a local national informant that has supplied credible and accurate information in the past; the information is considered reliable.

Credible information has been received that Subject 1, Subject 2, and Subject 3 have been assembling improvised explosives and hiring third-party individuals to emplace the devices, targeting U.S. military and host nation convoys throughout Hostile Province.

Subject 1 has been known to use the aliases Alias 1 and Alias 2.
Subject 2 has been known to use the aliases Alias 1 and Alias 2.
Subject 3 has been known to use the aliases Alias 1 and Alias 2.

Police intelligence indicates that Subject 1, Subject 2, and Subject 3 have been manufacturing improvised explosive devices in a mobile facility, most likely a modified panel van. Police intelligence further indicates that they consistently use electronic triggers supplied by a foreign source and that their devices are consistently radio frequency detonated using components from a single source supplier. When on the move, Subject 3 typically drives, while Subject 1 and Subject 2 work in the back of the van. Subject 3 is described as 6'6' tall, weighing more than 300 pounds, with a large, heart-shaped tattoo with "MOM" on his left forearm. There are currently no descriptions for Subject 1 and Subject 2.

Units operating in the area should be alert for suspicious activity, particularly at vehicle checkpoints and when involving paneled vans transiting the area of operations. If the suspects are encountered, detain if possible; however, exercise extreme caution. Additional intelligence indicates that their van is often "booby-trapped." If Subject 1, Subject 2, or Subject 3 are detained, notify the 50th Military Police Brigade as soon as possible to facilitate law enforcement of the suspects. Incident sites should be searched for remnants of trigger devices and other material to be collected for forensic evaluation.

The point of contact for this alert is Major Jane Surname, Military Police Operations Officer, 50th Military Police Brigade, XXX-ZZZ-1234.

This alert is intended for dissemination to all units operating in Hostile Province.

Figure 6-5. Example of a police intelligence alert notice

6-31. The police intelligence alert notice informs the recipients of criminal activity, specific actions required to interdict or mitigate the stated activity, and specific evidence collection and preservation priorities. The police intelligence alert notice is an action document, not an informational report. Police intelligence alert notices produced by USACIDC are referred to as criminal alert notices. Police intelligence alert notices and criminal alert notices follow the same basic format. They will typically include–

- The source and reliability of the information.
- Entities involved.
- Any known aliases.
- Known personal identification numbers (such as social security or driver's license).
- A summary of all pertinent information developed to date on the subject or suspect.
- Actions that the recommending unit wishes to be taken by the activities and agencies receiving the bulletin (such as detain subject or suspect and notify LE authority).
- Points of contact, including names and contact numbers from the issuing unit.
- Distribution and dissemination instructions and restrictions.

STATISTICAL DATA

6-32. Statistical data can be drawn from diverse sources and can be depicted in numerous manners. Statistical data may be presented in charts displaying–

- Frequencies (through the use of bar, pie, and Pareto charts).
- Trends (through the use of bar and line charts).
- Distributions (through the use of GIS, trend lines, or other formats).

6-33. Different audiences and types of data require different types of statistical tools to present data in a manner that is clear and concise. Data placed into a table or other database can be rapidly retrieved and manipulated into a presentation. The ways in which statistical data can be displayed are numerous. The next three figures show examples of statistical data in different formats and related to crimes in an AO. Figure 6-6 displays the number of burglaries, robberies, and larcenies for each quarter of a given year. Figure 6-7 shows the trend for larceny through the use of a run or line chart. Figure 6-8 displays a pie chart showing the percentage of occurrences (out of 100 percent) for each crime depicted on the chart.

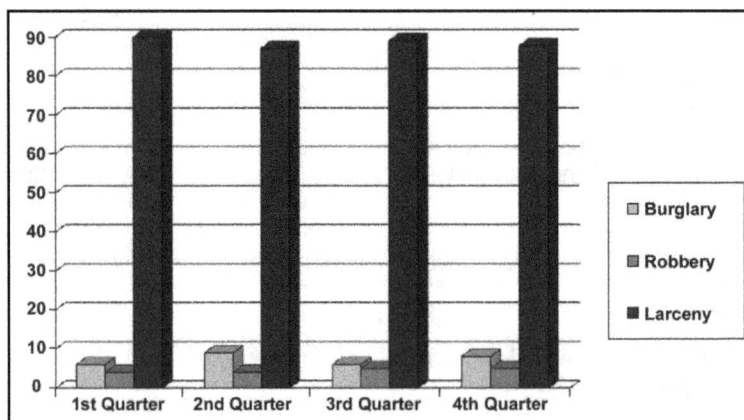

Figure 6-6. Example of a bar graph showing the rate of select quarterly offenses

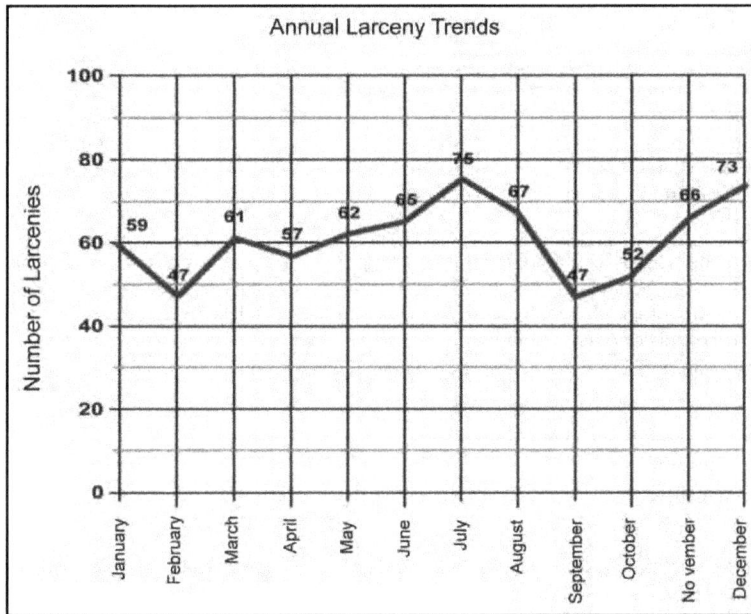

Figure 6-7. Example of a line chart displaying annual larceny trends

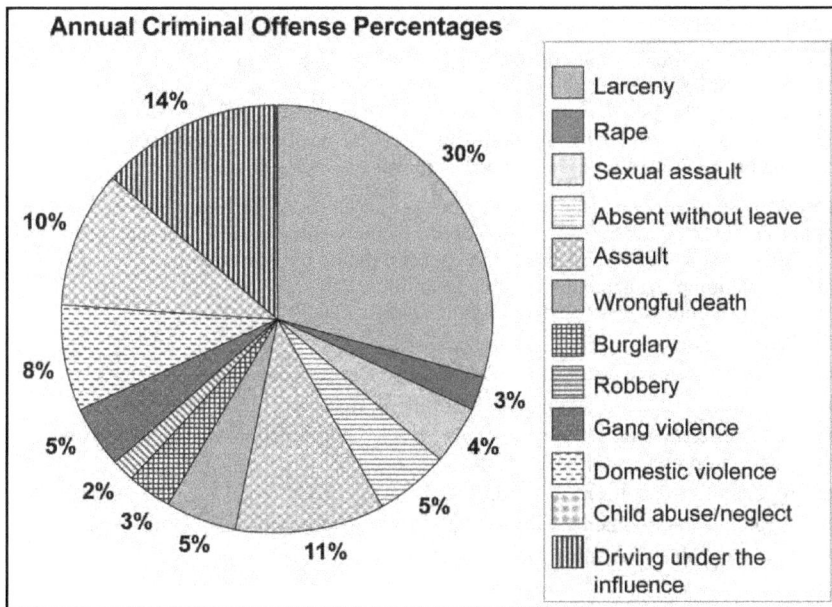

Figure 6-8. Example of a pie chart showing crime percentages over a one-year period

WANTED AND REWARD POSTERS

6-34. Wanted posters are clearly intended for public distribution and viewing. Formats typically vary, depending on the amount of information known, specific information sought, and the LE agency producing the wanted poster. Wanted posters are posted by local, state, and federal agencies (to include Army LE). The LE agency or military unit that has the investigative lead for the incident should be the final approval on the wanted poster. This allows the lead investigative agency an opportunity to review the poster to ensure that information about an individual or crime that police are withholding for investigative purposes is not inadvertently released.

6-35. Wanted posters may contain the names, descriptions, and pictures of one or more individuals known to LE. A picture can be an artist's sketch (a rendering of the suspect through the eyes of a witness) or a photograph. Any photograph should be as recent as possible. Below the sketch or photograph, there will typically be a short history of the criminal, including information such as the–

- Age and/or date or place of birth.
- Sex, height, weight, and hair and eye color.
- Known identifying scars or marks.
- Occupation.
- Nationality.
- Any known aliases.

6-36. In some cases, little is known about the criminal being sought. In these cases, the wanted poster may simply provide information about a specific crime or an unknown perpetrator and request additional information. Posters may contain instructions on what to do when an individual observes the wanted person. If a reward is offered, the poster should state how much money is offered and the individual or agency providing the reward. Wanted posters will also provide points of contact for persons with potential information.

6-37. Wanted posters used in support of full spectrum operations in OCONUS environments or in areas within the United States where English is not the primary language must have the information released and the translation carefully screened. It is important to have a native speaker review the wanted poster for accuracy of the translation and the cultural context of the poster for unintended word use or messages. Figure 6-9 and Figure 6-10, page 6-16, provide examples of wanted posters.

6-38. Reward posters are generated to notify the public that a reward may be available for information specific to a crime or criminal. They are a variant of the wanted poster. Like the wanted poster, reward posters are used to solicit information from the general public but may also include a tangible incentive in return for information provided under specified conditions (figure 6-11, page 6-17, provides an example of a reward poster). Reward posters typically contain specific details, to include–

- Reward amounts.
- Specifics about the crime or criminal for which information is sought.
- Pictures (if available) pertinent to the crime or criminal.
- Specific requirements that must be met (such as information leading to recovery or information leading to prosecution).
- A point of contact for the reward.
- A confidentiality statement from the provider reference information received.
- Any applicable expirations of the reward offer.

Wanted

ARMED AND EXTREMELY DANGEROUS

PHOTO:

NAME: SUBJECT NAME

DOB: NOVEMBER 29, 1985

SEX: MALE

HEIGHT: 6' 1"

WEIGHT: 195 POUNDS

HAIR: BROWN

EYES: BROWN

RACE: WHITE

Insert photo (if available)

SCARS OR MARKS: BULLET WOUND ON THE LOWER THIGH AND ON THE RIGHT ARM; SCAR ON RIGHT WRIST, SCAR ON THE LEFT THIGH, AND SCAR ON THE LEFT ANKLE. ALSO HAS TRACK MARKS ON HIS RIGHT ARM AND BETWEEN HIS TOES.

OCCUPATION: CONSTRUCTION

SSN USED: XXX-XX-XXXX

NATIONALITY: AMERICAN

PLACE OF BIRTH: MIAMI, FLORIDA

ALIAS: ALIAS #1; ALIAS #2

IF YOU HAVE ANY INFORMATION CONCERNING THIS CASE, CONTACT YOUR LOCAL FEDERAL BUREAU OF INVESTIGATION FIELD OFFICE.

THE CRIME: UNLAWFUL FLIGHT TO AVOID PROSECUTION – ATTEMPTED MURDER. SUBJECT IS BELIEVED TO BE CONNECTED WITH THE ATTEMPTED MURDER OF A STATE TROOPER WHEREIN A .357-CALIBER PISTOL WAS USED.

REWARD: YOUR LOCAL FEDERAL BUREAU OF INVESTIGATION FIELD OFFICE IS OFFERING UP TO $50,000 FOR THE APPREHENSION OF THE SUBJECT.

REMARKS: SUBJECT HAS BEEN KNOWN TO BE ASSOCIATED WITH THE KLU KLUX KLAN AND OTHER RACIST GROUPS.

SOURCES: PODUNK COUNTY SHERIFF DEPARTMENT

FBI HOMEPAGE: <http://www.fbi.gov>

WRITTEN BY: INVESTIGATOR DOE

Figure 6-9. Example of an FBI wanted poster

WANTED
BY CID

Information concerning the offense of Larceny of Government Property from the 29th Sustainment Brigade, Camp Doha, Kuwait APO AE 09090.

USACIDC Report of Investigation (ROI) 0092-96-CID987-20973-7F9A.

On 1 April 1996, the USACIDC initiated an investigation into the Larceny of Government. Property from the 29th Sustainment Brigade. Between 1800, 29 March 1996 and 0530, 30 March 1996, person(s) unknown stole one M998 HMMWV, bumper number "SVC 4 29TH SB", serial number 044308, from the parking lot adjacent to Building 1013A (Headquarters, 29 Sustainment Brigade), Camp Doha, Kuwait.

IF YOU HAVE ANY INFORMATION ABOUT THIS INCIDENT, PLEASE CONTACT THE CID OFFICE AT DSN 111-2222/2223, COMMERCIAL 0101-9992222/2223, OR CALL YOUR LOCAL MP STATION.

Legend:
APO	Army Post Office
CID	criminal investigation division
DSN	Defense Switched Network
HMMWV	high-mobility multipurpose wheeled vehicle
MP	military police
USACIDC	United States Army Criminal Investigation Command

Figure 6-10. Example of a USACIDC wanted poster

Figure 6-11. Example of a reward poster

DISSEMINATION OF POLICE INFORMATION AND POLICE INTELLIGENCE

6-39. Dissemination is the activity that delivers an analyzed product into the hands of commanders, PMs, staff, and LE investigators to answer IR, enabling decisionmaking and action. It is critical that dissemination occur as early in the process as practical and possible. The need to balance speed with thoroughness should be weighed throughout the process. Commanders and analysts should consider interim reports to provide key data to end users as it becomes available. Oftentimes, waiting for complete information may delay product dissemination so long that the product, although accurate, is too late to be useful to the Soldiers and LE investigators who need it.

COMMAND AND STAFF CHANNELS

6-40. PIO, in support of full spectrum operations, leverages command and staff channels to ensure timely and accurate reporting of police intelligence that answers IR, CCIRs, exceptional information identified by the staff or commander that is unforecasted but of immediate value to the command. Command and staff channels will also likely be used to distribute other products, such as wanted posters, spot reports, I&Ws, and BOLOs. This is likely the most efficient method to provide information to every member of a unit or organization. Products disseminated through command and staff channels should clearly articulate the purpose for distributing the product and what action is required or being requested.

FUNCTIONAL CHANNELS

6-41. Functional channels include military police and LE channels and other groups that operate along functional lines. The LE and intelligence networks are examples of functional channels. Oftentimes, police intelligence is maintained in LE functional channels. This is done to maintain control over sensitive information, as mandated by law, and protect information and intelligence critical to ongoing LE investigations.

POLICE INTELLIGENCE COLLABORATION AND FUSION

6-42. PIO networks in support of posts, camps, stations, and full spectrum operations are developed with the same overarching objective—to enhance police information and police intelligence sharing. Regardless of the OE, subtle influences will create variations in network memberships. Influences, such as the availability of agencies in the local AO, the varied personalities of organizational leaders, and cultural or operational differences between agencies, may influence membership participation and team dynamics. For example, military police and USACIDC personnel may not have a local FBI or Bureau of Alcohol, Tobacco, and Firearms field office in their immediate AO, or UN civilian police may be operating in your immediate AO with their headquarters and support elements hundreds or thousands of miles away. Despite local variations, general guidelines for developing, managing, and participating in police intelligence networks can be established.

6-43. Military police and USACIDC personnel may develop police intelligence networks anywhere in support of missions in any OE. Standardization provides a platform for tailoring staff, providing institutional training, and selecting the most appropriate resources (such as automation and other emerging technologies). The successful development of police intelligence networks may help enhance coordination and cooperation between local agencies and provide a springboard for developing vast regional, national, or international police intelligence networks.

DEFINING NETWORK PARTICIPANTS

6-44. A police intelligence network should be tailored to meet the requirements of the OE and the specific AO. Participation is influenced by threat assessments, IR, and specific needs of participating agencies. PIO collaboration and networking can occur in predetermined working groups with relatively set membership, structure, and function or in ad hoc venues created for a specific mission or event. A police intelligence network will typically consist of agencies located in the immediate AO; however, with the expansion of communications and internet technology, participation from outside the immediate AO is possible. This allows participation and sharing to occur between agencies located across the state, country, or world. Such arrangements may fill essential capability gaps in the PIO network. If particular agencies are not represented in the local environment (such as FBI or Drug Enforcement Administration field offices, MI, or host nation LE), military police and USACIDC personnel can add them to their network by either leveraging another LE PIO network or making direct contact with the agency using Internet-based intelligence services.

NETWORKS IN SUPPORT OF POSTS, CAMPS, AND STATIONS

6-45. Police intelligence networks established to support LE and security efforts at posts, camps, and stations can provide significant capability to address the complexities of the criminal threat to military assets and personnel. Cooperation between local, state, federal, and military agencies enhances LE and security operations for the military and local civilian community. Typically, networks in support of posts, camps, and stations are more static than those supporting full spectrum operations and provide continuity that builds institutional knowledge of crime and criminal threats, physical and social conditions, and long-term relationships with local, state, and federal LE agencies in the AO. Most police intelligence networks will typically have a core of constant participants and the flexibility to expand to form focused ad hoc, threat-specific cells to address, prevent, or react to a specific hazard, condition, or event.

6-46. Figure 6-12 provides an example of a police intelligence network supporting a typical Army post, camp, or station. Specific networks will differ slightly, based on available participants. Military police and USACIDC personnel are located in the center, post agencies are on the right, and agencies located off the installation are on the left. Typical LE agencies may include international, federal, state, and local LE, depending on whether the post is CONUS or OCONUS. Relationships between Army LE personnel and other police intelligence network members will differ. Some network members will require day-to-day working relationships, while others will be based on mutually supporting relationships for selected routine activities or occasional collaboration.

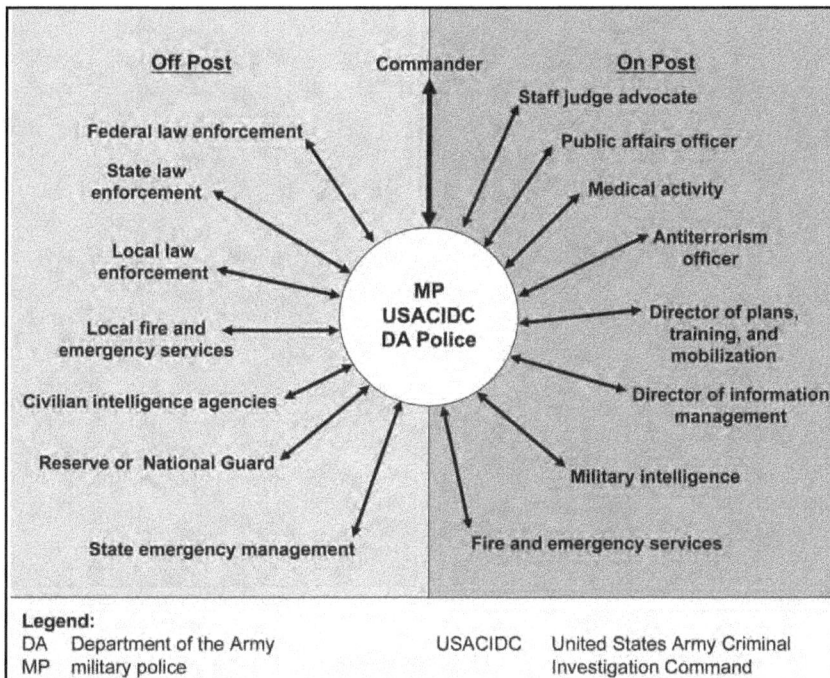

Figure 6-12. Typical police intelligence network in support of a post, camp, or station

6-47. Police intelligence network relationships between agencies will fluctuate, based on numerous factors in the OE. Relationships will also continue to develop as bonds are strengthened through joint ventures and as agencies expand their own operating networks. Missions and priorities of individual organizations will greatly affect participation and the level of sharing conducted.

NETWORKS IN SUPPORT OF FULL SPECTRUM OPERATIONS

6-48. Police intelligence networks are formed to support specific missions or operations during full spectrum operations. These networks are affected by unit deployments and rotations, governmental and civilian organizations operating in the AO, mission changes, and threat changes. These factors equal continuity that builds institutional knowledge of crime and criminal threats, improved physical and social conditions, and additional long-term relationships (often difficult to attain). Specific conditions or threats may bring additional resources and expertise to the AO and increase participation in the network. Similarly, mission changes and force reductions in the AO may reduce or shift the number of participating elements.

6-49. Figure 6-13, page 6-20, shows a typical PIO network in a deployed OE in support of full spectrum operations outside the United States or its territories. Like the previous example, these police intelligence networks will vary in composition, based on mission and operational variables in the OE. As with the example in figure 6-10, page 6-16, civil-military agencies are located on the left and military organizations are located on the right.

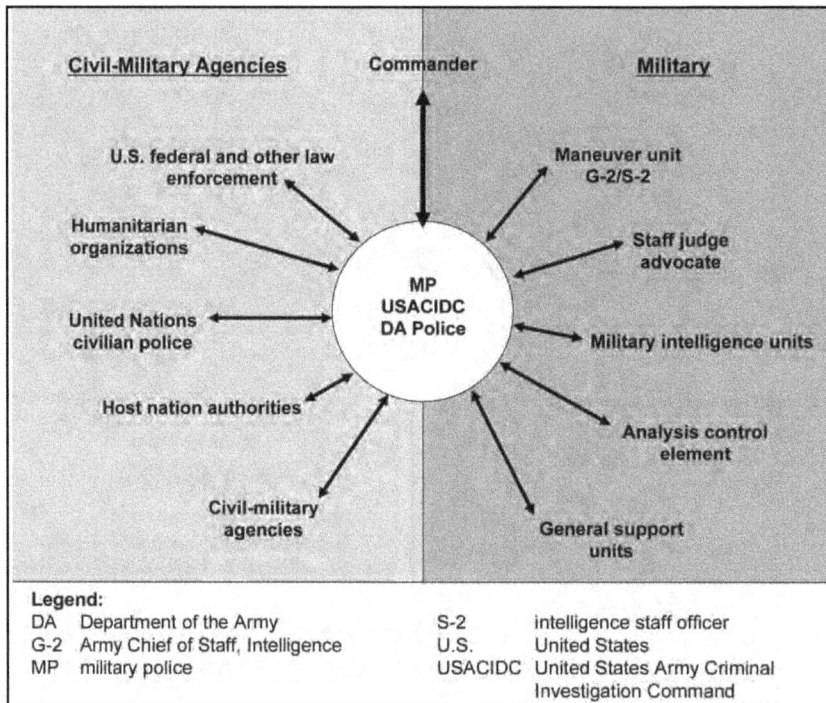

Figure 6-13. Typical PIO network in a deployed OE

6-50. The success of the police intelligence network depends on the mutual exchange of timely, relevant, and accurate police intelligence products prepared according to established laws and regulations. To accomplish this, military police and USACIDC staff should work closely with other agencies to thoroughly understand the strengths and weaknesses of each organization. This enables the organizations to capitalize on their respective strengths and compensate for organizational weaknesses, enabling organizational capabilities to complement each other. The respective staffs should understand each organization's vision, mission, goals, and objectives and identify and develop strategies to overcome cultural, organizational, and operational barriers.

APPROPRIATE COMMAND AND STAFF ALIGNMENT

6-51. Military police and USACIDC staff and commanders should identify and properly correlate their personnel with those of other organizations. This is important to ensure that coordination between staff and commanders from different organizations is conducted with counterparts operating at a similar level and span of control in other organizations. It is important to nest appropriately similar command and staff, levels of authority, and intelligence functions between agencies to increase interoperability. Similar terms for ranks or titles between organizations do not necessarily translate to the same management level. A lieutenant with the state police, for example, may be the equivalent of a military police colonel. A full understanding of the counterpart structure and appropriate staff alignment can avoid embarrassment and help to build personal working relationships with more effective interagency cooperation and intelligence sharing. Using a modified organizational chart, managers can identify comparable staff positions and existing gaps between organizations.

COMMUNICATIONS

6-52. A comprehensive communications system to support the police intelligence network will ensure uninterrupted contact between elements when necessary. Contact lists for all agencies should be disseminated throughout the network and routinely checked to validate less-frequent contacts and maintain personal working relationships. It is desirable that agencies have compatible communications systems for routine support. Communications systems between network organizations may include–

- Standard communications systems, such as–
  - Telephones.
  - Radios.
  - Facsimile machines.
  - Commercial e-mail.
  - Web sites.
  - Videoconferencing capability.
  - Computer databases.
- Nonstandard communications systems, such as–
  - SIPRNET.
  - Nonsecure Internet Protocol Router Network.
  - Electronic intelligence interface.
  - LE specific information exchange networks.

POLICE INTELLIGENCE FUSION CELLS

6-53. Fusion is a collaborative effort between two or more organizations working together and sharing resources, expertise, and information to enhance the ability of all participating elements to detect, investigate, and respond to prevent or mitigate crime and criminal activity. It involves the processing of information from multiple systems, assets, and sources, and translating that information into refined information and police intelligence products that increase situational understanding and knowledge. Fusion enables commanders and Army LE to have a significant "observe, orient, decide, and act" advantage over criminal networks and terrorist groups, cells, and individuals. This effort enables commanders, PMs, and LE investigators to guide and direct actions that achieve desired effects. The combination of trained and experienced staff, LE personnel, and police intelligence analysts, coupled with open information-sharing agreements and advances in technology, allows all elements participating in the fusion process to analyze a variety of information from different organizations, collection assets, and systems to more effectively produce actionable police intelligence for personnel making decisions.

6-54. In some cases, a police intelligence fusion cell may be formed to facilitate collaboration, integration, and fusion of police information and intelligence with other LE and intelligence agencies and organizations. The primary purpose of a police intelligence fusion cell is the collation, correlation, and fusion of data from multiple sources, enabling further analysis to produce actionable police intelligence and increased knowledge concerning police, crime, and criminal activities. This enables the military police and USACIDC staff and police intelligence analyst to build a coherent picture of the environment to increase SU and enable informed decisionmaking by commanders, PMs, and LE investigators regarding policing and investigative activities. Collaboration of LE and MI information and intelligence in a police intelligence fusion cell enhances the overall police intelligence effort.

6-55. Fusion cells are typically formed to support specific investigations, missions, and operations. They are also typically more focused and meet more frequently than working groups. These cells may be required to work continuously to support their assigned mission and purpose. Police intelligence fusion can provide police information and police intelligence to the operations process and supporting integrating processes. The CITF is an example of a fusion cell. In the United States, these cells may include local, county, state, federal, tribal, and all source intelligence agencies operating in or supporting policing and LE operations in the AO. Outside the United States, this agency interaction and coordination may include other military units, military and civilian U.S. and multinational organizations, host nation LE elements, and OGAs. The composition of the fusion cell in any environment is dependent on the specific mission of the organizations and agencies involved. Table 6-1 shows an example of the composition for a police intelligence fusion cell.

Table 6-1. Example of police intelligence fusion cell composition

In Support of Post, Camps, Stations, and Civil Support Operations	In Support of Full Spectrum Operations Outside the U.S. or its Territories
Military police (to include DA civilian police)	Military police (to include DA civilian police)
USACIDC	USACIDC
Local, state, and federal LE	Civilian police
902d Military Intelligence	902d Military Intelligence
	G-2 or S-2
	host nation police and security forces

Legend:	
DA	Department of the Army
G-2	Army Chief of Staff, Intelligence
host nation	host nation
LE	law enforcement
S-2	intelligence staff officer
U.S.	United States
USACIDC	United States Army Criminal Investigation Command

6-56. The employment of police intelligence fusion activities is applicable across the full spectrum of conflict. Fusion activities work well for analyzing complex criminal organizations and establishing trends, patterns, and associations from information gathered across a large AO and multiple organizational areas and jurisdictions. These activities can identify duplications of effort and enable participating elements to eliminate unnecessary duplications of collection and analysis activities. The effective application of fusion activities can facilitate the coordination and synchronization of local, state, national, international, service intelligence, and private-sector organization capabilities while simultaneously enhancing the commander's COP.

Appendix A

Police Intelligence Operations Briefing and Debriefing Requirements

Successful PIO require the commander and staff to establish, resource, and conduct mission briefing and debriefing activities. The PM section or S-3 should develop a mission briefing and debriefing plan for preparing mission elements to collect information supporting police IR and for gathering postmission information from individual collection assets. Ideally, the mission briefing and postmission debriefing are incorporated as an integrated part of standard mission briefings and synchronized, when appropriate, with any G-2 or S-2 intelligence briefing and debriefing requirements.

POLICE INTELLIGENCE OPERATIONS MISSION BRIEFINGS

A-1. The purpose of a PIO mission briefing is to ensure that all personnel conducting missions where collection of police information is likely or directed are sensitized to specific information and reporting requirements, information gaps, and unique mission requirements. PIO mission briefings may include updated intelligence assessments; a detailed briefing on current mission or investigative information and existing gaps; and specific information, material, or data that may assist police intelligence analysts and staff. These briefings may also include a review of collection objectives and methods to be employed.

A-2. The mission elements briefed may be restricted to a small number of investigative or LE personnel supporting a specific investigation, provided to all LE personnel operating in an area, or include all units operating in an AO. In addition, the exact subject matter depends on the nature of the mission, specific requirements, and the sensitivity or classification of known information and police intelligence. These specific content and dissemination decisions are based on operational considerations and classification restrictions that may apply to the information and police intelligence being disseminated.

A-3. PIO mission briefings may be conducted as separate presentations or, ideally, integrated in planned mission briefings. Mission briefings are informal briefings that occur during operations. Briefers may be commanders, staffs, or special representatives. The mission briefing format is determined by the nature and content of the information being provided but typically follows the OPORD format. These briefings are conducted to issue an order; provide more detailed instructions or requirements pertaining to the mission; review key points and considerations relevant to the specific mission; and ensure understanding of the mission objective, specific roles in the mission, and potential problems or threats required to overcome or mitigate those problems and threats. See FM 5-0 for more information on mission briefings.

KEY POLICE INTELLIGENCE OPERATIONS BRIEFING CONSIDERATIONS

A-4. Planning for PIO mission briefings requires consideration of several key elements. First, identification of the briefing audience is required, consistent with investigative requirements, operational objectives, and information dissemination restrictions. All identified mission elements operating in the area should be thoroughly briefed to ensure that maximum collection capability is leveraged and synchronized where appropriate. The PIO mission briefing should also provide criteria for reporting immediate time-sensitive information, reporting requirements for nonpriority reporting, and postmission debriefing locations and procedures. The PIO brief should include the following–
- Police and criminal environment (POLICE) update.
- Threat update, to include–
  - Route information and current available information and intelligence.
  - Information and intelligence identifying known and potential high-threat areas and specific threats in the area.

- Information and intelligence regarding individuals and groups operating in the area that poses threats to U.S. forces and interests.
- Specific types of criminal and threat activities identified in the AO.
- Focus areas for observation.
- Specific collection requirements, to include–
  - Evidence-collection priorities.
  - Requirements for the handling and disposition of collected documents.
  - Special requirements for the handling and disposition of captured detainee and enemy materials.
  - Specific requirements for use of digital photography.
- Specific personnel, activities, materials, data, or other evidence that should be reported immediately, such as–
  - Observed conditions inconsistent with normal events (such as an unusually high amount of traffic departing an area or a complete lack of activity by the local population).
  - Indications of an imminent threat to U.S. forces or interests.
  - Identification of specific persons wanted for specific criminal or threat activity.
  - Identification of material or information with strategic value or impact.
  - Time-sensitive information relative to specific criminal activities or investigations.

POSTMISSION POLICE INTELLIGENCE OPERATIONS DEBRIEFING

A-5. PIO debriefing is the process of questioning military police elements and other personnel returning from missions to collect information of potential value. The purpose of a PIO debriefing is to identify and record data collected by the mission element. This data may pertain to assigned IR, collection tasks, and any additional information and observations made concerning the AO or to identify and properly record any evidence gathered during the conduct of their mission.

A-6. Properly conducted, PIO debriefing operations ensure that all available police information is collected, collated, and assessed in an attempt to answer police IR and expand situational understanding. A comprehensive and systematic PIO debriefing program ensures that information from assigned collection tasks is gathered for analysis. It also allows staff and analysts conducting PIO to ask specific questions to pull information gained from observations made by military police elements to enhance situational understanding and fill gaps in current knowledge. When conducting debriefing operations, all mission elements should be debriefed, to include–

- Leaders returning from operational liaison positions or meetings.
- Military police and other LE elements (at the conclusion of all missions).
- Functional and multifunctional assessment teams (following missions in the AO).
- Other personnel exposed to persons or environments where they may have obtained information of intelligence value.

A-7. In conjunction with the S-2 or G-2, the S-3 or PM section and police intelligence analysis personnel should–

- Debrief personnel or provide specific guidance for unit level debriefs, to include reporting criteria.
- Collect, collate, and format reports, as required.
- Report police information and police intelligence through prescribed reporting channels, based on the information and applicable constraints.

KEY POLICE INTELLIGENCE OPERATIONS DEBRIEFING CONSIDERATIONS

A-8. After an element returns from a mission, the military police staff, unit leadership, or designated police intelligence debriefing team should conduct a thorough debrief. The debriefing should include all members of the mission element, including the leader, unit members, and any attached personnel. Missions should not be considered complete, or personnel released, until reports and debriefings are complete.

A-9. The PIO debriefing will typically follow the mission briefing format. This assists personnel conducting the debriefing and unit personnel by maintaining a standard format, thus helping to prevent exclusion of critical aspects of the mission. If possible, any reports generated during the mission should be reviewed by personnel conducting debriefing activities before any PIO debriefing to provide a measure of situational awareness and help in developing follow-on questions. A review of generated reports before conducting a debriefing of any element enables PIO debriefing personnel to concentrate on filling in gaps and following up on reported information. If the mission element used digital cameras (or other recording devices), it is helpful to use the photographs during the debriefing. A detailed sketch or map may also be useful for facilitating discussion and ensuring understanding by all parties.

A-10. During the PIO debrief, avoid "yes" or "no" questions or questions framed in a way that lead the respondent to a particular answer. The goal of debriefing proceedings is to gain information from the mission element that is not currently available or that corroborates existing information. PIO debriefing personnel should also ask questions that may extract information from observations or other input that the mission element may deem as unimportant but, in fact, may provide police intelligence analysts, staff, and investigators with critical pieces of the police intelligence picture. For example, debriefing personnel should—

● Ask the mission element "What did you see (or hear or learn about)?" rather than "Did you encounter any criminal or threat activity?"

● Avoid asking questions only for the published police IR. This may limit answers obtained from mission personnel, causing valuable information to be missed.

● Use follow-up questions to get complete information, such as "What else?" or "Is there anything else you remember?" before leaving a specific discussion point.

● Refrain from focusing only on visual observation; ask questions relating to all the senses, such as "Were there any smells that were particularly noticeable or out of the normal?" or "Were there any unusual sounds (or lack of sounds)?"

A-11. At the conclusion of the PIO debriefing, all collected observation and material evidence should be documented. A PIO debriefing report should be completed and include—

● The size and composition of the mission element.

● The mission type, location, and purpose.

● The departure and return date-time groups (DTGs).

● The specific AO on which the mission was conducted, including routes, engagement areas, and the locations of specific observations and evidence collection sites.

● A detailed description of the terrain in which threat elements were documented or suspected.

● The results of any police engagement with the local population, host nation police, or host nation officials.

● The unit status at the conclusion of the mission, including the results of any physical engagements with threat elements (include the exact site locations, disposition of dead or wounded Soldiers, and disposition of any dead or wounded civilian and threat persons).

● A description of any physical evidence or materials collected during the mission (including photographs or other recorded materials).

● Conclusions or recommendations.

RESPONSIBILITIES

A-12. The S-3 section or PM section responsibilities include–

- Providing tasking and guidance on specific areas and objectives for police engagement and tactical questioning, based on unit PIR and specific police IR.
- Synchronizing police intelligence collection requirements with G-2 or S-2 military intelligence collection requirements.
- Providing relevant background police information, police intelligence, or military intelligence and information (to include open-source information) to mission elements to improve their cultural knowledge and situational awareness, thus facilitating effective police engagement, tactical questioning, and protection efforts.
- Establishing procedures to ensure that all mission elements are debriefed at the end of the mission.
- Establishing and emphasizing procedures for immediate reporting of information of critical or time-sensitive tactical value (such as a spot report in the size, activity, location, unit, time, and equipment format).
- Establishing procedures and disseminating special requirements for proper evidence collection and handling of captured equipment or media (such as cellular telephones, documents, or computers).
- Coordinating for any additional assets required to support police information collection requirements (such as HUMINT collection teams, civil affairs, engineer support, and other support requirements) and fill military police capability gaps.
- Identifying and briefing units and mission elements (such as multifunctional site exploitation teams) regarding any expedited reporting requirements for specific critical information or high-value targets.

A-13. Unit commander responsibilities include–

- Training and integrating specific collection techniques in the planning, preparation, and execution of military police missions.
- Providing tasking and specific planning guidance to subordinate leaders to ensure adequate understanding of police IR and collection requirements.
- Reviewing IPB, police intelligence products, and other available data to ensure situational understanding and situational awareness, and passing information specific to the unit AO to personnel in the S-3 or PM section (and the G-2 or S-2 when applicable) to improve their knowledge of the AO.
- Providing full support to unit PIO debriefing activities and compliance with established briefing and debriefing procedures by all military police elements.
- Reinforcing the importance of the procedures for immediate reporting of information of critical or time-sensitive value.

A-14. Platoon, squad, section, team, and mission leader responsibilities include–

- Training and integration of specific collection techniques in the planning, preparation, and execution of military police missions.
- Providing tasking and specific mission guidance to platoons, squads, or sections to ensure adequate understanding of IR, collection, and other specific mission requirements.
- Reinforcing the importance of the procedures for immediate reporting of information of critical or time-sensitive value to all personnel.
- Preparing for (and participating in) the unit debriefing activities after all military police missions. Reporting information based on visual observations and police engagement during the debriefing or through immediate reporting of critical or time-sensitive information.
- Carefully conducting evidence collection and documentation and compiling written reports during military police missions.

Appendix B

Legal Requirements and Authorities

The number of agencies involved in police intelligence and the array of applicable laws, regulations, and directives can make negotiating the various authorities and restrictions complex. Military police and USACIDC personnel leverage the expertise and advice of an SJA to ensure compliance with all legal parameters in which military police and USACIDC personnel must operate. This is especially true when planning and conducting PIO in support of domestic antiterrorism, civil support, and homeland defense programs or foreign stability operations where rule of law is established and enforced. Military police, DOD police, and USACIDC personnel collect, manage, analyze, produce, and disseminate police information and police intelligence under the legal instruments of national and international laws, federal statutes, DOD and DA directives and regulations, and SOFAs. Military LE personnel are governed by information acquisition regulations, most notably DODD 5200.27, and not intelligence regulations. This appendix addresses those documents most prevalent to the PIO collection efforts. A summary of each document (with respect to its relevancy and applicability to the PIO function) and its restrictions and provisions to Army LE to conduct PIO are described.

AUTHORITY TO CONDUCT POLICE INTELLIGENCE OPERATIONS

B-1. While the following authoritative documents do not specifically use the term police intelligence operations, they do provide the authority and the premises on which to conduct PIO on installations. It is the police information and police intelligence that results from the activities described in these documents that comprise PIO activities. DODD 2000.12 directs commanders to ensure that they have a capability to collect, receive, evaluate, analyze, and disseminate all relevant data on terrorist activities, trends, and indicators of an imminent attack. It also requires commanders to fuse suspicious activity reports from military security, LE, and counterintelligence organizations with national level ISR collection activities.

B-2. Department of Defense Instruction (DODI) 2000.16 directs commanders to task the appropriate organizations under their command to gather, analyze, and disseminate terrorism threat information, as appropriate. It requires the Army to ensure that forces are trained to maximize the use of information derived from LE liaison and intelligence and counterintelligence processes and procedures. This includes intelligence procedures for handling PIR or in-transit units and the implementation of procedures to conduct IPB and mission analyses.

B-3. AR 525-13 directs commanders to ensure that the appropriate intelligence and LE organizations in their command collect and analyze criminal threat information and that the collection operations are being conducted according to applicable regulations and directives. This AR also requires commanders to ensure that threat information prepared by the intelligence community, USACIDC, PMs, and other organizations or sources be used when conducting threat assessments.

EXECUTIVE ORDER 12333

B-4. EO 12333 provides direction to U.S. intelligence activities and is intended to enhance human and technical collection techniques. While serving that purpose, nothing in the order is to be construed to apply or interfere with authorized civil or criminal LE responsibility of any department or agency.

B-5. This order provides for nonconsensual physical searches in the United States by the FBI and other LE activities in specific situations, such as "searches by counterintelligence elements of the military services directed against military personnel in the United States or abroad for intelligence purposes, when authorized by a military commander empowered to approve physical searches for LE purposes, based upon a finding of probable cause to believe that such persons are acting as agents of foreign powers" (see EO 12333).

B-6. National foreign intelligence collected at OCONUS locations is coordinated with the Central Intelligence Agency (if not otherwise obtainable). Collection procedures performed at CONUS locations are coordinated with the FBI.

B-7. EO 12333 allows intelligence agencies to–

- Cooperate with appropriate LE agencies for the purpose of protecting employees, information, property, and facilities of any agency in the intelligence community.
- Participate in LE activities to investigate or prevent clandestine intelligence activities by foreign powers or international terrorist or narcotics activities, unless otherwise precluded by law or this order.
- Provide specialized equipment, technical knowledge, or assistance from expert personnel for use by any department or agency or, when lives are endangered, to support local LE agencies. The provision of assistance by expert personnel is approved by the general counsel of the providing agency on a case-by-case basis.
- Render any other assistance and cooperation to LE authorities not precluded by applicable law.

DEPARTMENT OF DEFENSE DIRECTIVE 3025.15

B-8. DODD 3025.15 establishes DOD policy and assigns responsibilities for providing military assistance to civilian authorities. It establishes the procedures and reporting requirements for DOD assistance to civilian authorities.

B-9. This directive does not apply to the Inspector General of the DOD, the Defense Criminal Investigative Service, or military criminal investigative organizations (such as the USACIDC, the Naval Criminal Investigations Service, and the Air Force Office of Special Investigations) when they are conducting joint investigations with civil LE agencies pertaining to matters in their respective jurisdictions and using their own forces and equipment. It also does not apply to support to authorized inspector general or military criminal investigative organization investigations by elements in the DOD.

DEPARTMENT OF DEFENSE DIRECTIVE 5200.27

B-10. The purpose of DODD 5200.27 is to establish the general policy, limitations, procedures, and operational guidance pertaining to collecting, processing, storing, and disseminating information concerning persons and organizations not affiliated with DOD. This directive pertains to the acquisitioning of information concerning the activities of individuals and organizations (not affiliated with the DOD) in the U.S., the Commonwealth of Puerto Rico, and U.S. territories and possessions. It also applies to non-DOD affiliated U.S. citizens anywhere in the world. While serving this purpose, nothing in this directive–

- Prohibits the prompt reporting to LE agencies of any information indicating the existence of a threat to life or property, a violation of law, or the prohibited use of record keeping on such a report.
- Restricts the direct acquisition of information by overt means. Information acquired under this directive will be destroyed in 90 days unless its retention is required by law or is specifically authorized under criteria established by the Secretary of Defense or his designee.

B-11. DOD policy prohibits the collecting, reporting, processing, or storing of information on individuals or organizations not affiliated with the DOD, except in limited circumstances where such information is essential to the accomplishment of DOD missions. Information-gathering activities will be under overall civilian control, with a high level of general supervision and frequent inspections at the field level. Where collection activities are authorized to meet an essential requirement for information, maximum reliance will be placed on domestic civilian investigative agencies—federal, state, and local. In applying the criteria for the acquisition and retention of information established pursuant to DODD 5200.27, due consideration will be given to the need to protect DOD functions and property in the different circumstances existing in OCONUS geographic areas. Relevant factors include the–

- Level of disruptive activity against U.S. forces.
- Competence of host nation investigative agencies.
- Degree to which U.S. military and host nation agencies exchange investigative information.
- Absence of other U.S. investigative capabilities (such as in the unique and vulnerable positions of U.S. forces abroad).

B-12. DODD 5200.27, paragraph 4, authorizes Army LE personnel to gather information to accomplish the following missions–

- Protection of DOD functions and property. Information may be acquired about activities threatening defense, military, and civilian personnel and defense activities and installations, including vessels, aircraft, communications equipment, and supplies. Only the following types of activities justify the acquisition of information under the authority of this paragraph:
  - Subversion of loyalty, discipline, or morale of DOD military or civilian personnel by actively encouraging the violation of law, disobedience of lawful order or regulation, or disruption of military activities.
  - Theft of arms, ammunition, or equipment or the destruction or sabotage of facilities, equipment, or records belonging to DOD units or installations.
  - Acts jeopardizing the security of DOD elements or operations or compromising classified defense information by unauthorized disclosure or by espionage.
  - Unauthorized demonstrations on Regular Army or reserve DOD installations.
  - Direct threats to DOD military or civilian personnel in connection with their official duties or to other persons who have been authorized protection by DOD resources.
  - Activities endangering facilities that have classified defense contracts or that have been officially designated as key defense facilities.
  - Crimes for which the DOD has responsibility for investigating or prosecuting.
- Personnel security. Investigations may be conducted in relation to the following categories of personnel–
  - Members of the armed forces, including retired personnel, members of the reserve components, and applicants for commission or enlistment.
  - DOD civilian personnel and applicants for such status.
  - Persons having need for access to official information requiring protection in the interest of national defense under the DOD Industrial Security Program or being considered for participation in other authorized DOD programs.
- Operations related to civil disturbance. The Attorney General is the chief civilian officer in charge of coordinating all federal government activities relating to civil disturbances. Upon specific prior authorization of the Secretary of Defense or his designee, information may be acquired that is essential to meet operational requirements flowing from the mission assigned to the DOD to assist civil authorities in dealing with civil disturbances. Such authorization will only be granted when there is a distinct threat of a civil disturbance exceeding the LE capabilities of state and local authorities.

B-13. DODD 5200.27 identifies instances in which Army LE personnel are prohibited from collecting information on individuals and organizations. The prohibitions state that–

- The acquisition of information on individuals or organizations not affiliated with the DOD will be restricted to what is essential to the accomplishment of assigned DOD missions under this directive.
- No information will be acquired about a person or organization solely because of lawful advocacy of measures in opposition to government policy.
- There will be no physical or electronic surveillance of federal, state, or local officials or of candidates for such offices.
- There will be no electronic surveillance of any individual or organization, except as authorized by law.
- There will be no covert or otherwise deceptive surveillance or penetration of civilian organizations unless specifically authorized by the Secretary of Defense or his designee.
- No DOD personnel will be assigned to attend public or private meetings, demonstrations, or other similar activities for the purpose of acquiring information—the collection of which is authorized by DODD 5200.27—without specific prior approval by the Secretary of Defense or his designee. An exception to this policy may be made by the local commander or higher authority when, in his judgment, the threat is direct and immediate and time precludes obtaining prior approval. In each case, a report will be made immediately to the Secretary of Defense or his designee.
- No computerized data banks will be maintained relating to individuals or organizations not affiliated with DOD unless authorized by the Secretary of Defense or his designee.

DEPARTMENT OF DEFENSE DIRECTIVE 5240.1 AND 5240.1R

B-14. According to EO 12333, DOD has established procedures in DODD 5240.1 and DODD 5240.1R for the collection, retention, and dissemination of information concerning U.S. persons. Special emphasis is given to the protection of the constitutional rights and the privacy of U.S. citizens. DODD 5240.1 and DODD 5240.1R apply to all DOD intelligence components and activities. It does not apply to authorized LE activities carried out by DOD intelligence components having an LE mission.

ARMY REGULATION 190-24

B-15. This regulation establishes policy and procedures for the establishment and operation of Armed Forces Disciplinary Control Boards (AFDCBs). AFDCBs are established by installation, base, or station commanders to advise and make recommendations to commanders on matters concerning eliminating conditions adversely affecting the health, safety, welfare, morale, and discipline of the Armed Forces. AFDCB composition typically includes representatives from the following functional areas–

- LE agencies. Typically, on an AFDCB where an Army installation is the senior service, the PM will serve as the senior Army AFDCB representative.
- Legal counsel.
- Health.
- Environmental protection.
- Public affairs.
- Equal opportunity programs.
- Fire and safety programs.
- Chaplains' services.
- Alcohol and drug abuse programs.
- Personnel and community activities.
- Consumer affairs.

B-16. Civil agencies or individuals may be invited to board meetings as observers, witnesses, or to provide assistance where they possess knowledge or information pertaining to problem areas in the board's jurisdiction. Typically local LE agencies regularly participate in AFDCB proceedings.

B-17. In support of AFDCB mandates, Soldiers, military, or DA civilian police may be required to perform off-installation operations. These LE personnel must be thoroughly familiar with the applicable agreements and constraints of 18 USC 1385 and U.S.-host nation agreements. In the U.S or its territories, U.S. military and/or DA civilian police assigned to off-installation operations have the sole purpose of enforcing regulations and orders pertaining to persons subject to their jurisdiction. When accompanying civilian LE officers, these policing forces remain directly responsible to and under the command of their military chain of command. Military and DA civilian police may come to the aid of civilian LE officers to prevent the commission of a felony or injury to a civilian LE officer.

B-18. The constraints on the authority of Soldiers and/or DA civilian police to act on off-installation operations (and the specific scope of off-installation operations) will be clearly delineated in all authorizations for off-installation support. Off-installation operations will be coordinated with the local installation commander through the SJA or higher authority and the appropriate civilian LE agencies.

B-19. AR 190-24 establishes the primary objectives of any off-installation operations as—

- Rendering assistance and providing information to service personnel.
- Preserving the safety and security of service personnel.
- Preserving good order and discipline among service personnel and reducing off-installation incidents and offenses.
- Maintaining effective cooperation with civil authorities and community leaders.

ARMY REGULATION 190-45

B-20. This regulation establishes LE reporting requirements for Army LE organizations. It also establishes geographic areas of responsibility for reporting incidents involving Army personnel and assets. The regulation—

- Prescribes policies and procedures for submitting criminal history data (biometric) to the Criminal Justice Information Systems (CJIS).
- Provides policies and procedures for Army participation in the CJIS, NCIC and supplements standards and procedures established in the FBI NCIC Operating Manual and the National Law Enforcement Telecommunications System.
- Mandates the use of COPS and the Military Police Reporting System as the automated reporting systems to standardize LE reporting throughout the Army.
- Prescribes responsibilities and updates policies and procedures for reporting serious incidents in DA. The Serious Incident Report System—
  - Provides early notice to Headquarters, Department of the Army (HQDA) regarding serious incidents.
  - Provides the chain of command with timely information enabling an informed response to queries from DOD, news media, and others.
  - Meets LE reporting requirements for selected criminal incidents and provides LE personnel, such as the DHS and Transportation Security Administration, the most current information available.

B-21. In referring specifically to PIO, AR 190-45 states, in regard to garrison LE operations, that the purpose of gathering police intelligence is to identify individuals or groups of individuals in an effort to anticipate, prevent, or monitor possible criminal activity. Police intelligence that is developed and factually establishes that a criminal offense may have occurred results in initiation of an investigation by military police and USACIDC or other investigative agencies.

B-22. AR 190-45 affirms the importance of establishing agreements between military LE and civilian LE counterparts to facilitate improved information sharing, especially concerning investigations, arrests, and prosecutions involving military personnel. This regulation provides policy guidance regarding the establishment of formal memoranda of understanding with civilian LE agencies to establish or improve the flow of information between agencies. The regulation establishes policy regarding the–

- Active exchange of police intelligence between DOD LE; military police; USACIDC; and local, state, federal, and international LE agencies.
- Transmission of written LE-related documents. Written extracts from local police intelligence files provided to an authorized investigative agency must have the following statement included on transmittal documents: THIS DOCUMENT IS PROVIDED FOR INFORMATION AND USE. COPIES OF THIS DOCUMENT, ENCLOSURES THERETO, AND INFORMATION THEREFROM, WILL NOT BE FURTHER RELEASED WITHOUT THE PRIOR APPROVAL OF THE INSTALLATION PM.
- Public dissemination of police intelligence files. Local police intelligence files may be exempt from certain disclosure requirements, as outlined in AR 25-55 and the *Freedom of Information Act*.

ARMY REGULATION 195-2

B-23. AR 195-2 prescribes responsibilities, missions, objectives, and policies pertaining to USACIDC. This regulation requires commanders to report suspected criminal activity to Army LE personnel and notify investigative services. Criminal incidents in the Army are reported to the military police. Serious criminal incidents, as defined in AR 195-2, are reported to USACIDC personnel. AR 195-2 requires that the focus of the police information program be to detect, analyze, and prevent criminal activity from affecting the Army. In part, the purpose of this program is to conduct criminal investigations, crime prevention, and police intelligence activities, to include personnel security, internal security, and criminal and other LE matters, all of which are essential to the effective operations of the Army. This regulation, like AR 190-45, requires close coordination between DOD LE agencies; military police; USACIDC; and local, state, federal, and international LE agencies and that police information and police intelligence be actively exchanged between them. This interaction between different agencies allows for the creation of networks, forums, and fusion cells that are described in chapter 4. These shared, fused systems enhance the ability of Army LE personnel to produce timely, accurate, and relevant intelligence that is crucial to the commander's decisionmaking ability.

ARMY REGULATION 380-13

B-24. AR 380-13 implements DODD 5200.27 and establishes policy and procedures governing the acquisition, reporting, processing, and storage of information on persons or organizations not affiliated with DOD. It does not apply to authorized criminal investigations and LE information-gathering activities, which are the responsibilities of military police and the USACIDC Investigation Command. Such activities will continue to be conducted according to applicable regulations. It states that no information will be acquired about a person or organization solely because of lawful advocacy of measures in opposition to U.S. government policy or because of activity in support of racial and civil rights interests. It provides other restrictions on the types of information that may be collected as they apply to the intelligence community. This regulation allows for prompt reporting to Army LE personnel any information that indicates the existence of a threat to life or property and the violation of a law. Paragraphs B-10 through B-13 provide detailed information on requirements and restrictions for storing various categories of information.

ARMY REGULATION 381-10

B-25. AR 381-10 is an MI community regulation. However, to clarify what Army LE personnel can expect in terms of assistance from MI, the following information is provided. It is important for Army LE personnel to understand that the procedures of this regulation do not apply to them. If, during an Army intelligence component investigation, evidence surfaces that provides reasonable belief that a crime has been committed, details of the investigation will be relinquished to the USACIDC or the appropriate military police investigating agency, according to AR 195-2, AR 190-45, and AR 381-20.

B-26. Agencies within the MI community are authorized to–
- Cooperate with LE agencies for the purpose of protecting the employees, information, property, and facilities of any agency in the intelligence community.
- Participate in LE activities to investigate or prevent clandestine intelligence activities on foreign equipment or technical knowledge, provide assistance from expert personnel for use by any department or agency, or, when lives are endangered, support local LE agencies (unless otherwise precluded by law or AR 381-10). The provision of assistance by expert personnel will be approved by general counsel of the providing agency on a case-by-case basis.
- Render other assistance and cooperation (not precluded by applicable law) with LE authorities.

B-27. Army LE personnel can expect cooperation (consistent with DODD 5525.5) from the MI community for the purpose of–
- Investigating or preventing clandestine intelligence activities by foreign powers, international narcotics activities, or international terrorist activities.
- Protecting DOD employees, information, property, and facilities.
- Preventing, detecting, or investigating other violations of law.

B-28. A significant item that AR 381-10 highlights is the definition of "collect." In the text of this regulation, its definition is different from the everyday, common definition of "to assemble or to gather." In AR 381-10, collect includes the intent to use or retain information received and include information received from cooperating sources in the collection effort. The intent of this definition, although not stated in this regulation, is also the intent of information collection efforts by Army LE personnel.

ARMY REGULATION 525-13

B-29. AR 525-13 is the regulation that establishes and provides implementation guidance and requirements for the antiterrorism program. The antiterrorism program's purpose is to protect personnel, to include–
- Soldiers.
- Members of other Services.
- DA civilian employees.
- DOD contractors.
- Family members of DOD employees.
- Information.
- Property.
- Facilities (including civil work and like projects).

B-30. Military police and USACIDC elements hold critical responsibilities due to their LE function and ability to collect, analyze, disseminate, and manage police intelligence. Specific responsibilities are given to the Provost Marshal General and USACIDC commander for implementation. The Provost Marshal General, acting in direct support from the HQDA Deputy Chief of Staff (DCS); G-3; Assistant Chief of Staff, Civil Affairs (G-5); and information operations staff officer (G-7) in the management and execution of the Army antiterrorism mission, is responsible for–

- Staffing and providing an antiterrorism branch to serve as the functional proponent and to establish policy and objectives regarding the antiterrorism program.
- Operating an antiterrorism operations intelligence cell (ATOIC) in close coordination with the Office of the DCS, G-2 to–
  - Issue early warning of criminal and terrorist threats to Army commands, Army Service component commands, direct reporting units, and other senior Army leaders and organizations.
  - Coordinate analyses and reporting of terrorist-related intelligence with appropriate intelligence and LE agencies to provide warnings and maintain visibility of threats to senior Army leadership; all major commands (Army major commands, Army Service component commands, and direct reporting units); and threatened installations, activities, facilities, and personnel.
  - Fuse criminal and terrorist threat information to form a single threat picture.
  - Assess terrorist and criminal threats to Army forces and publish an annual comprehensive DA threat statement and daily DA force protection memorandum to disseminate potential and future threats, thereby enhancing threat awareness at all levels.
  - Publish DA antiterrorism travel advisories (as required) to inform commanders of DOD-designated HIGH or SIGNIFICANT threat level countries, cities with high crime rates, and travel advisories.

B-31. AR 525-13 also outlines specific responsibilities for the Commander, USACIDC, as the senior commander responsible for Army criminal investigations. USACIDC is responsible for–

- Ensuring a sufficient USACIDC police intelligence capability to monitor and report on the activities, intentions, and capabilities of domestic threat groups (according to applicable regulations and directives).
- Collecting, analyzing, and disseminating police intelligence to affected commands pertaining to threat activities (in the provisions of applicable statutes and regulations).
- Providing appropriate threat-related police intelligence to HQDA ATOIC, the Intelligence and Security Command, and Army Counterintelligence Center (ACIC).
- Maintaining a capability to analyze and disseminate collected, time-sensitive information concerning the criminal threat against Army interests.
- Investigating threat incidents of Army interest and to monitor such investigations when conducted by civilian, host nation, military, or other police agencies. Providing applicable results of terrorist-related investigations to ATOIC, ACIC, and CALL.
- Providing trained hostage negotiators to support Army antiterrorism operations worldwide.
- Planning and coordinating the protection of HRP for DOD, DA, and foreign officials as directed by HQDA.
- Serving as the Army's primary liaison representative to federal, state, local, and host nation agencies to exchange police intelligence.
- Establishing procedures to ensure appropriate liaison at all levels between USACIDC, the Intelligence and Security Command, and PM elements operating in support of the antiterrorism program.
- Immediately notifying the affected installation PM and HQDA on receipt of time-sensitive threat information.
- Ensuring that criminal activity threat assessments and personal security vulnerability assessments are conducted for Army personnel, installations, systems, operations, and other interests as directed by HQDA and/or based on Army commander's operational requirements.

- Providing technical personnel support to DCS and designated G-3, G-5, or G-7 assessment teams, as required.
- Investigating all incidents of suspected terrorism as criminal acts, to include safeguarding evidence, collection testimony, preparation of investigative reports, and presentations to appropriate judicial officials. Investigations are conducted jointly with federal, state, local, and foreign LE agencies, as appropriate.
- Providing appropriate terrorism analyses and threat assessments to the ATOIC in support of Army requirements and the antiterrorism program.

B-32. The regulation also outlines responsibilities for installation and garrison commanders. These commanders are required to–

- Ensure that LE and intelligence organizations in their command collect and analyze criminal and terrorist threat information.
- Develop a system to monitor, report, collect, analyze and disseminate terrorist threat information.
- Identify a focal point for the integration of operations and local or host nation, intelligence, criminal investigations, police information, and police intelligence.
- Coordinate LE support with their higher headquarters in case organic LE is not available.
- Ensure that appropriate connectivity to receive threat-related information from all available sources (such as ATOIC, FBI, ACIC, USACIDC, PM, local LE, Intelink-S, and Intelink).
- Ensure that collection operations are being conducted consistent with the requirements and restrictions of AR 381-10, AR 381-12, AR 380-13, DODD 5200.27, and other applicable regulations and directives.
- Establish an antiterrorism program supported by all-source intelligence, with PIR, CCIR, and focused collection, analysis, and dissemination to protect personnel and assets in the AO.
- Ensure that products and analyses are focused and based on their PIR and CCIR. Review PIR and CCIR for currency and revalidate at least annually to update changing threats and/or requirements.
- Ensure that information and intelligence regarding terrorist activity is developed, collected, analyzed, and disseminated in a timely manner. Current intelligence will be integrated into the antiterrorism training program.
- Ensure that LE and intelligence organizations in their command collect and analyze criminal and terrorist threat information.

B-33. In reference to terrorist threat assessments, the regulation specifically addresses the LE and intelligence community as follows–

- Threat information prepared by the intelligence community, USACIDC, and the Provost Marshal's Office will be used when conducting threat assessments and technical information from information management.
- Threat assessments will serve as a basis and justification for antiterrorism plans, enhancements, program and budget requests, and the establishment of force protection conditions.
- Threat assessments will be part of a leader's reconnaissance, in conjunction with deployments and follow-on threat and vulnerability assessments (as determined by the commander).
- Consolidated MI and police intelligence data identified in threat assessments (on U.S. personnel) cannot be filed, stored, or maintained as an intelligence product (as directed in AR 381-10). These assessments must be filed, stored, and maintained in operational channels.

JURISDICTIONAL AGREEMENTS BETWEEN THE UNITED STATES AND A HOST NATION

B-34. SOFAs are typically established when a long-term U.S. presence is required or anticipated. While this is typical, some AOs in which U.S. forces operate do not have established SOFA agreements between the U.S. and host nations. This is common in an AO experiencing MCO or significant instability. As the theater matures and a stable host nation government establishes control, a SOFA will typically be developed if an enduring U.S. presence is required.

B-35. These SOFAs play a vital role in preserving command authority and the protection of military personnel. The purpose of such an agreement is to set forth rights and responsibilities between the U.S. government and a host nation government on such matters as criminal and civil jurisdictions, uniforms, arms possession, tax and customs relief, entry and exit procedures of personnel and property, and resolutions to damage claims. SOFAs define the legal status of U.S. personnel and property in the territory of another nation.

B-36. All SOFAs are unique and reflect specific considerations based on the countries entering into the agreement and other factors. SOFAs establish guidelines for civil and criminal jurisdiction. This process is critical to ensure that the U.S. and DOD can protect, to the maximum extent possible, the rights of U.S. personnel who may be subject to criminal trials by foreign courts and imprisonment in foreign prisons. Typically a SOFA will recognize the right of a host nation government to primary jurisdiction, allowing jurisdiction for all cases in which U.S. military personnel violate host nation laws. Most SOFAs will provide two exceptions where the U.S. may retain primary jurisdiction. These two exceptions are for offenses committed–

- By U.S. personnel against U.S. personnel.
- In the performance of official duties.

B-37. In some AOs, agreements between the United States and host nation countries may establish legal parameters regarding U.S. authority over host nation personnel. The host nation typically retains jurisdiction over its citizens; however, in some cases, the host nation government may be nonfunctioning or incapable of maintaining security and control over the population. These environments may require U.S. military forces to establish and maintain control over the population until the host nation can assume authority and control. This may be particularly true as operations transition from MCO to stability operations and the OE becomes stable enough for the host nation to implement the rule of law in dealing with the population and maintaining order. The OE immediately following a major disaster, either natural or man-made, may also cause conditions in which U.S. military forces are required to restore order and maintain control over a host nation population.

B-38. As the OE becomes stable and the host nation begins to reestablish the rule of law, U.S. military forces may still be necessary to assist the host nation in policing activities. This is only done pending full assumption of control by the host nation. During the interim, legal agreements between the host nation and the United States may be established to ensure that the U.S. military and its Soldiers act in the rule of law established by the host nation and that the rights of the local population are maintained.

Appendix C

Police Intelligence Initiatives

The LE community in the United States is universally committed to the timely and seamless exchange of terrorist and criminal information and intelligence. In light of the tragedy on 11 September 2001, it is absolutely critical that all LE personnel work together to protect the nation. This appendix identifies some of the key civilian agencies participating in PIO and identifies initiatives and coordination venues used by other LE agencies in an effort to facilitate interagency coordination. The civilian LE community typically uses the term *criminal intelligence* to refer to all police intelligence, whereas the Army uses the term *police intelligence* as the overarching term and criminal intelligence to refer specifically to police intelligence specific to criminal threats and vulnerabilities (typically associated with criminal investigations).

OVERVIEW

C-1. In the civilian police community, there are several definitions and processes describing criminal intelligence and the criminal intelligence process. Two of the most prevalent variations of the definition of criminal intelligence are "the product of an analytic process that provides an integrated perspective to disparate information about crime, crime trends, crime and security threats, and conditions associated with criminality" (see *Criminal Intelligence Sharing: A National Plan for Intelligence-Led Policing at the Local, State, and Federal Levels: Recommendations from the International Association of Chiefs of Police (IACP) Intelligence Summit)* and "information compiled, analyzed, and/or disseminated in an effort to anticipate, prevent, or monitor criminal activity" (see *Law Enforcement Intelligence: A Guide for State, Local, and Tribal Law Enforcement Agencies).* The civilian law enforcement community typically defines the criminal intelligence process as consisting of six basic steps–

- Planning the gathering of information.
- Gathering the information.
- Processing the information.
- Analyzing the information to produce an intelligence product.
- Disseminating the intelligence product.
- Evaluating the usefulness of the intelligence product.

C-2. The term *intelligence-led policing* enjoys wide currency among criminal justice researchers and national policymakers, although there is vigorous debate regarding a definitive description or definition. Regardless of their positions, most officials agree that intelligence-led policing integrates easily with other popular policing models, including community policing and problem-oriented policing. *Law Enforcement Intelligence: A Guide for State, Local, and Tribal Law Enforcement Agencies*, a 2004 Community-Oriented Policing Services publication, describes intelligence-led policing as "the integration of community policing and LE intelligence." The report *Intelligence-Led Policing: The New Intelligence Architecture,* issued by the Bureau of Justice Assistance and their partners in 2005, calls it "a collaborative enterprise based on improved intelligence operations and community-oriented policing and problem solving."

INITIATIVES AND PROGRAMS

C-3. The sharing of police information has received significant emphasis since the terrorist attacks on 11 September 2001. Several initiatives by the federal government to improve information-sharing capabilities between federal, state, local, and tribal agencies have been implemented. Beyond simply sharing information, standardization of training to develop a common language and understanding of police information and police intelligence and development of fusion centers will enable timely exchanges and transmission of police information. The following paragraphs provide information of some of the civilian LE initiatives and programs that enable interagency cooperation and standardization of police intelligence training. These initiatives, while developed in the civilian LE community, are open to Army LE and a thorough understanding of civilian standards, policies, and procedures is critical in successful interagency cooperation between Army LE and federal, state, local, and tribal agencies operating in the same AO.

OneDOJ

C-4. The United States Department of Justice (DOJ) system known as OneDOJ (formerly the Regional Data Exchange) is a repository for LE information shared with other federal, state, local, and tribal LE agencies through connections with regional information-sharing partnerships. OneDOJ is used to share LE information internally across investigative components and provide regional connectivity for authorized users to conduct searches of OneDOJ information and share LE information. Additional information on OneDOJ can be accessed at the following Web site: < http://www.justice.gov/jmd/ocio/leisp/onedoj.htm>.

C-5. All DOJ LE components—the Bureau of Alcohol, Tobacco, and Firearms; Bureau of Prisons; Drug Enforcement Administration; FBI; and the United States Marshal's Service—participate in OneDOJ. Criminal information shared includes open- and closed-case documents, investigative reports, witness interviews, data on criminal events, information on criminal histories and incarcerations, and information about individual offenders. Outside agencies connect with OneDOJ through regional sharing systems using a standard secure platform developed through the Law Enforcement Information Sharing Program (LEISP). The DOJ, through the OneDOJ system, shares information with the Military Criminal Investigative Services (USACIDC, Naval Criminal Investigative Service, and Air Force Office of Special Investigations).

Law Enforcement Information Sharing Program

C-6. The LEISP is an effort by the DOJ to improve LE information sharing between state, local, tribal, and other federal LE partners. The objective of the program is to share LE information across jurisdictional boundaries to prevent terrorism and to systematically improve the investigation and prosecution of criminal activity. Sharing of LE information with agencies outside DOJ is accomplished through regional sharing centers. Additional information on the LEISP can be accessed at the following Web sites: <http://www.justice.gov/jmd/ocio/leisp/> and <www.usdoj.gov/jmd/ocio/onedoj_strategy.pdf>.

National Information Exchange Model

C-7. The National Information Exchange Model (NIEM) is a national information framework that eases cross domain exchanges. It allows transfer of information using standard language and protocols enabling information sharing between various agencies involved in LE, emergency management, homeland security, and other specific domains. The Law Enforcement Exchange Specification (LEXS) (pronounced "lex") is the specific domain in the NIEM that enables DOJ and other federal, state, local, and tribal LE organizations to establish LE information exchanges. LEXS is the basis for the OneDOJ regional LE information sharing partnerships. Additional information on the NIEM can be accessed at the following Web site: <http://www.niem.gov/>.

NATIONAL CRIMINAL INTELLIGENCE SHARING PLAN

C-8. The *National Criminal Intelligence Sharing Plan,* published in October 2003, resulted from an effort to close identified gaps in police intelligence capability in the aftermath of the terrorist attacks of 11 September 2001. The plan outlines 28 recommendations for implementation by LE agencies to improve sharing of police information. The recommendations covering areas, such as fusion centers, security clearances, core training standards, and technology emphasize the need to engage every LE agency (regardless of size and type) in the sharing of police information. See the following Web site for additional information on the *National Criminal Intelligence Sharing Plan* and associated recommendations: <http://it.ojp.gov/documents/National_Criminal_Intelligence_Sharing_Plan.pdf>.

Criminal Intelligence Coordinating Council and Global Intelligence Working Group

C-9. The Global Intelligence Working Group (GWIG) is composed of state, local, tribal, and federal justice; homeland security; and public safety representatives. The GWIG has the capability of drawing on subject matter experts external to the working group as needed. It operates in partnership with the Criminal Intelligence Coordinating Council (CICC). The CICC was formed in 2004 to provide recommendations regarding the implementation and refinement of the national criminal intelligence sharing plan. The CICC membership represents law enforcement and homeland security agencies at all levels of government. It serves as an advocate for LE agencies at all levels in the effort to develop and share police intelligence to promote public safety and national security. The CICC is a policy-level organization involved in setting priorities, directing research, and preparing advisory recommendations. The GWIG and CICC operate in the framework of the Global Justice Information Sharing Initiative.

Global Justice Information Sharing Initiative

C-10. The Global Justice Information Sharing Initiative is a federal advisory committee advising the U.S. Attorney General regarding LE related information sharing and associated initiatives. It was created to support the development of LE information exchange applied across all LE agencies and levels of government. The organization promotes standards-based electronic information exchange to provide the justice community with timely, accurate, complete, and accessible information in a secure and trusted environment. Additional information of GWIG, CICC, and the Global Justice Information Sharing Initiative can be accessed at the following Web site: <http://it.ojp.gov/global>.

NATIONAL STRATEGY FOR INFORMATION SHARING

C-11. The *National Strategy for Information Sharing* was published in October 2007 to address a capability gap focused on the sharing of homeland security information, terrorism information, and law enforcement information related to terrorism from multiple sources. It calls for a national information sharing capability through the establishment of a national integrated network of fusion centers. Sources of information addressed in the plan are interdisciplinary. They are from multiple sources, at all levels of government, and include private sector organizations and foreign sources. The *National Strategy for Information Sharing: Successes and Challenges in Improving Terrorism-Related Information Sharing* can be accessed at the following Web site: <http://georgewbush-whitehouse.archives.gov/nsc/infosharing/index html>.

C-12. In addition to traditional LE uses, such information is used to–
- Support terrorism prevention efforts.
- Develop critical infrastructure protection and resilience plans.
- Prioritize emergency management, response, and recovery planning activities.
- Develop training and exercise programs.
- Allocate funding and other resources.

C-13. The *National Strategy for Information Sharing* identifies baseline capabilities requirements for fusion cells. Defining these operational standards enables federal, state, and local officials to identify and plan for the resources needed—including financial and technical assistance and human support—to attain the baseline capacity required for successful information fusion cells. The baseline capability ensures that fusion cells have the necessary structures, processes, and tools in place to support the gathering, processing, analysis, and dissemination of police information, to include information and police intelligence in support specific operational capabilities; suspicious activity reporting; alert, warning, and notification reporting; risk assessments; and situational understanding reporting.

REGIONAL INFORMATION SHARING SYSTEMS

C-14. Regional Information Sharing System® (RISS) networks are conduits for the exchange of criminal information and criminal intelligence among participating LE agencies. The RISS program is composed of six regional centers that share intelligence and coordinate efforts against crime and criminal networks operating in many locations across jurisdictional lines. Typical targets of RISS activities are terrorism, drug trafficking, violent crime, cybercrime, gang activity, identity theft, human trafficking, and organized crime and criminal activities. Each of the centers, however, selects its own target crimes and the range of services provided to member agencies. Additional information on RISS can be accessed at the following Web site: <http://www.riss net/>.

Glossary

Acronym/Term	Definition
	Definition
ACI2	Army Criminal Investigative Information System
ACIC	Army Counterintelligence Center
AFDCB	Armed Forces Disciplinary Control Boards
AO	area of operations
APOD	aerial port of debarkation
AR	Army regulation
ARNG	Army National Guard
ARNGUS	Army National Guard of the United States
AS	area security
ATOIC	antiterrorism operations intelligence cell
ATTP	Army tactics, techniques, and procedures
BOLO	be-on-the-lookout
CALL	Center for Army Lessons Learned
CARVER	criticality, accessibility, recuperability vulnerability, effect, and recognizability
CCIAC	Crime and Criminal Intelligence Analysts Course
CCIR	commander's critical information requirement
CICC	Criminal Intelligence Coordinating Council
CITF	Criminal Investigation Task Force
CJIS	Criminal Justice Information Systems
COA	course of action
CONUS	continental United States
COP	common operational picture
COPS	Centralized Operator's Police Suite
CPS	crime prevention survey
CRM	composite risk management
CVB	Central Violation Bureau
D3A	decide, detect, deliver, and assess
DA	Department of the Army
DC	displaced civilian
DCGS–A	Distributed Common Ground System–Army
DCS	Deputy Chief of Staff
DHS	United States Department of Homeland Security
DNA	deoxyribonucleic acid
DOD	Department of Defense
DODD	Department of Defense directive
DODI	Department of Defense instruction

DOJ	Unites States Department of Justice
DSCA	defense support to civilian authorities
DTG	date-time-group
ECTA	economic crime threat assessment
ELINT	electronic intelligence
EO	executive order
F3EAD	find, fix, finish, exploit, analyze, and disseminate
FBI	Federal Bureau of Investigation
FM	field manual
FMI	field manual interim
G-2	Army Chief of Staff, Intelligence
G-3	Assistant Chief of Staff, Operations and Plans
G-5	Assistant Chief of Statt, Civil Affairs
G-7	information operations staff officer
GCC	geographic combat commander
GIS	geographic information system
GPS	global positioning system
GWIG	globel intelligence working group
HLS	homeland security
HQDA	Headquarters, Department of the Army
HRP	high-risk personnel
HUMINT	human intelligence
I/R	internment and resettlement
I&W	indications and warning
IACP	International Association of Chiefs of Police
IED	improvised explosive device
IGO	intergovernmental organization
IPB	intelligence preparation of the battlefield
IR	intelligence requirements
ISR	intelligence, surveillance, and reconnaissance
J-2	intelligence staff section
JP	joint publication
JWICS	Joint Worldwide Intelligence Communications System
KM	knowledge management
L&O	law and order
LE	law enforcement
LEISP	Law Enforcement Information Sharing Program
LEXS	Law Enforcement Exchange Specification
LOC	line of communications
LSTA	logistics-security threat assessment
MCO	major combat operations

MEB	maneuver enhancement brigade
MDMP	military decisionmaking process
MI	military intelligence
MMS	maneuver and mobility support
MSHARPP	mission, symbolism, history, accessibility, recognizability, population, and proximity
MSR	main supply route
NAI	named area of interest
NCIC	National Crime Information Center
NGO	nongovernmental organizations
NIEM	National Information Exchange Model
OCONUS	outside the continental United States
OE	operational environment
OGA	other governmental agencies
OPLAN	operation plan
OPORD	operation order
PCA	Posse Comitatus Act
PDTT	police development and transistion team
PIA	police intelligence advisory
PIO	police intelligence operations
PIR	priority intelligence requirements
PM	provost marshal
POLICE	police and prison structures, organized criminal elements, legal systems, investigations and interviews, crime conducive conditions, and enforcement gaps and mechanisms
PSVA	personal security vulnerability assessment
R&S	reconnaissance and surveillance
RFI	request for information
RISS	Regional Information Sharing System
ROE	rules of engagement
S-2	intelligence staff officer
S-3	operations staff officer
SAC	special agent in charge
SARA	scanning, analysis, response, and assessment
SIGINT	signals intellegence
SIPRNET	Secret Internet Protocol Router Network
SJA	staff judge advocate
SOFA	status-of-forces agreement
SOP	standing operating procedure
SPOD	seaport of debarkation
SRT	special reaction team
TC	training circular

TRADOC	United States Army Training and Doctrine Command
U.S.	United States
USACIDC	United States Army Criminal Investigation Command
USACIL	United States Army Criminal Investigation Laboratory
USAMPS	United States Army Military Police School
USAR	United States Army Reserve
USC	United States Code

SECTION II – TERMS

*criminal intelligence

Criminal intelligence is a category of police intelligence derived from the collection, analysis, and interpretation of all available information concerning known and potential criminal threats and vulnerabilities of supported organizations.

*police information

Police information is all available information concerning known and potential enemy and criminal threats and vulnerabilities collected during police activities, operations, and investigations. Analysis of police information produces police intelligence.

* police intelligence

Police intelligence results from the application of systems, technologies, and processes that analyze applicable data and information necessary for situational understanding and focusing policing activities to achieve social order.

References

SOURCES USED

The following sources are either quoted or paraphrased in this publication.

Intelligence-Led Policing: The New Intelligence Architecture, September 2005.
Military Police and Counterinsurgency Operations, Operation Iraqi Freedom Initial Impressions Report, 22 July 2008.
National Criminal Intelligence Sharing Plan. October 2003.
National Strategy for Information Sharing: Successes and Challenges in Improving Terrorism-Related Information Sharing. October 2007.

ARMY PUBLICATIONS

AR 10-87. *Army Commands, Army Service Component Commands, and Direct Reporting Units.* 4 September 2007.

AR 25-55. *The Department of the Army Freedom of Information Act Program.* 1 November 1997.

AR 190-24. *Armed Forces Disciplinary Control Boards and Off-Installation Liaison and Operations.* 27 July 2006.

AR 190-30. *Military Police Investigations.* 1 November 2005.

AR 190-45. *Law Enforcement Reporting.* 30 March 2007.

AR 190-53. *Interception of Wire and Oral Communications for Law Enforcement Purposes.* 3 November 1986.

AR 190-58. *Physical Security.* 22 March 1989.

AR 195-2. *Criminal Investigation Activities.* 15 May 2009.

AR 195-6. *Department of the Army Polygraph Activities.* 29 September 1995.

AR 380-10. *Foreign Disclosure and Contacts with Foreign Representatives.* 22 June 2005.

AR 380-13. *Acquisition and Storage of Information Concerning Nonaffiliated Persons and Organizations.* 30 September 1974.

AR 381-10. *US Army Intelligence Activities.* 3 May 2007.

AR 381-12. *Subversion and Espionage Directed Against the U.S. Army (SAEDA).* 15 January 1993.

AR 381-20. *The Army Counterintelligence Program.* 26 May 2010.

AR 525-13. *Antiterrorism.* 11 September 2008.

FM 1-02. *Operational Terms and Graphics (MCRP 5-12A)* 21 September 2004.

FM 1-04. *Legal Support to the Operational Army.* 15 April 2009.

FM 2-0. *Intelligence.* 23 March 2010.

FM 2-22.3. *Human Intelligence Collector Operations.* 6 September 2006.

FM 3-0. *Operations.* 27 February 2008.

FM 3-05.40 . *Civil Affairs Operations.* 29 September 2006.

FM 3-07. *Stability Operations.* 6 October 2008

FM 3-19.13. *Law Enforcement Investigations.* 10 January 2005.

FM 3-34.230. Topographic Operations. 3 August 2000.

FM 3-39. *Military Police Operations.* 16 February 2010.

FM 3-39.40. *Internment and Resettlement Operations.* 12 February 2010.

FM 3-34.170. *Engineer Reconnaissance.* 25 March 2008.

FM 3-90. *Tactics.* 4 July 2001.

FM 3-90.31. *Maneuver Enhancement Brigade Operations.* 26 February 2009.

FM 3-100.21. *Contractors on the Battlefield.* 3 January 2003.

FM 5-0. *The Operations Process.* 26 March 2010.

FM 5-19. *Composite Risk Management.* 21 August 2006.

FM 6-0. *Mission Command: Command and Control of Army Force.* 11 August 2003.

FM 6-22. *Army Leadership.* 12 October 2006.

FM 7-15. *The Army Universal Task List.* 27 February 2009.

FM 19-10. *Military Police Law and Order Operations.* 30 September 1987.

FMI 2-01.301. *Specific Tactics, Techniques, and Procedures and Applications for Intelligence Preparation of the Battlefield.* 31 March 2009.

TC 2-22.303. *The 2X Handbook.* 31 July 2006.

TC 2-33.4. *Intelligence Analysis.* 1 July 2009.

JOINT PUBLICATIONS

JP 1-0. Personnel Support to Join Operations. 16October 2006.

JP 1-02. *Department of Defense Dictionary of Military and Associated Terms.* 12 April 2001.

JP 2-0. *Joint Intelligence.* 22 June 2007.

JP 3-0. *Joint Operations.* 17 September 2006.

JP 3-16. *Multinational Operations.* 07 March 2007.

JP 3-28. *Civil Support.* 14 September 2007.

MISCELLANEOUS PUBLICATIONS

DD Form 1408. *Armed Forces Traffic Ticket.* 1 December 1987.

DOD O-20012.H. *DOD Antiterrorism Handbook.* 1 February 2004.

DODD 2000.12. *DOD Antiterrorism Program.* 18 August 2003.

DODD 3025.15. *Military Assistance to Civil Authorities.* 18 February 1997.

DODD 5200.27. *Acquisition of Information Concerning Persons and Organizations Not Affiliated With the Department of Defense.* 7 January 1980.

DODD 5240.1. *DOD Intelligence Activities.* 27 August 2007.

DODD 5525.5. *DOD Cooperation with Civilian Law Enforcement Officials.* 15 January 1986.

DOD 5240.1-R. *Procedures Governing the Activities of DOD Intelligence Components that Affect United States Persons.* 11 December 1982.

DODI 2000.16. *DOD Antiterrorism Standards.* 8 December 2006.

EO 12333. *United States Intelligence Activities.* 4 December 1981.

Freedom of Information Act. 6 September 1966.

USC Title 10. Section 16. *Armed Forces.*

USC Title 18. Section 1385. *Crimes and Criminal Procedure. Use of Army and Air Force as Posse Comitatus.*

USC Title 32. *National Guard.*

READINGS RECOMMENDED

These sources contain relevant supplemental information.

DHS and DOJ, Global Justice Information Sharing Initiative, *DHS/DOJ Fusion Process: Technical Assistance Program and Services.* February 2009.

DOJ, FBI, *Protecting America against Terrorist Attacks: A Closer Look at the FBI's Joint Terrorism Task Forces,* 1 December 2004.

DOJ, Global Justice Information Sharing Initiative, Counterterrorism Training Coordination Working Group, *Minimum Criminal Intelligence Training Standards for Law Enforcement and Other Criminal Justice Agencies in the United States: Findings and Recommendations,* October 2007.

DOJ, Global Justice Information Sharing Initiative, *Fusion Center Guidelines: Developing and Sharing Information and Intelligence in a New Era,* August 2005.

DOJ, Global Justice Information Sharing Initiative, *Law Enforcement Analyst Certification Standards,* August 2006.

DOJ, Global Justice Information Sharing Initiative, *Law Enforcement Analyst Certification Standards,* August 2006.

DOJ, Global Justice Information Sharing Initiative, *Privacy, Civil Rights, and Civil Liberties: Policy Templates for Justice Information*, February 2008.

DOJ, Global Justice Information Sharing Initiative, *Privacy Policy Development Guide,* October 2006, <http://www.search.org/files/pdf/Privacy_Guide_Final.pdf>, accessed on July 2009.

DOJ, Office of Community Oriented Policing Services, *Law Enforcement Intelligence: A Guide for State, Local, and Tribal Law Enforcement Agencies,* November 2004.

DOJ, Office of Justice Programs, Bureau of Justice Assistance, *Intelligence-Led Policing: A New Architecture*, in the series *New Realities: Law Enforcement in the Post–9/11 Era,* by IACP with the National Sheriffs Association, Major Cities Chiefs Association, Police Foundation, and National Organization of Black LE Executives, September 2005.

Findings and Recommendations of the Suspicious Activity Report (SAR) Support and Implementation Project. June 2008.

Law Enforcement Intelligence*: A Guide for State, Local, and Tribal Law Enforcement Agencies,* David L. Carter, November 2004.

Crime Analysis: From First Report to Final Arrest Steven Gottlieb, Sheldon Arenberg, and Raj Sing, 1998.

Criminal Intelligence Sharing: A National Plan for Intelligence-Led Policing at the Local, State, and Federal Levels: Recommendations from the IACP Intelligence Summit. August 2002.

LE Intelligence Unit, *Criminal Intelligence File Guidelines.* March 2002

Part 23, Title 28, Code of Federal Regulations. *Criminal Intelligence Systems Operating Policies.*

The National Security Act of 1947.

USC Title 50. Section 401a. *War and National Defense, Definitions.*

DOCUMENTS NEEDED

These documents must be available to the intended users of this publication. Department of the Army (DA) forms are available on the Army Publishing Directorate (APD) web site (www.apd.army.mil).

DA Form 2028. *Recommended Changes to Publications and Blank Forms.*

This page intentionally left blank.

Index

By order of the Secretary of the Army:

GEORGE W. CASEY
General, United States Army
Chief of Staff

Official:

[signature: Joyce E. Morrow]

JOYCE E. MORROW
Administrative Assistant to the
Secretary of the Army
1018203

DISTRIBUTION:

Active Army, Army National Guard, and U.S. Army Reserve: To be distributed in accordance with the initial distribution number (IDN) 115970, requirements for ATTP 3-39.20 (FM 3-19.50).